Sure, It's Funny Now
Volume I

Alan Gorsuch

Author of
All the Ways I Found To Hurt Myself , Volume I
and
All the Ways I Found To Hurt Myself , Volume II

Puddy Muddle Press
Tacoma, Washington

Sure, It's Funny "Now"

Alan Gorsuch
Puddy Muddle Press

Published by Puddy Muddle Press, Tacoma, WA

Publisher's Cataloging-in-Publication
(Provided by Cassidy Cataloguing Services, Inc.).

Names: Gorsuch, Alan, author.
Title: Sure, it's funny now. Volume I / Alan Gorsuch.
Description: Tacoma, Washington : Puddy Muddle Press, [2024]
Identifiers: ISBN: 979-8-9891869-0-7 (paperback) | 979-8-9891869-1-4 (ebook) | LCCN: 2023917864
Subjects: LCSH: Gorsuch, Alan--Humor. | Washington (State)--Biography. | LC-GFT: Humor. | Autobiographies. | Essays. | BISAC: HUMOR / Form / Essays. | LITERARY COLLECTIONS / Diaries & Journals. | BIOGRAPHY & AUTOBI-OGRAPHY / General.
Classification: LCC: F895.22.G67 A3 2024 | DDC: 979.7044092--dc23

DEDICATION

To Cheryl,
my wife and fellow traveler
also the love of my life

the thoughtful hauntings that memory brings
and the careful covering of them the
winds of time lay bare
our carefully planned wanderings we
have roamed this earth
on the wings of time we share
dare we agree it's all been worth
pains and miseries
sunshine shadow and mirth
on the winds of time we've sailed skies and seas upon
this globe and girth
there's more worth seeing and knowing
let's go while the wind is still blowing for
over a far distant future hill
the winds will stop and be still

MY FAVORITE ENDORSEMENT

A few years ago I was delivering my second volume of "All the Ways I Found to Hurt Myself" to my friend, Kim, owner of "Nisqually Auto Wrecking" in Lacey, Washington; she informed me her dad had borrowed Volume I and wouldn't give it back.

A thirty-something attractive female employee-friend of Kim's sat on a stool behind the counter. As I handed the new book over to Kim, the other young lady leaps off her stool and snatches it from my hand, hollering, "Wait a minute! *YOU* wrote this book?!?'

"Unh, yes."

YOU wrote these books?!"

" . . . Yeah." Having *no* idea where this is going.

"I love these books! These are the best books *EVER!* All my friends *FIGHT* over these books! These books have been in every *jail* I have *EVER* been in – in my entire *life!!!*"

Thank you, Kailie N-----!

Alan

Contents

Preface   ix

Introduction   xi

1   Paranormal Triangle   1

2   My Three Amigos   5

3   Winter Olympics   9

4   Swimming Eagle The Face Eater   13

5   Trolls   23

6   Emotionally Over Rotten   31

7   Scrufalumpus Hopalong Kerplop   35

8   My Thoughts On The Plague   41

9   Battle Of The Little Bighorns   45

10   Interruptive Personality Disorder   49

11   Shrunken Drawers   53

12   Town Without Pity   57

13   Slideshow   63

14   I See Naked People   67

15   Think, Man, Think!   73

16   Three Weeks On The Road, Act One   79

17   Three Weeks On The Road, Act Two   87

18   Three Weeks On The Road, Act Three   93

19   Three Weeks On The Road, Act Four   99

20   Three Weeks On The Road, Act Five –
The Curtain Falls   113

21   Mischief Framed By Decree   121

22   Seabeck   127

23   Camping With Cheryl   131

24   Meese   135

25   Mom Was Right   139

26 Transformers   143
27 The Claw Machine   147
28 Tacoma Washington Area Two Dollar Bill   153
29 Marines!   165
30 GOOD CITIZEN   171
31 Newly Acquired Information   175
32 Power Bill   177
33 Scotch Tape Store   181
34 What Are The Odds?   185
35 Coco   191
36 The Farm   195
37 Topsy Turvy   201
38 Olympic Club   207
39 Tin Men   213
40 The Spar   217
41 Regrets   223
42 Nyet   231
43 A Right Fine Time   235
44 Fork In The Road   245
45 The Lost City   251
46 Appleknockers   257
47 Cat And Mouse   265
48 Clark And The Kitchen-Aid   271
49 Curse Of The Mummy   275
50 Hilda Peach – Revisited   281
51 Naked And In Tears   285
52 Tijuana Toothache   289
53 Malrobe Wardfunction   293
54 Old Bones   295
55 Cowpies And Indians   299
56 Chessmaster   303
57 Nisqually Wreck   307
58 The Rodeo Comes To Town   311

59   Hhhaaats!   315

60   Wasting Away   319

61   Man-Eating Horses   323

62   Horse Piss   327

63   The Raft   331

64   The Backbar   335

65   Act I – Soccer Hooligans   341

66   Act II – Let's Make A Deal   345

67   Scrufalumpus Interruptus   353

Acknowledgements: 359

Preface

Dear Reader:
What you are about to read is, among other things, an unauthorized autobiography and it is dedicated to all people who never had a book dedicated to them. In the space below please fill in your name, social security number, as well as a phone number where i can personally reach you at 4:00 A.M.

All names have been changed.
Any similarities are purely coincidental.

If anyone objects to any material in this book,
I hereby retract it.

INTRODUCTION

My first trip across the U.S. from west to east and back again six months later did not involve the pursuit of antiques. Of the hundreds of thousands of miles of cross country and international trips that I've made since then, it's almost the only one that didn't.

While on vacation from working construction in upstate New York and camping at the Rocky Neck campground in Connecticut, I was on a grocery run to buy some bacon for our campfire meal when I stumbled onto a yard sale and became hopelessly hooked by the charm and allurement of the tables full of colorful old bottles for sale.

I think the gentleman's name was Albert Corey. Whatever his name was, however, he was the next-door neighbor to one Charles Gardner, who Mr. Corey explained, was the dean of American bottle collecting. Albert had become infected through this neighbor's passion for old bottles. Albert then effectively infected me when he offered me fifty dollars for the applied handle A.M. BININGER glass jug I told him I had back home in Washington State.

The rest is history.

Bottles led to bottle shows. Bottle shows led to tobacco tins and old wood telephones. Whiskey signs and crockery. Country store advertising and soda fountain dispensers. Slot machines and saloon stuff, such as swinging saloon doors, slate pool tables with cast iron fullbodied lions for the bases, back bars, front bars, giant stained and beveled glass windows and nickel-plated based-burner coal stoves. Anything that weighs around two-and-a-half tons. And it all started with one bottle, one yard sale and the man who ran it, and his next-door neighbor who wasn't home and whom I have never met.

But it didn't happen overnight. It took years to blossom into the full-blown disease of the magnitude and proportion it is now. I remained in the construction trade as a reasonably acceptable member of society while I merely *collected* bottles and dabbled in learning about other antiques for the first couple of years.

As a child, I was addicted to heights, danger of all kinds, especially the possibility of falling from a considerable distance onto a pointed object, so I quite naturally fell into the roofing trade, the application of cedar shakes and shingles my specialty.

My small roofing business afforded me enough opportunity to embezzle from myself money to pay for my newly acquired collection addiction. I remained in the roofing and construction trade while I opened, in 1972, a small antique shop on Olympia's eastside. The two overlapping careers would symbiotically coexist and nurture each other for a few more years. On the occasion of an older home's roof needing to be torn off in preparation for the new roof, for example, I'd sometimes spot a pile of nineteenth century picture frames, or a couple of old trunks squirreled away in the rafters, forgotten by the previous homeowners and ignored by the present ones. So, while buying the contents of an attic, my reroofing opportunities had sometimes fed my need for an antique fix, while my fledgling antique shop had paid some of the bills when construction and roofing was slow.

I was married by now and unfortunately by this time, kids were beginning to pile up in all the corners, which I thought was quite annoying. Although I didn't actually dislike any of them personally, I found them to be noisy, expensive and distractive. Some of them, because of their being somewhat cute and cuddly, were robbing me of the valuable time I needed to spend in the pursuit of something meaningful in life, like rooting around rural areas for cool old tin cans and coke machines or oak furniture. I still love American Oak rolltop desks, secretaries, curved glass china cabinets and the like, and none of those kids are cuddly anymore, let me tell you. In fact, they all remind me of how I used to be bullied and shoved around back in Lacey grade school; only now, it's my own grown kids that push me down and take my lunch money. I have no idea how I came to command such little respect from my own children; I often wonder where they went wrong. I've always tried to set what I thought was a stellar example.

Roofing and rooting, and they went hand-in-hand for some time before I thought maybe it was a good idea to give one of them up. It wasn't a hard decision to make. After many years as a roofer, I had managed to acquire a "housemaid's knee," along with more than a few scary and oddball experiences while roofing.

1

PARANORMAL TRIANGLE

I'd like to tell you about, not the first roof I ever worked on, but it was the first western red cedar shake *tear off* and *reroof* I had ever done. I was nineteen.

On the eastern shore of Thurston County's Lake St. Clair, my partner, Larry Ross, and I were hired to reroof an old summer home one hot summer long ago. It was Larry's job, and I was working for him, learning as I went, having never done a shake tear off before, although I had installed lots of new shakes before this job. The roof itself was at least a 12-12 pitch: very steep; essentially a triangular-shaped top structure. It was also two stories high, and even more so up near the peak. Adding in the difference at which point the lake's bank sloped away where the house was situated on and in the embankment, the total distance from where I was when something supernatural nearly took my life, was around nearly sixty feet. I was up at the peak and almost done peeling all the old splintery cedar shakes from that side of the ancient wooden pyramid-shaped structure which was old enough that it may have been built and deposited there by the Pharoah himself, when it happened.

Larry was nowhere to be found; he had disappeared a couple of hours earlier, and it had nothing to do with anything supernatural. Anybody that has ever hired a roofer will tell you that's quite natural and predictable. They all disappear. That's what they are paid to do. That way you will appreciate them that much more when they reappear early the next morning, slamming bundles of material onto the rooftop, knocking plaster onto you as you sleep. That's their job. Then, once they tear off the old roof and the open rafters are exposed while thick, ominous, black clouds loom on the horizon, they evaporate again.

I didn't know any of this yet, though. I didn't yet understand that part of my job description was to suddenly transmutate from the roof job and reconfigure somewhere else like, say…the local pool hall or tavern. Eventually I would learn. In my case, though, once I did learn how to disappear by quietly coasting down the driveway and popping the truck's clutch at the end of the street, my reconfigurations usually involved an old farm or neighborhood where I might root out a Hoosier kitchen-queen or maybe a double-barreled cider press.

But there I was, not knowing any better than to keep on working, with Larry off chasing materials, turning in bids, collecting money, or any of the other excuses roofers invent in order to slide off the jobsite.

I had only one small patch of the ancient cedar to pry off the roof's sheathing to say that half of the house was ready for its new roof. The small patch was at the junction where the sixty feet of towering brick chimney rose from the fireplace footing and was connected to the gable's peak. It was attached to the end of the house, on my left as I faced the lake. Over the ridge was now a gentle, welcome, unobstructed southwest summer breeze.

Earlier, when swinging my pickaxe into the old roofing between the spaces separating the one by eight-inch-wide sheathing, the old house vibrated with each swing. By now, I had several throbbing blisters. I was also covered in sweaty black dust and nicely sunburned.

Carefully pulling the nails around the chimney's metal flashing, I also had to peel away the last remnants of original shakes from under the flashing and under the heavy large Ushaped bracket that wrapped around the chimney, and which was secured to the roof. I was done.

"He'd better show up with lunch," I mumbled to myself as I rose to my feet to inspect the cool lake water over the peak below me. It was beckoning.

When I hung my hammer in my tool belt to count my blisters, I had barely noticed at first, but something new began to register; although it was hardly detectable, I could see what was happening. The rickety old house was slowly collapsing! Just barely leaning at first, it was worsening, clearly listing more and more to the right—it was going over and it planned on taking me down with it! I stood there for a moment, hoping for it to stop—but it was no use. In the next second or so, it silently continued in its slow inch by inch accelerating lean.

Watching the wobbly balloon-framed structure separate from the stalwart towering rigid brick chimney, which evidently was going to be the only thing left standing when Larry got back or when the owners came home, I made my decision. I decided to outsmart the murderous house and jump onto the sturdy brick tower. They'd have to devise some way to get me down later. Although panicky, I pictured myself sitting atop the giant chimney when everybody would return. Knowing I'd most assuredly be blamed for the collapsed skeletal house of sticks lying in shambles in the side yard, I considered surf-riding it down and hoping for the best. Maybe I'd survive the descent. If so, then I could disappear into the sticker bushes as I had always done as a kid. I decided it was a bad idea. I remember I was hollering and yelling a buncha stuff, although I'm sure it made no more sense than did the situation I was in.

Hoping to outlive, as well as outsmart, a suicidal and apparently haunted house, I readied myself to jump onto the top of the sooty old smokestack. As the gap slowly widened to about three feet between the chimney and the ill-fated abode, I made a sudden unconscious observation. EVERYTHING was sliding to my right! Everything except the chimney! The lake! The opposite shore! The sky and clouds in it! Everything! That's not right!

With my panicked right hand, I quickly grabbed a roof rafter through the space between the sheathing and lunged out with my blistered left hand, just in time to catch the leaning sixty-foot Tower of Babble by a top black brick of the chimney's rim. With one finger. My middle finger. With surprisingly very little effort, I then slowly guided back the standing tower of what was nearly a noisy pile of broken bricks, brick dust and black soot soon to be lying in the opposite side yard from where I was only a moment before, *convinced* the house was crumbling.

It quietly clunked back into place, and I immediately reaffixed the iron girdle that had bracketed the eighty-year-old square brick pillar to where it had always been—'til I got near it. And to think, in my supernatural confusion, I had nearly jumped on top of it and rode it down to be embedded dead into the damp lake bank. Where, if they had any sense, they would've left me. Talk about learning as you go.

Soon, Larry returned with a box of eight-penny galvanized nails and lunch.

"Looks good—how'd it go?" he asked, while I picked slivers out of my open blisters.

"Fine. Did'ja get anything to drink?"

2

My Three Amigos

Every fifteen seconds someone in America falls down and gets hurt. You'd think that guy would eventually learn to just stay on the floor.

Most people that hurt themselves in a simple fall do so only because they've not yet learned *how* to fall, whether falling off a log or bicycle, tripping while running, falling off the edge of a normal nine-foot-high roof, and so forth. In most cases, if an alert person keeps his head, he can protect it, as well as other fragile body parts, by employing basic survival techniques. Screaming at the top of your lungs all the way to the ground doesn't count; all that does is alert bystanders to the fact that you are a clumsy and careless knucklehead. T u c k and roll: If when on a bike, running, or falling face first downstairs into a moldy cellar or *any* similar head-first fall, *never* attempt to break your fall with your hands. If unable on your way down, to snatch up a family pet or a small child to wrap around your head for protection, for heaven's sake, learn how to tuck your head down, curl up *one* shoulder, and *roll into* the fall, shoulder first—tuck and roll.

A slightly, if at all, bruised shoulder, is better than two broken wrists, flattened nose, missing teeth and possibly a dislocated appendage. And that's just some of the stuff that can happen to you when your wife comes home to find out you drug the family dog or little Suzie with you when you pitched yourself down the cellar stairs on your way to go get more beer. Dog bites, by the way, are painful and take time to heal. Especially so it seems, if they're inflicted by one's *own* dog and are in the tender-most facial area. Which is one more reason why I prefer cats. I always encourage our cat to sleep on the top step of our stairs. What few teeth she has left are loose and smaller than those of most dogs.

It's just better all the way around to tuck-and-roll; similar to how a football player throws a shoulder block.

Or pick a *place* to land. When an unanticipated sudden journey earthward presents itself, and an impending fall is apparent and ninety-five percent unavoidable, always turn yourself into the fall and pick your landing spot. Learn to abandon that last—nearly hopeless—five percent, grasping at straws possibility; instead pick a spot to plant both feet and land safely—relatively safely anyhow. It's much better to land on your feet and then to tip over, than to land on your back off the ladder, roof, or barstool. If you're pretty sure you are going down anyway, stop clawing at shingles, branches, passing fowl or swizzle sticks and sticky straws stuck to the bar top. Never, under any circumstances, grab the handle of the beer mug belonging to the guy next to you. The much better option is to turn, if you can, and face your fate. Rather than panicking, take control of your descent and bring yourself to a smooth landing. Act as if you've done it on purpose. If you were graceful enough, most bystanders will assume you just realized that you left the stove on at home or had forgotten something in the car, and that you were departing the premises.

Way back when I actually thought I had friends, I made the simple mistake of visiting "Casey's Tavern" in downtown Lacey with three of them one afternoon after work.

Dave Demuro ("Curly"), Dick Knapp ("Moe") and Rick Crawford ("Larry") sat together at the bar, guzzling beer with their backs to me, while I played pool and semi-guzzled behind them.   As the afternoon wore into evening, my three stool stooges had soaked up enough suds to need to visit the small room necessary for such occasions several times per stoolie. An innocent sipper sitting alone and silently minding his own business now occupied the previously empty stool at the end of the bar, and at the far right of my string of stooges. Little did he know that at the hands of these other three stool pigeons he was gonna take a fall. A loud one. While I was concentrating on pocketing a reasonably difficult eight-ball, a noisy conflab began to override all other conversations and scattered gurgling within the tavern's interior. Missing my shot because of the sudden eruption of racket near me, I looked up to see what the outbreak of what sounded like violence, was.

It was my three idiot friends. And they were clustered together, in dominoes fashion, each of them having a firm and desperate grip on the collar of the other. They were halfway between their empty bar seats and the dirty tavern floor when I had looked up. All three of them were falling over backwards off their barstools, together.

With a loud synchronized thud-like "OOF" my three thug-like dunderheads thundered over and onto their backs and flat onto Casey's floor. and one-third of the three had dragged the poor innocent sipper down with them. He, the innocent sipper, quickly rose to his feet and suddenly remembered that he had indeed left the stove on at home and threw some money on the bar.

My three stoolies squirmed around on the floor for an embarrassing amount of time, trying to untangle themselves from each other's clutches, while loudly proclaiming it was the other one's fault. By the time they were done, they'd all agreed to blame the poor guy they yanked down with them.

"Are they friends of yours?" asked the guy to whom I was about to lose my eight-ball game.

Shaking my head sadly while digging in my pocket for some quarters, I answered, "Nope, never saw'm before."

3

WINTER OLYMPICS

Years before that tale of a brawl on the barroom floor, myself and three other young, sober and hardworking apprentices partook of a not-too-dissimilar aerial plummet earthward. Rather than it being the end of the workday, it was the very beginning of it; in fact, it was the first ninety seconds on the job.

The three guys I refer to—Bill Warner, Lowell Smith and Ron Hoyt—weren't inebriated or even clumsy. Quite the contrary, all four of us were bright-eyed and bushy-tailed young roofers starting up the ladder to begin the day's work. I was about to be the first up the ladder and to step onto the plywood sheathing of one of Al Thompson's fine new homes in the "Tanglewilde" addition subdivision.

The house itself was an average single-story, configured in a u-shape, creating a semienclosed courtyard within the "U", a very popular design in the late seventies. It was spring. It was sunny. It was frosty. It was early. It was time to get started. I put my nail belt on and headed over to the ladder, to be the first one up.

As we ascended the ladder, one after the other and maybe twenty or thirty seconds apart from each other, the welcome morning sun slightly warmed our backs, as it had already warmed the side of the roof I stepped onto. Dew covered the plywood slant that faced the eight o'clock sunrise.

Unknown to me, only minutes before I stepped off the ladder and onto the wet wood, the wood had been white with frost. When I climbed up the wet wood slant and stepped over the roof's peak onto the other side, the still dark and shady side, and the side not yet warmed by the morning's rays, I became even more bright-eyed and bushy-tailed.

The shadowed side of the house's plywood roof, where we were all headed, was a nice even slick ski-slope of *frozen* dew; but I had no way of knowing that until I confidently placed my first foot onto it. Even then, not until I had put *all* of my weight onto that foot. And *by then*, it was too late.

Like an arrow suddenly released from a crossbow, somebody seemed to pull the invisible trigger as soon as my weight shifted onto my first foot over and when I had lifted the second foot. I shot down the slanted slope of thin frost over plyboard toward an unknown target. No time to yell. I felt cool air whistling past my face; my eyes watered. I could hear my shoes sizzling through the thin snow. Soon I saw the cold courtyard of construction mud, also covered in frosty dew—the mounds of muck I knew I was soon to be implanted into. The only question was: will I be installed into the thick mud with its frosty topping face first? Or feet first?

This was a perfect example of how a person *experienced in falling* on his face, back, butt, side, elbows, knees or crown-of-the-head *should by now* have skilled himself to the point he's able to avoid killing himself in a fall. Only by maintaining my balance for the duration of my slide would I be able to pick-my-place-to-land; and I knew that.

Without screaming profanities or warnings to anybody below, or hollering for my mommy, I zipped down the roof and off of it. Soon my feet and legs were plugged into the mud as if I was a big electrical fitting jammed in a 220 wall socket. Although unharmed, I was plenty muddy; the deep mud was reasonably soft and because I had successfully remained upright, I was therefore able to avoid injury.

Naturally, Al Thompson, the head honcho of the Tanglewilde Development, was standing only a few feet away, on the entryway with the new homeowners. Embarrassed, I quickly unsocketed my feet, pretended like nothing happened and briskly left the courtyard to start back around and over. I also needed to warn the others of my crew about the ice on the shaded side of the roof.

I trotted around the house, scaled the ladder, and ran up the sunny side of the house's sheathing. When I looked over the peak, I was greeted with four sets of ski tracks in the frosty coating. I had heard nothing, nor seen anything, but each of the other three—Bill, Lowell, and Ron—had obviously followed me over, also to an unknown fate below. I remained there, listening for sounds of people writhing around in mud—and in pain.

I could hear unintelligible conversation from voices I didn't exactly recognize, possibly because of having too much mud in their mouths. I did recognize Al Thompson's. I couldn't make out what was being said, but he sounded exasperated and possibly even apologetic to whoever else it was that was with him.

One by one, my entire Olympic ski jump team reappeared at the top of the ladder, each separated from the other by around a half-minute. Wide-eyed and muddy-tailed, we each asked the other what had happened to them.

Our quick comparison of each other's story soon bore out that exactly enough time had lapsed between the ascent—and sudden descent of one-before-the-other, that none of us had seen or heard the other's unexpected snow slide. Not one of us had known what had happened to the other three.

And that's because my crew had fallen silently, as I had always recommended, thereby not alerting more witnesses to our lack of proficiency. Also, each of them was too busy to scream because they were trying their best to stay on their feet and PICK-A-PLACE-TO-LAND! as I had also taught them. So, to that degree anyway, I was proud of my young, eager—just tryingtomake-a-living crew, that they had at least learned how to fall correctly.

By eight-fifteen the roof had thawed, and we stopped laughing and went to work. Al Thompson always looked at me funny after that, as if he wanted to ask me something. But he never did.

I only relate these roofing stories because if I didn't record and tell them, who else would? Not only are most of us old roofers only half literate in the first place; our heads and fingers are too gnarled up from years of roofing to write. Not to mention our inability to form clear thought caused from too many bad falls off rooftops, ladders, scaffolding and barstools.

4

SWIMMING EAGLE THE FACE EATER

Today, as I sit aboard the "Chelan" San Juan Island to Anacortes ferry, trying to stop the bleeding from a multitude of fresh wounds incurred only hours ago, more or less at the hands of a giant bird, I feel like a country kid again. Thanks to the Andersons.

Although I am seventy years old now and live in our downtown Tacoma antique shop, I feel as if I've worked hard my whole life to— at heart at least—remain the country boy I once was. I've successfully avoided education of any kind, been an ardent technophobe—even avoiding cell phones, and I can proudly state that I am roadkill lying in the ditch *alongside* the information super-highway. But, up until today, I would have admitted that time, circumstances, city life, and the changing world around us had drained most of the country out of this boy.

The last three days spent at Jim and Mimi Anderson's second home, on San Juan Island, have reinfused me and re-enthused me. Especially on this, the last of the three days of country/ island living. Today I had a huge infusion of life-in-the-wild, overlooking Haro Strait in Puget Sound ("The Whulge" the Indians used to call it). We now call it "The Salish Sea," in honor of our first peoples.

Because of all the very recent lacerations on my body, especially the lower half, if the bleeding doesn't soon stop, I may require a saline solution transfusion due to my weekend infusion and recent injection of country enthusion. But it was worth it. And I can already taste that fresh salmon I fought so hard—and nearly died for—the salmon we'll eat tomorrow night at Jim and Mimi's north-end Tacoma home.

One of us was gonna get it, that was clear. The Harbor Seal, the Bald Eagle, the Turkey Vultures, or Jim and I. Neither Jim nor I wanted the damn salmon in the first place. We only wound up with it because we were innocent spectators that got drug into the picture through a quarter mile of blackberry thorns, and were awarded a freshly-caught big fish. Bigger than any I ever caught when I was a kid. (If, at this point, you are alarmed by anything you have read, or *think* you *might* read, pretend this is simply a work of fiction, and please keep reading.) The biggest complaint I have about life on the San Juan Islands is that you can't get anything done. Life here in the Islands is far too distractive. I came here to relax and write. Everybody and everything teamed up to make sure that wouldn't happen.

As soon as you get to the Islands for a visit you have to listen to the Island residents babble on and on about whales and whatnot. They prattle on endlessly about Orcas and Eagles, Seals and Sea Lions, Herons, Deer, Fox, Oysters, and the Andersons' all-time favorite: Bats. As if living an island-country-type life was something special. I didn't want to hear about it. I didn't need the distractions. But no matter *where* I went to hide and write, deer were staring at me, including while in Jim's bathroom.

So, I cloistered myself in the kitchen, close to the fridge, where Mimi kept her yummy food and Jim had poorly concealed his beer behind a lot of organic milk and other wholesome stuff. No sooner had I settled into writing a long overdue story of "How-to-Fall" (and avoid serious injury) when everyone upstairs starts shrieking and squealing something about a "Pod." I thought they maybe were watching "Invasion of the Body Snatchers" or a pea shellers challenge. So, I tried to ignore them. That was becoming increasingly difficult as the three of them—Jim, Mimi and now my wife Cheryl—bounded from room to room and deck to deck, up and down the stairs, colliding into my chair and table. Brandishing binoculars and flailing around while hollering something about "breaches" and "tail-slaps." Defiantly, I would glare at them. But it was no use.

I've seen whales before, here in the Islands, and on the coast. And it was always cool. But these fanatics had now set their hooks in my wife; she was hopping around, waving her binoculars like a newly "healed" previously crippled person does their crutches during one of those faith healing conventions. They made me look.

And it was cool. Dorsal fins, blowholes, big males, big females, and big babies. Big deal. Within half an hour, however, I was running breathlessly with my pod of people along the shore at Lime Kiln Point, screaming, "Look!" Another breach! They're headed into the kelp beds! Here come three more! Run! Run!" Tears welled up in my eyes, all the while jumping up and down in a state of gleeful over-reactionary emotionalistic ecstasy that would have caused even the most zealous Pentecostal preacher to tell me to sit down and shut up. Now they had *me* hooked on whale watching. And I have no idea how they did it.

Every time I sat down to write during the next two days, I'd write approximately three words and then my eyes would lift themselves off the page and wander over to the window, crawl over the sill onto the deck. There they would climb the railing and leap out at the salt water below, searching for signs. Signs of an approaching pod. These damn whales were ruining my weekend. I'd look out another window. More deer. I'd go hide in the backyard. Quail stampede.

But the final straw was this morning.

After creeping outside with my second cup of coffee, hopefully before any creatures of the forest, sea or my wife figured out I had eluded them and slipped away to write something on my nearly blank paper, the screeching started. *Immediately* after I sat down. Only this time, the screeching involved *my* name. "ALAN! GET IN HERE! It's a Bald Eagle! And he's in the water! He's hurt! Oh, no!" my wife was screaming at the top of her lungs.

I don't know about you, but whenever my wife screams like that at me, I do exactly what *all* small prey is meant to do when a lion roars. I panic and run around in circles until she smacks me in the snout with a rolled-up newspaper.

So, into the house I ran, after knocking my coffee cup over into my entire weekend's useless attempts at writing. Looking out the window onto the water far below, I saw an eagle in the water, just as she had so succinctly proclaimed. I've seen lots of eagles in my life, including bald eagles. I've never seen an eagle in the water, swimming. And I don't mean swimming like a duck, either. This eagle was doing the breaststroke and he was doing it well; better than I ever could.

"He's hurt! He's hurt!" Threateningly she held the big binoculars behind her head, ready to bring them down onto the top of mine. "*Do something!*" Not wanting to be bludgeoned by Mimi's new spyglasses, I began to negotiate by taking stock of the situation.

"He's *not* hurt! He's swimming for shore!" Which was one-hundred to one-hundred-fifty yards away from him. "He's probably towing a salmon."

"No, he's NOT! He's hurt! LOOK? Now there's a SEAL after him!"

Sure enough, *now* he was being trailed by what appeared to be a Harbor Seal, which probably wanted *something*. I assumed it was the salmon the Olympic marathoner, Swimming Eagle, wearing the white swim cap, towed in his talons. The salmon my wife knew wasn't there. I longed for my safe quiet home in the city. I decided to go get Jim, who had only ten minutes before, announced that he was "going upstairs for a shower."

I ran up the stairs, hollering, "Jim! Jim! There's an eagle in your water!" I heard the bathroom door lock. *Just as I thought—he's had-it-up-to-here with island life, too.* Not thinking for a moment that possibly he'd just had-it-up-to-here with us, my wife and myself, I went back downstairs to console the distraught women and see *what else* was on the Discovery channel. There appeared to be little change. Swimming Eagle vs. charging seal. Cheryl threatened me again. Then she chased me back up the stairs to the upper deck. Mimi was already there and within a few minutes Jim arrived in his bathrobe with a sour look on his face, as if he'd been robbed of some precious quality time alone. "Now you know how I feel," I said.

"Do something," was his retort after staring out at the scene one-third of a mile below us.

Less than a minute later, I found myself bounding wildly down a 35% grade gravel driveway and thrashing through thickets, meadows, stands of small trees and into a forest of giant blackberry vines. On my way to save the day. wearing my new green open-toe Nordstrom's Huarache sandals and my best white linen shorts, without even so much as the San Juan Island "Journal" newspaper rolled up in my hand to defend our great American icon. As if when I got there I was going to swat a sea lion or harbor seal or island kelp monster or whatever the hell else it was that was after Swimming Eagle.

"Turn right!" Jim yelled from the mountain top. As soon as I would, he'd holler, "Turn left!" and then laugh.

I did my best to ignore the tatters of skin dangling from the blackberry blades in the swath behind me. Thorny talons dove into my city flesh as if I was fresh sushi. Like a lone salmon encircled by a large, tangled net, I swam into the jungle of ubiquitous blackberry cables, their saberous incisors feeding on me as I fought. *Save our national symbol—the Great American Swimming Bald Eagle*, the only thing on my mind. I still had two hundred yards to go when I hurdled the last roll of concertina vegetation and landed in the ditch by the side of the road. No traffic—thanks to what *they* call "Island time," everybody else on the island was still at home counting how many deer were in their resident pod.

Across the road to the dry meadow and into an acre or so of *dead* blackberry vines—the light leafless colored tan ones you can't see because in death their coloration matches the tall dead grasses that conceal them—ensuring even in their afterlife, anybody treading upon their grave will emerge looking as if he was attacked by a pack of wild dogs.

Loping down to the edge of the bluff and nearly falling over the cliff onto the rocks below, I see Swimming Eagle on a rock eight feet up out of the slurping and gurgling surf. He's slurping and gurgling on the salmon that I *told* my wife he was towing. The seal was gone. Swimming Eagle was fine. The seven- or eight-pound salmon and I both were bleeding badly. I left.

After leading Jim who deftly pranced in Gazelle form, over or around the dry but slobbering dead incisors of Hades down to where we could see Feeding Eagle and the saddened Silver, we saw that the eagle had flown. The salmon was still there, most all of it. That's when the turkey vulture, which I had earlier seen annoying Feeding Eagle, arrived for the second time and swooped near the altered salmon. By this time, Jim was already below me, by one rock shelf, and therefore that much closer to the sleeping Silver. So I said to him, slowly, "Jim? How many people on earth can say that they've watched an eagle swim? Not only that, but how many people can say they've eaten *fresh* salmon—*caught and delivered* to their doorstep by a giant American Bald Eagle?"

To which Jim answered, "Ooooh, man! Whad'ja hafta go and say *that* for?" A rhetorical question at best, because soon Jim was on his way down the cliff to examine the corpse.

"All he ate was the fish's face?" Jim exclaimed.

The huge turkey vulture that had been circling overhead grew smaller in the distance. A Bald Eagle landed in a far tree, a half mile or so north. I excitedly yelled at Jim hoping he'd fall into the water. "Look! An Eagle! And he looks pissed!" Jim ducked and I laughed. When Jim finally saw the Eagle on a branch, he moaned, "He's miles away and not even looking this direction. You're just trying to scare me."

I was examining all the dripping thin red ribbons which festooned my bare legs and ankles. "Salmon just doesn't get any fresher than that," I said matter-of-factly. "Pick him up."

"How?" Jim asked.

"By his gills, what kinda city kid are you, anyway?"

"He doesn't have any gills. They're gone."

"The eagle ate his gills?"

"I told'ja his whole face is gone."

"Well, just pick him up and let's go and eat him."

So Jim did. With both hands Jim picked up the salmon without a face and even less of a future. And that's precisely when a squawky seagull just overhead let out three shrill shrieks. I jumped on the opportunity.

"The eagle! The eagle! Look out! He's back! He's right above you! He's headed for your face!"

Jim dropped that fish and positively flew like an eagle across the numerous rock tops to implant himself onto the side of the cliff, like thistledown stuck on Velcro, covering his head, especially his face, the whole way. I was ecstatic. I was laughing so hard I thought I felt thorns squirt out of my shins, "Swimming Eagle the face eater *almost* gotcha!"

"YOU JERK!" (not his exact word) Jim hollered, loud enough I might've heard some faraway seals hit the water. I kept laughing. And bleeding.

Jim was successfully negotiating the rocks, after again snatching up the slippery shimmering silver salmon of serendipity, while looking over both shoulders at the same time.

That's when I gave him useful instructions on what to do, should he lose his balance and fall.

"If you start to fall, throw me the fish."

"If I fall, the salmon comes with me."

"Yah, you're right. If you're layin' down there with a buncha broken legs and whatnot, you'll need to cover your face with that fish; Swimming Eagle only dines on faces." I pulled a thorn out of my knuckle with my teeth, laughing as I did so.

Jim made his way to the rock shelf below where I stood, leaking from my wounds. "I can't climb this spot without getting rid of the fish; even then, I'm gonna need a hand, "he whined.

"Okay, hand up the fish, then I'll help you up." Which he did. I was surprised how slippery the salmon was. It did indeed require both hands because of its size and the fact Swimming

Eagle had made off with its handles. I turned and left.

Halfway through the blackberry cemetery Jim caught up with me. "Hey, thanks for all the help back there."

"Both of us now have hands so slimy you *would* have landed on the rocks. We couldn't have maintained a hand grip." Which was true. But the real truth was, I had forgotten, once I glommed my hands onto that big fish. Like Golem, that's all I could think about. My *Precious*. Yah, I guess you're right," Jim conceded, sniffing his hand.

Cheryl was sitting below the house on a bench when we came crawling up the hill, so she saw us first. "You TOOK the salmon away from her?" she hollered incredulously, jumping to her **feet**.

"He ate what he wanted, then left," I felt like a little kid going, "*He followed us home. Can't we just keep him? Please?*"

"You STOLE HER SALMON from her? After she worked so hard for it?" Somehow Swimming Eagle had found the time to undergo a sex change while all this was going on. This was a busy bird.

"He left it, and then the turkey vultures were gonna get it," I reasoned. "YOU'RE who's gonna get it—LOOK!" Pointing out at the water. "Here comes the Fish and Wildlife boat! They saw the whole thing!" I dropped the fish. Jim and I both wheeled around. There was no boat. Cheryl threw her head back and started laughing like Long John Silver.

As we made our way near the backside of the house, Mimi looked out through the kitchen door screen and hollered, "Whooohooo! Fresh salmon!" She immediately started rattling sabers and other kitchen utensils.

While I readied the silver for its final insult, other than being cooked and eaten, Cheryl reappeared near the rock I had chosen for the purpose of cleaning our…umm…catch. "Look, Honey," I began plaintively, "I'm bleeding to death," pointing at my shredded, bleeding and mangled legs, hoping for a shred of sympathy.

"I can't *believe* you stole her salmon!…. What on earth did you *do* to that poor fish? *Where's* her face?"

* * * * * *

Mimi knows how to cook a great bourbon-based salmon. Especially fresh salmon. And, as it turned out, it was a King, not a Silver.

'Course Cheryl took most of the credit for our delicious meal because, as she put it, she "was the one who saw the drowning eagle in the first place."

Jim and I may be a lot of things, but one thing we are not, is fish pirates. Not intentionally, anyway. So if anybody is even thinking about pressing charges in relation to this story, consider it only a work of fiction. Nothing more than a fish story. Jim and I are both big liars when it comes to some things; just ask our wives.
Future Epilogue:

Jim lives on the Island full-time now. Not San Juan Island. McNeil Island, where we have our federal prison. By the time he's released back into the wild, he'll be partially bald, but otherwise well-quaffed as always, now sporting a fine crown of pure white hair. His hair color turned while serving his residency on McNeil.

I turned state's evidence because, after all, I saw the whole thing.

If you visit Jim, don't bring him any snacks that contain seafood. Especially salmon. Says it turns his stomach.

And if he asks you, "Does eagle taste just like chicken?" Say yes.

5

TROLLS

One of the darkest chapters of my life occurred when I was only fourteen and a freshman at North Thurston High School. The darkness descended during art class, quite suddenly and, as usual, was delivered to me by my own hand—my right hand. I've never told anybody this story—I'm only telling *you* because you seem to have an understanding and forgiving attitude about you—well, we'll just see about that, won't we?

It's the end of art class and Miss Briton has us (me) sweeping up all the loose clay pellets that have been dropped (thrown) by the entire class (mostly me) within the last hour. Soon, I'm all done sweeping, and now I'm walking to the supply room to replace the broom, by preparing to put it, handle first, back into the large cardboard barrel where they're kept.

Because of the earlier years I'd spent as an only child in the woods playing with myself and what with the only materials around to entertain me being: sticks, rocks, trees, branches, water and bees' nests, I had, over time, become quite adept at throwing sticks and rocks at all the bees' nests that were to be found at water's edge, hanging in the branches of trees. I was an ace—A-number-one— spear thrower. And I'd only been stung four thousand one hundred thirtyseven times in the process of honing my superior spear hurling capabilities. Although I spent several of my summers quite swollen from all the wasp and hornet venom I'd absorbed, I was dead eye when it came to chucking a spear; when the swelling around my good eye didn't interfere with my aim, that is. My other track and field abilities improved greatly during those years as well. After impaling a large hanging paper-wasp's nest with a perfectly thrown spear, for example, one quickly learns not to stand around and gloat; unless particularly enamored by those pictures of a beekeeper with his head and face covered with his pet honeybees. One learns that, unless he turns and runs like the wind, he'll soon have a helmet and mask of hornets clinging to and covering his head and face. My frequent 100-yard dash wind-sprints built up my ability to eventually run even greater distances and away from even greater perils, such as: auditors, adult responsibility, big guys with blackjacks/guns/knives, large dogs, jury duty, offspring and Claudia Kimble.

Not only was it the end of art class on that fateful day, it was also nearly the end of the spring quarter and in a few days spring vacation would commence. So I was feeling frisky. And at the exact moment I felt the most frisky, my most treacherous, although infrequent companion that I've ever had, paid me a short but memorable visit: confidence. My confidence in my truly remarkable spear chucking abilities kicked in and told me that *I could do it*. I could spear-toss that broom—handle first—into the crescent-shaped barrel's opening that could be seen from where I stood, listening, listening to those same treacherous lies that once again, confidence whispered into my ear, filling my otherwise hollow head with the desire to do something noteworthy, impulsive, and cool.

Skillfully, I took aim and drew my right arm back, masterfully balancing while leveling the broom spear into a perfect horizontal alignment, pointing at the slim crescent. With the narrowed concentration, eye-of-the-tiger focus willfully possessed by only the most remarkable warriors within the annals of accomplishment in the art of spear/javelin and broom tossing, I sailed, with complete follow-through and shoulder rotation, my missile of skill. Though the opening of the barrel was larger than any wasp's nest, the angle and trajectory from where I threw my broom/javelin narrowed it down to where my throw did indeed require all the ability I could muster. It was a perfect toss. It was only off by, maybe, one inch. And that's all it took. Instead of the wooden end of the broom sliding smoothly INTO the slim fertile crescent opening of both the barrel and the related noteworthiness and cool remarkability that would most assuredly follow, it missed by one inch, grazed the OUTSIDE of the rim, and when the heavier end of the broom—the broom end—kept going forward and over, it created a lever-action change of angle in my missile of misdirection.

How in living hell a broom traveling at, say, twenty-five miles per hour, can, after contacting the outside edge of a barrel, change not only direction, but somehow accelerate its speed to that of an Intercontinental Ballistic Missile is still beyond me.

My narrowed eye-of-the-tiger, just on-the-brink-of-extinction outlook immediately and instantaneously widened to that of a horror-stricken and incontinent cow-eyed beast of burger about to gasp its last breath in its final step on the ramp of the packing house.

The bell rang at the same exact moment the devil spear from Hades took its ninetydegree left turn and flew across the room towards Claudia Kimble who, up 'til my hell-broom had located her, by its automatic built-in face location system device impacted itself, handle first, directly onto the side of her nose, *had* been one of the most beautiful girls in our school.   In that instant I introduced to Claudia, single-handedly, the face of change. The bell continued clanging away, drowning out the screaming and carnage that followed. As I bolted for the door—*well*, class *was* over!—I may have detected the fine crimson mist of spray that seemed to dim the lights—as well as my future—and Claudia's.

School was out, in more ways than one, for me at least. Art class was the last period before boarding the bus for safety and that day

I was, for the first time, the first one on ours. Soon, the bus began filling up with those less damned than myself. One of the earliest to board was Janice Worden, a most kind and pleasant fellow graduate of Lacey Grade School, whom I had known since third grade. "Did you see Claudia Kimble's nose?!?" The first thing out of her mouth, after taking the seat directly behind me. "I heard some shithead in art class went crazy and tried to beat her to death with a barrel or a fire extinguisher, or a shovel or something." "Yeah, me, too," while trying falsely to hum some imaginary and nonexistent tune to myself and hopefully thereby drown out the near-distant but still audible conversations about the evil bastard that had unsuccessfully tried to butcher Claudia and in his failure had disfigured her greatly. Blood. Gore. Vengeful retaliation.

As quickly as I had become disinterested in javelin tossing and had abandoned all hope of any future Olympic recognition, I became interested in something I had inadvertently learned about ancient Jewish history. Specifically, pertaining to accidental but possibly negligent, homicide.

In ancient Israel, let's say as an example, a couple of guys are out in the woods, falling timber—yes, they actually *had* timber back then—one guy's axe head flies off the handle and kills his buddy. An accident, to be sure. However, the guy with the headless axe *should have* soaked, swelled and better bound his axe together. But because he bore culpability in the death of his coworker that now wore an axe head in his skull, the family of the deceased then had every right, should they choose to do so, to track down the bad-ass with the bad axe and kill him. If they had an axe to grind, it was up to them to exact an "eye for an eye"—recompense for his bloodguilt.

That was ancient Mosaic Hebrew law. The only recourse the woodcutter with the faulty equipment had was to run like hell to what was called a "City of Refuge," of which, if memory serves, and because I'm not the type of person to go look it up, there were in the land of Israel or fertile crescent if you like, four such cities. Once within the walls of the City of Refuge, the family wasn't allowed to touch him. But he had to stay there. He wasn't allowed to venture outside the city's walls for fear of running into Zeke, or Obadiah, the brothers of the deceased; the ones that had loaned the former woodsman the money to start a pickle factory. The biblical connection was very easy for me to make because of the fact that not only was Claudia Kimble's father a pastor in one of the local churches, she was going steady with an athletic tree of a guy whose name, I think, was Darrell Fast, and *his* dad was pastor of *yet another* local and, if I'm not mistaken, Pentecostal church.

So, I was about to be tracked down and executed by all the religious factions Lacey had to offer. If nothing else, I, and I alone, had contributed, or was about to contribute my life to rural religious reunification and ecumenical edification, with the possible exception of the local Catholic contingency who, as I had heard it, probably only wanted to fondle me, although it sounded tempting. It certainly was not enough reason for me to attend, I had already decided long before. The Protestants, on the other hand, were without a doubt after me and wanted my head. Thanks to me, they now had plenty to protest. Retribution was near at hand, I was sure of it.

There was no "City of Refuge" for me to run away to; truancy was the closest thing to it in my case. Only a few days left before spring vacation, after which I hoped the worst of it may be over, I rationalized, telling my mom the school had let us out a little early for a three-day workshop, or some lame-assed lie, was the only thing I could think of. She only bought it because after taking her up on an offer she had made a few days earlier, I cheerfully agreed to spend my next few days, and then my entire vacation, digging, splitting, pulling and burning the copious amount of Douglas fir tree stumps that infested our entire property on Kinwood Road, at the rate of fifty cents each. They'd made the offer months before, knowing full well I was far to lazy to take them up on it.

Every time I threw another stump onto the roaring bonfire, my folks exchanged worried glances, wondering where they would come up with the small fortune I was accumulating, along with the mountain of blisters and splinters to testify to my secret self-imposed penance. After two weeks of shoveling and chopping, regularly checking and soaking my axe head as I did so, my folks informed me that they'd never be able to pay me the hundreds of thousands of dollars I had earned while laying low, something I already knew, so I told them to forget about it—a statement that nearly sent both of them to an early grave. *Just wait until you get the bill for Claudia's nose*, is what I thought, silently, hoping they'd never know I had, in *art class*, mind you, rearranged a girl's face to resemble a Picasso.

By the way, did I somehow forget to mention that Claudia Kimble was not only beautiful, blonde, intelligent, popular, and deeply loved by Jesus, she was ALSO an identical twin? Oh, yes, Claudia had an identically beautiful SISTER, named Carol. Except now, they weren't twins anymore. Not when I was through with one of them, anyway. Let me just tell you something about myself right now. If I'm going to bludgeon a perfectly and previously handsome young woman into unrecognizability with a blunt wooden instrument, I'm not going to pick out a single example. Why no, I'd much rather go for a pair, maiming for life only one of the matched set, so that society can always compare and thereby see for itself what she would have looked like, had it not been for my artistically Olympic onslaught (think Ethan Frome). Also ending once and for all, any sibling rivalry arising from which one was the prettiest. I was there to settle that question forever. Carol wins. Claudia loses. Thanks to Alan, Claudia, much like Alan himself, is now doomed to the life of a troll; each for a different reason banished from the gaze of normal folks to go off and live under a bridge somewhere. Bridges, plural, certainly not the *same* bridge, that would be *too* cruel. Although there were no bridges in Lacey proper, there was a culvert under Martin Way that I mentally claimed for my own, where I knew it was dark and safe.

So, for the rest of the year in school, I did my utmost to remain as inconspicuous as possible, transferring out of art class into wood-shop, where I quickly proceeded to maim only myself. Wearing clever costumes, such as a tie and sport jacket, while also changing lockers and traveling alternate routes between classes helped, maybe, in my cowardly attempt to save my sorry, scared, scrawny—but never actually *apologetic*—neck.

For the last fifty-five years, whenever I've seen a lovely adult blonde head of hair heading in my direction, I'll to this day dart into the shadows of an alley, a darkened hallway, shrouded doorway or sleazy tavern to avoid any possible confrontation or eye contact. If unable to scurry off to any of those places—or under a nearby underpass, or worse yet, should I become trapped in some such place as an elevator with a female blonde, I break down and begin spewing and blathering forth a stream of compulsive nonsensical meaningless blanket apologies for everything I've ever done. Especially anything that in the most remote way may have involved a blonde female, real or imaginary. After which I'll scamper away into the underbrush and dingleberries underneath the closest train trestle until there are no blondes in sight. Only then will I slither out into the light of day to further inflict myself upon the general population.

* * * * * *

Claudia's nose was never really mentioned to me, anyway. And although I can't say for sure, whenever I drive over the old Nisqually Bridge, I glance down at the abutments where, more than once, I'm certain I caught a glimpse of a small patch of matted golden hair half covering the face of a frail gnome-like creature with a huge, offset nose skittering around amongst the undergrowth.

Because this unfortunate incident happened over a full half-century ago, I may also be mistaken about whose nose I broke; it may have been Carol's; I don't know anymore; in fact, I'm not sure I knew then, because whenever I heard even the slightest murmur of either

name, or if I thought I caught sight of either glisteningly golden—
Breck Shampoo ad—head of hair coming down the crowded hallway, I evaporated. But I'm pretty sure it was Claudia's. Either way,
I'm still a sorry fugitive with a sincere apology to offer; along with
two questions: Can Darrell Fast still swing a baseball bat like he did
back in high school? And, may I please be allowed to come out from
under this moldy old culvert?

6

EMOTIONALLY OVER ROTTEN

I was older than I care to admit when the following took place; by this time I had my second car, a '55 Plymouth. I'd bought it from my friend, Bob Richards, who would later also sell me his '63 Chevy pickup, neither of which I would finish paying for. I gave each of them back to Bob, in good condition with an apology and explanation of why I couldn't come up with the money. I was born irresponsible, shiftless and lazy; I did my best to stay that way forever. Eventually I would fail at this, too. I'm not really sure of what "crossroads" are in life or if we even know when we're in one, but it might have happened around this time.

Living alone in my tiny Hick's Lake apartment with no money to chase girls, out of work and not much to do (no T.V.), driving around at night was a pastime. A few times the old YelmOlympia Highway called. It's no longer the dark quiet country road, and lonely, it was then. There was this one old abandoned two-story farmhouse which maintained its own personal deliberation on whether or not to stay upright—or admit defeat and collapse. If it was the latter, I wanted to be there when it happened; to say goodbye. This old house looked much the same as the one in Andrew Wyeth's painting—"Lisa's World"— only in sad shape, dark and forlorn.

Sometimes in the rain, I chose to stay in my car and watch this house—my house—although I was not connected in any real way to it or this property, I had decided we had something in common and that it became emotionally somehow attached to me. A one-sided decision to be sure. I'd sit and watch a dark empty house and imagine former occupants and struggles.

And I'd wonder why I was doing this.

* * * * * *

A well-lit summer night once found me in the waist-high yellowed tall mixed grasses swishing my way around the dark looming structure of other people's dead memories. Lifeless, sad, mute glass eyes in moonlight stared at the young interloper standing in the dry wreath which encircled it, as if asking—"Why are you here?" to which I would say, "I don't know."

And I knew if those black glass flat eyes were asking, "*Who* are you ?" and "What do you want?" I had only the same empty answer, "I don't know."

It's beginning to rain. One of these dry deep summer rains with large loud drops which start out slow and then stop. I felt the change. The rain has ceased. It has barely sprinkled but it changed everything just now. I remember this smell. I recalled summers like this when I was a kid—not so long ago—when everything around me was bone dry and dusty, and when it began to rain. And how much I loved this odor. Much later in my life I will learn the word for it—"petrichor." But for now it is just a memory and I savor it as I walk around this hollow shrine, doing backstrokes in my own melancholia. Teasing from it its memories—summer droughts and not much crop—a son lost in one war or another—six children born upstairs and one still-born—birthdays, funerals in this parlor through the tattered paper shades. And I am crying and I know why.

Because I want to. I am saying goodbye. Not to a home that was never mine—but through it. I am emotionally "laying my hands upon" this house, so to speak, and "setting it free into the wilderness."

Now maybe this old wreck does not agree, but over these visits I've decided I am this house. And this house is me. This frame of sticks is saying goodbye to anybody who will stop and listen. I am simply, finally, I guess, saying goodbye to my childhood.

The heavy dank air is still filled with the nostalgia-soaked welcome smell of what I will later learn is a known chemical of its own—"goesmin." But I don't need a name for it; why can't it just be a memory? Why do these people gotta show up and ruin everything?

I left that night knowing I probably would not be coming back. I did say goodbye. I needed to get my ass a job. Maybe it was then that I *began* to be hurled into adulthood and responsibility. But I doubt it—in fact I still fight it.

Couple years before this, a lotta classmates were pinpointed before graduation and hurtled towards Viet Nam. Now there's some kinda adulthood.

When it came down I don't remember, but I do recall many times driving my roofing truck past that small forgotten farm and watching it go by, and smiling as I did so.

Over the years as I witnessed the remnants of structure slowly steep into eternity, I realized the simple truth in the old adage, "You can't turn back the clock." More than once I waved at the rotting remnants.

Its purpose had been served.

7

SCRUFALUMPUS HOPALONG KERPLOP

On the occasion of a rare and somewhat recent north wind polar ice storm we received, unbeknownst to us, a desperate visitor. He would remain unnoticed for well over a month. When paw prints repeatedly appeared on the toilet seat in our antique shop's bottom floor of three, we assumed we had been adopted by another "possum." When Wes, who worked for us, told us he'd seen a skinny filthy white cat down there, we grew quickly concerned. We knew he'd been living on fish food near our indoor Koi pond, for over a month (not Wes—the poor kitty).

For the next three weeks Cheryl, my wife, ever the cat savior, was down there with her morning coffee and some more kitty treats and fresh water for yesterday's now empty bowls. Then she sat on an oak twenty-four-foot backbar and talked in a high-pitched, singsong voice to an invisible hungry scared hidden refugee.

Then, one day, he appeared: skinny, filthy and injured. His right "arm" was evidently broken. Not only abandoned, he had been severely abused. We would later deduce he'd been kicked—hard—more than once. By a male, because of his reaction when an unknown pair of shoes would enter the room, coupled with a masculine voice. He would dive for cover. But right now all he could do was hop and hobble over to the food Cheryl had brought. He ate and drank while she sing-songed in her kitty voice, telling him it was all going to be okay—bad stuff will never happen again. When he'd finished eating he would disappear among the inventory. She'd keep on talking sweetly and slowly withdraw up the carpeted ramp to go home, happy to have seen him.

It was not long when the day came, after she'd said her routine morning "goodbye," that, near the top of the ramp, he called her back. A mournful pleading—"Yeeoooow!"—*puhleeze* come back— supplication. Of course she complied.

They met halfway down the ramp when he came hopping up and head-butted her extended hand. Both in tears. Although I was not there, I can say now it was at that moment, my wife the cat whisperer won for us, the three of us, one of the most prized moments of our lives. And for the three of us, possibly the most rewarding.

For weeks he hid up on our top floor, under a mass of empty showcases on wheels, the ones we used for antique auction displays. Eating, drinking and using the littler box. He'd come out for Cheryl *if* no one else was around; the time now had come for *me* to be his hero. I soon learned how happy he was to risk his life for...*turkey* meat! Throwing a piece near the edge of a showcase wheel to watch a quick white feline arm snatch and gobble. Soon a yellow green eyeball would leer out from the darkness in anticipation of a replay. The next one caused him to crawl out from under, grab the meat and slither back to safety. We did this, he and I, for maybe a month.

Soon enough, though, he'd limp up to my chair and "kerplop" his dirty broken white carcass over onto his left side waiting for a treat and some attention. Because he was in such condition, I named him "Scruffy." Formally, Cheryl said it must be "Scrufalumpus." It was official—everybody was now adopted. Scrufalumpus Hopalong Kerplop was family.

* * * * * *

Within a couple years he thought he ran the place—all three floors. When six o'clock came—closing time, and someone outside approached our front door to come in, Scruffy would rise up off the stool or showcase he'd been napping on and would start growling at them. As in, "Ya just better get the hell away from that door, buddy. We're *closed!*"

But he was a lot of fun. One of his most favorite games ever was "fetch." Not like a dog and a stick—other way around—*we* "fetched." He had a favorite small red ball that he'd go get if we were down on the bottom near the ramp. Pretty soon, here it comes, and if we missed it, we had to find it, to toss it back up to him so we could do it all over again.

And he would be thrilled. He found other ways to order us around also, and he did it silently. I don't mean he was quiet. He *talked.* He did not whine. And this was a cat that'd *had* plenty to complain about. No, he pushed us around other ways—literally. When finished with a hot bath I would come to our carpeted two-step drop into our living room. He was no longer a dirty-white cat. We had moved him into our apartment in the back of our shop. He took that over, too., and he was *pure* white.

At the bottom of the two steps, he'd stop me, look up into my eyes and put a paw on my knee—and push me down! Scruffy would keep his hand (paw) on my leg until I sat down on the steps and put my warm dank bath towel on my lap for him to curl up on. And he was happy!

Then there was "Bug." Bug was a small stuffed—grinning from ear to ear—ladybug type toy that he *worshipped.* We couldn't get anything done. *This* toy he did fetch—over and over—nonstop, until someone passed out from fatigue. Or if Bug got lost behind something, he'd find Bug later that night and put him in my shoe or drown him in Scruffy's water bowl. His punishment for getting lost, I guess.

Another toy was a small ugly leather doll which he dearly loved.

Scruff was patrolling the middle floor of our store, with Cheryl in the lead, when she was stopped by Peter, one of our vendors. He owned the "Ugly Doll Shop."

"Hey, Cheryl, I thought Scruffy might like to have this –" WHAM! *and it was gone*—"doll."

As soon as Scruffy had heard his name, he was airborne, and that doll was down the road! He'd snatched it right out of Peter's hand because he heard him *say* it was for him. This cat understood *everything*. "Wow! I guess he *likes* it."

"Sure looks like it. Thank you, Peter. But don't ever say something like that if you're holding a turkey sandwich; you might lose an arm."

* * * * * *

He understood every word, every nuance of ours—he learned to *spell*!

In our apartment we have an upper floor which includes a greenhouse on our roof and a sliding patio door out to our roof garden.

Whenever I was on my way upstairs from the kitchen area I'd alert Scruff. "Scruff! I'm goin' *up*. Wanna go UP?" And he'd *streak* over to the stairs, put one paw on the bottom step, and freeze, wide-eyed in excitement, waiting for me to go up and get him some *grass*— his favorite.

We know he loved his grass. But we think he loved this, his "little ritual," more. And God help me if, after watering, I *forgot* his green treat! He wouldn't let me back in. I'd be greeted with a death glare and an immovable cat. I'd have to go back out and find some.

The very word "grass" became problematic. If Cheryl said, in a whisper, "Gonna go get our boy some grass?" to me, chances are *I* didn't hear her—I don't hear whispers so good—but Scruff would come tearing into the room in eager anticipation. So we started spelling it out. "Didja get his G-R-A-S-S- today?"

Within a few weeks, it was more like "did he get any G-R…" and there he was, sliding up to us on our oak floor, eyes ablaze.

And as far as his voice-word recognition goes, I tested it from time to time. If I said his name, barely in a huff *or* in conversation with someone, he'd light up. He could be in another room talkin' to a house finch on our windowsill and he'd stop to go find out why we were gossiping about him. And if he didn't like what he was hearing or if we weren't paying enough attention to him, one of us might get swatted. He was feisty and we loved every minute we had with him. Even when he'd bite us.

It took us awhile to realize if you stroke them *too* long, repeatedly, in certain weather conditions, the static electricity may build up in their fur and shock them. We may not feel it—but *they do.*

He would also punish us for being gone too long. Once every two months we went to Europe on a two-week antique gathering-buying trip. He was *sooo happy* when we came home. Within a couple days, though, he might be in my lap, everything fine, and he'd bite my wrist. He'd just haul off and bite me. When he let go, he'd sit there and glare at me—punishment for being gone so long. He had warned us before we left by peeing on our luggage when it was near the front door for the next morning's departure. This is how he rolled—or is that—"ruled"?

* * * * * *

My favorite "shop" story was the time he, as always it seemed, occupied the top of a large glass showcase near the cash register, bathing in peace. By this time he was no longer afraid of most *all* customers—he was nice to everybody—but Scruffy did not suffer fools.

Enter my friend, Dave Meconi.

Dave is a really good guy, but he is well known for making the wrong decision every time he has a chance. Today would be no different. Dave is at our place paying his tab for a recent antique auction where he'd purchased more than a few quality pieces of *old* pewter—something he knew nothing about and still does.

Scruffy has one rear leg pointed straight up while he bathes some of his more intimate features, exposing his nice round fluffy tummy. Dave stares down at the peaceful sweet bather and says, "Ohhh, nice kitty. Boink." And pokes him in the tummy. Dave giggles as Scruffy stops bathing, slowly lowers his leg and lifts his gaze up to meet Dave's.

In slow motion, Scruffy—eyes locked onto Dave's—rises to his feet. Up until now, Dave, as usual, was unable to conceptualize the gravity of the situation. As Scruffy takes his second slow "birdstalk" step toward Dave, I see Dave's dim flicker of intelligence ignite into a solar flare. "Uh-oh," is all he says, and he takes off running into the auction room, knocking over chairs. Scruff is right on his heels. Dave is screaming like a little girl, "Call him off! Call him off! That cat is possessed! Eeek!"

Now they're back in here, Dave is white as a sheet.

"Get 'im, Scruff! Kick his ass!" and off they go into the auction hall again. Satisfied, Scruff relents after awhile, and Dave comes back in, wheezing, face no longer white.

"Hey, Dave. I got a question for ya."

"What's...that?" leaning on a showcase.

"Didja *learn* anything?"

"What the hell's wrong with that cat?"

"People like you."

The taverns are full of gadabouts making merry this eve and though I may press my face against the window like an urchin at a confectioner's, I am tempted not by the sweetmeats *within. A dram in exchange for the pox is an ill bargain indeed.*

8

My Thoughts on the Plague

Not the one in 1665; the one we're enjoying *now*. And first of all, if they had just *called* it that in the beginning, exactly what it is, *a plague*, even the *dumbest* American might have sat up and paid attention and followed the rules! But we didn't wanna scare people too much, so we called it a *pandemic*. Sounds like a new pizza crust or something. Nobody knew what a pandemic was. Okay, show of hands—who knew? Look around and—see? Nobody knew. *Plague?* Oh, yeah, *we all knew!*

I'm only writing this because I'm the last one to do so. All of 2020 was consumed with people stuck at home sharing the great American pastime: feeling sorry for oneself. I feel sorry for myself no matter where I am. So I guess I'm lucky.

People are afraid of vaccines because they heard they can cause infertility. IF ONLY! Let's hope they do! Now you can't have any kids? Go get some kids out of the foster care merry-go-round; you know, the kids nobody wants? They'd love to live in a nice, educated home like yours. You know who has their fingers crossed that vaccines cause infertility? ALL OTHER LIFE on this earth, as well as EARTH itself! Me, I've had all four vaccinations, and two vasectomies. My wife wanted me to get a "booster" for that, too.

The highest paid person in Washington State was paid 3.5 million dollars a year! To coach football. And he gives that up because of his religion. What religion says you can't get vaccinated and coach football? In any case, *just change religions*! For 3.5 million a year I'd become a Catholic and join the Vatican choir as a castrato; I'm already halfway there. People don't get the shots because they don't want to be told what to do. Your wife has been telling you what to do for years and you do it, because you have to, if you KNOW WHAT'S GOOD FOR YOU! But a lot of them don't and now they're sick. These are the idiots in the ICU clogging up our hospitals. REFUSING the correct treatment because another moron on the internet told them it was a joke. A hoax, or a trick, or they're after a body part. They also believe the earth is flat, the moon landing was fake, Elvis is alive and the Clintons ran a child sex ring out of a Washington D.C. pizza parlor! EVERYBODY knows it was a donut shop! So, there they are on the gurney: "I changed my mind. Can I have my vaccine now?"

"No."

"Why not, I don't feel so good."

"It's too late."

"Can I just have the booster then? I feel really icky."

"No. We need to save these for people with brains. I'm putting this mask on you now. We're gonna try to get you through the night."

"Oh, no. I'm not wearing that. It'll make me look dumb. Plus, I don't know where that's been. Can I have some candy?"

"No. Well, you're probably going to choke to death tonight anyway…"

"PAMELA! We've just lost three more doctors, fifteen nurses and thirty-two more technicians. Can you go to the other ward and roll all fifty-eight of the covids onto their left side and change their diapers? When you come to any cold ones, here is a stack of post-its. Just stick one on their nose, okay?"

"I was hoping to go have some lunch when I was done dealing with this fool."

"Pamela—you had lunch three weeks ago; what is *he doing?*"

"He's sucking his thumb. Because forty years ago his mommy told him he was special. I'll be right there after I tell him he'll be dead by morning. I don't really have an appetite anyway. I can't taste anything."

9

Battle of the Little Bighorns

The Game Department:

Now, these people work in mysterious ways, as well as in mysterious reasonings. When first in the antique business I heard stories about how some *new* law had been passed to protect our bald eagles. To the point of enforcement that the feds were going into museums and confiscating historic native chieftains' headdresses and *burning* them! An eagle, *sacred eagle*, which had been dead for the better part of two centuries! Begs the question: who committed what crime?

Three years ago, I acquired a pair of *very* large storage units from a former customer of mine, Richard Spence, through his out-of-town daughters. They included a pair of "Little Bighorn" mountain sheep; one shot *by* Richard in Arizona and the second in the Sierras. All legal, with "papers," which I had. Both were in full form, and in calm repose, each with a separate "rock" which the taxidermist had constructed to hang on the wall for each sheep to "rest" on. And that is how I displayed them, on each one's rock, on my wall. Although I don't like hunting or taxidermy, they were cool. Beautiful, even, in unnecessary death. Maybe he ate 'em, but I doubt it.

So a guy named "Jeff" comes in and wants to buy one. I told him one thousand each, but he hasta take both. Said he'd talk to his wife. (First red flag—most women hate taxidermy.) When he called back a month later, he said she now agreed to *both*. (Second red flag.) Arrangements were made for a pickup, so we took them and their "rocks" off my wall.   When he showed up for pickup I had the receipt made out in advance, "$2,000 cash for two artificial wall hung *rocks*, $1,000 each." And I read the receipt to him, with the words "just to clarify, I am selling you these 'rocks,' *only*. These two critters are free to go. I will put them outside on the sidewalk and tell them they are free to romp in the ocean or wander the hillsides, but when I close my overhead door I don't care where they go. I will have set them free."

He sat on the hood of his small S.U.V. and with a slight smile and a twinkle in his eye, handed me a roll of hundreds. I gave him his paperwork. I'm sure he was "wired."

"Can't take'm now; couple weeks maybe." (Third red flag.)

When two months pass, I am by then positive that this was a "sting." At least I have the two grand of taxpayers' money. I had heard about these "stings" before and that the process goes on for about two years and $20,000 before you are released back into the wild. With a record. Of course I understand the logic behind penalties for trafficking in any endangered species, but you are *not* allowed to sell or barter any part of *legally* obtained game animals, either? Why? You *can* own it, but not sell it. I think you can pass it on in your will. Or take it with you.

On a quick sidetrack, I recently heard on N.P.R. that last year two dozen species were just removed from the endangered list. "Well, that's good news," I said into my morning coffee cup. Then Scott Simon, host of "Weekend Edition" added: "The reason? They're extinct." Another month goes by and even though I have explained this "sting" thing to everyone here in my camp, including our cats, *somebody* here phones this Jeff guy to come get his stuff! Unbelievable! I used to tell people that you have to be brain-dead to work here. My wife made me stop saying that, so I've changed it to "*half* brain-dead ´ as an upgrade. They now view it as a promotion.

I was unaware they had invited the devil back into the house until, while conducting a small estate sale across the street, I see Monica helping "Jeff" carry a Little Bighorn sheep to his car! Now I expected the worst. A "transaction" had been finalized that did indeed involve the actual animal, *not* a rock. I readied myself for handcuffs, fines, lawyers, news scandals, and bread-and-water. And a bad haircut. Never mind, I already have that.

That was a year and a half ago and I still have my Little Bighorn buck and two fake boulders. No handcuffs in sight, yet. But they *have* tried. I put a "not for sale" sign on the big boy in case they sent in another "agent" to "buy" him *again*.

About six weeks ago a dude asks Monica if I was willing to trade him for *other* mounts. He said he had a lot of it to trade. I'll just bet "he" does, and I know where "he" gets them; from other confiscations. She said, "I don't know. Talk to Alan." Remember, you *cannot* barter (trade) wild legal game, so this was another trick. "They" have not called.

* * * * * *

My wife was running the store years back when a mixture of people: old lady, college guy, middle-age mom and a construction worker milled around the shop. Each one left their card—they were *all* game department.

I think I'll just make soup out of him.

10

Interruptive Personality Disorder

Whether we are born with the natural ability to distinguish right from wrong, and good from bad, or moral acceptability from that which is unacceptable and carries with it a lengthy prison term, I don't know.

Whether we learn through the guidance of parents, peers, parochial or private educators, police officers, priests or through just plain living what is and isn't right, is a matter for people more qualified than I to address.

These types of philosophications are far better left to folks with credentials in those areas, people who know what they're talking about. I seldom am able to keep track of what *I'm* talking about, let alone be expected to follow along with what someone else, especially someone of virtuous high principle, is saying; and with good reason. The first simple fact is that I have most likely already made up my mind whatever it is they or you are about to say is probably of no useful interest to me. I'm already thinking about what I'm going to say next; therefore I have no time or power of concentration left over to pay attention to what you're prattling on about. This is also why I'm likely to interrupt you, so that you can just save your breath.

If, for some inexplicable reason after I've made a point (and after I had interrupted you three times) determine through your partial and incomplete sentence that you agree with me, I'll look surprised and ask you to repeat yourself, allowing you to finish this time. By the end of your response, if it still seems to align with my opinion, grievance, outlook, intellect, fantasy or ranting, I'll immediately congratulate you for being so well informed and intelligent. If, in the course of conversing with me that ever happens, which isn't very likely, you should feel and act highly honored for displaying what I have recognized and judged to be superior cognitive brilliance. The chances of this taking place, however, are slim, not because you might think I had earlier doubted your intelligence before we'd even met or spoken, which is something I would never do, but because *nobody* ever agrees *with anything* I have to say. This brings me to the second reason for my conversational inefficacy and ineptitude.

My head's always been too full of other stuff. I've been distracted by *something else* my entire life. As a child it was bad enough. By the time I became a teenager and was already worn out from dragging into adolescence all the unsolicited emotional baggage that came with it, I had by then lost any ability to form clear formative and constructive thought.

Impure thinking?—Now *that's* a different matter.

After being approached, when I was younger, by someone of unquestionably very high moral fiber, and then asked the question, smugly but concernedly, "Son, are you troubled by impure thoughts?"—a fair enough question given my daily agitation, my destructive impulses, and my blossoming facial blemishes. Oh, and the secret constant collaboration my hand had with my...but he couldn't possibly have known about that...so I answered him. "*Troubled* by impure thoughts? Well, no. Up till now, I've always rather enjoyed them. I mean, that's the whole point, isn't it?"

From all appearances it seemed as though my honest response was as unexpected as it was unwelcome. I'm telling ya, the sour look that some people get on their faces whenever I speak has always annoyed me; you'd think I'd be used to it by now.

So, as if natural impurity of thought coalescing with my congeniality accrued personal moral standards of questionable value and crudity of virtue weren't enough to drive me to interruptive distraction, the problem of properly expressing myself when in the company of others was yet another issue. I've never had any trouble expressing myself when I'm alone.   Because my grandmother had lied to me when I was small, about what she considered to be my superior intelligence quotient, thereby misleading me into believing that I was a clever kid, the harsh reality that I was, in actuality, dumber than a box of rocks, hurt my feelings. Initially, though, my extremely well-honed coping skills of adaptability and blame shifting had helped me to persevere and to finish my first day of school in the first grade, but I was deeply scarred; however, don't think for a moment I didn't scar them as well. Forever I would carry the permanent newfound knowledge that I am stupid—the majority of my teachers, wives, friends, police, imaginary friends and children have been more than happy to help reinforce this conclusion.

Believing, as a prepubescent child, that my contribution to any given conversation would likely be ignored or, at the very least, discounted as infantile babble, I spent most of my time talking to myself, my desk, or to the little face and stick figure I'd drawn on my palm. (Her name was Tammy. And she developed breasts *waaay* earlier than most girls. We still keep in touch.)

Then one day, while shopping with my mom, salvation arrived in the form of a single statement made by one of the pair of ladies sipping coffee near me at the downtown Olympia's three-story Woolworth's lunch counter; overheard by me while I finished my cherry milkshake. As I listened to my mom arguing with and swearing at a clerk halfway on the other side of the store, one lady said to the other, "Yes, that's right, all profanity is, is a weak mind trying to express itself." And they nodded to each other in apparent concurrence.

What in livin' hell are they talkin' about? I asked myself in disbelief. *Is that right? How come I never knew about that before? So there's hope for me yet!* The entire school system and life itself had been effectively teaching me that I was indeed weak minded. Therefore, I qualified. *"Well, that's for me."* I silently hollered to myself, slamming down my glass. "Dammit—Milkshake's all gone. Well, I'll be go-to-hell!" Swinging my leg off the red swivel barstool and standing upright, facing away from the bar and into the direction of my mom and the escalating skirmish she was inciting with the clerk and store manager, I hitched up my pants. "Guess I better go'n see what all the pissin' n' moanin's about." Not bothering to look at the coffee klatch pair of lady linguists on my left, I had just used up my entire vocabulary of curse words, such as it was at my young age. So I had no more saucy, provocative, or profound speech with which to confound their afternoon coffee chatter. Swaggering away I heard their heavy cups clatter onto their thick saucers' underplatters.

As sad and pathetically unprincipled as my life was back in those days, I suppose I should at least seek comfort in the consistency I've maintained over the last seven decades. Still void of virtue, value, morals, principles, and any ability to decipher right from wrong, I have at least added a couple more colorful words of cursedness to my slurred speech. Therefore, I'm more conversationally fluent and expressive. Mostly, though, our cat has been the sole recipient of any of my expressions of color. Lately especially. Our cat has been interfering with my sex life.

That damn cat.

11

SHRUNKEN DRAWERS

A few months back, after liquidating a sizable estate–collection by public auction on the premises, in the nearby town of Ruston, fortune smiled upon me. Briefly.

In the alley behind the large old house where we had held the estate auction, my wife, while parking her car, ran over something. After exiting her vehicle and preparing to lock it, she looked down at what she had crushed; this was not something she normally would do. Usually she just keeps right on driving in these cases, not looking back; sometimes she'll turn the radio on way up to drown any wailing or loud threats of retribution.

Upon inspecting the space just behind the driver's front tire for the wheezing remains of whatever slow-witted, small creature had been stupid enough to get in her way, she saw a rather large orange plastic pharmaceutical container semi-squashed into splinters. Still full of pills while held together by its RX label, she was able to pick up the once round and full container that was now sorta flat. The myriad of blue pills within were also all squashed up and crushed like, themselves being in splinters. Reading the label—"Viagra," she quickly inserted the flattened orange package of fantasy into her purse and later presented it to me (I refuse to even imagine the circumstances surrounding how a jarful of Viagra came to be lying in the alley in the first place).

Over a year before, we'd had a blistering first-time experience with the "Big V" as Cheryl now refers to it. We were in Mexico at the time, vacationing with our dear friends, Ray and Deena. While skipping the principles involved in acquiring a prescription related to the very same pharmaceutical and after consuming exactly the correct amount of cervezas in order to get my nerve up, I purchased one pill. I now know they manufacture them in twenty-five, fifty, and one-hundred milligrams. All the nice lady at the small wharfside Puerto Vallarta had for sale that day was the full-scale one-hundred-watt size pill. Looking back on it—I should have waited until Cheryl and I were alone to take it. Months later, Deena's exact words were: "Jeeze, we all could'a just camped under that thing."

At this point, I realize that the reader may be fearful that I have meandered away from the story, or that I have forgotten what it was that I was originally talking about, which is only partly true. But please don't wander off while I'm talking to you. I hate that. Anyway, I'm simply making a point: the point being that I'm just as pathetic and morally squalid now as I was when I was a kid.

So these misshapen and broken up little shards of magic blue pellets were thrown into my nightstand drawer, which has a crack in it—like me, it too is an antique and therefore has shriveled up and shrunk in some places, especially in the joint, right inside the front of its drawers.

Occasionally, I'd find out that small slivers of my little blue pill stash had dribbled out through the crack in the bottom of the drawer. I knew this because there they'd be, on the brick floor of our bedroom, or kicked by one of us, or the cat, clear into the living room, lying on the dark blue carpet. Sometimes I'd find one on the white tile of our bathroom floor. Or maybe on the kitchen's oak floor. Always grateful to have rediscovered my partial pill of pleasure each time, I'd snatch it up and gulp it down.

Only after several months of scouring the floor for blue tidbits of erectitude did I realize that I still seemed to have most of them in my drawer. My original supply had hardly dwindled; just then the cat came tearing out of the bathroom.

Now, I don't know about all cats, but I do know that when our cat finishes her business in our bathroom, where her littler box is kept, she celebrates by sprinting throughout the whole house at the speed of a cheetah—about seventy miles-an-hour. Then she sets about trying to shred our eight-dollar-a-yard carpeting. That's when I noticed a good-sized chunk of one of my pills stuck between her toes. And there's another one—lying on the rug! I promptly swallow the loose one as I always do, then I dive for the cat in a futile attempt to dislodge my partial pill. While calling down profanities on her because of the new toothmarks in my thumb, from my vantage on the floor I'm then able to distinguish, even with my poor eyesight, a couple more of the bright blue gravel-like pebbles on the bricks. Laying in the same path the cat had taken when streaking out from…the bathroom…and her…litter box…?!?

If, for any reason you should find yourself slipping into the depths of utter depravity as have I, and if you have a legitimate prescription for Viagra, and if you have bad eyes and shaking hands—or a crack in your nightstand drawer—and if you own an indoor cat, there are two brands of cat litter that you must never buy. Unless, of course, you're looking forward to groveling behind your cat while ingesting crystal kitty litter. Fresh Step™ and Tidy Cat™ both exhibit the same exact brilliant blue coloration as the real thing.

Now, whenever the cat pees and then roars around the house sprinkling little blue boulders, I get a sudden erection and take off after her while shaking my fist and swearing out loud. That's usually when my wife intervenes.

"Stop cursing at that kitty! And just what the hell is your problem anyway?"

Now then…what was it we were talking about, just before you interrupted me?

12

Town Without Pity

By 1972, I had opened a small and modestly successful antique shop on Olympia's Fourth Avenue hill. I stole the name, "Sanford & Son," from Redd Fox, while also stealing one of his best lines: "We buy junk and sell antiques." By now I was addicted to not only the antiques themselves, but the buying and selling of antiques and "junkin'" trips, which was what we called them back then.

My first few junkin' trips hardly radiated more than twenty miles from my home—or the jobsite where I was supposed to be installing a roof. Sliding quietly off the rooftop and slithering down the ladder and away in order to feed my addiction to antiques became a common occurrence. One minute I'd be hammering away, the next I'd be stealthily driving my truck off the jobsite and down some winding back road, looking for my next fix. Maybe a nice, old farmstead that had seen better days; with the possibility of procuring for myself the relics contained within the embraces of its outbuilding, unpainted and weather worn walls. Plus, it looked like it was gonna rain anyhow. I never did like pounding nails in the rain, and in Washington State, it's always raining or getting ready to rain, so everything worked out just right. 'Cept maybe for the owner of the house I should'a been protecting from the elements by installing the roof I'd been hired to.

The thrill of discovering a barn owned by an agreeable farmer willing to part with old furniture and whatnot that might have been "ratholed" since the Depression became also quite addictive. The adrenaline rush far offset the negative rantings I'd have to face upon returning to the worksite.

Back in the early seventies, many times I scored nineteenth-century cast-iron cider presses, nickel-plated cookstoves, oak ice boxes, sets of Victorian wicker and loads of whoknows-what that I packed home from "work." Before long—an eternity of three years—my love of antiques and my antique finding "highs" overshadowed my adornment for purple fingernails acquired from misapplying my roofing hammer to my left hand's digital extremities. My excitement from discovering a nice, shiny, domed-top trunk far exceeded the thrill received when "housemaid's knee" cause one of my lower extremities to swell up to a nice, painful, shiny dome.

Besides, it got to the point that I was making more money by accident, while out scrounging around for junk, than I could make on purpose when actually working for a living. It was clear which had to go. My business cards and checking account heading evolved from reading "Cedar Roofing" to "Sanford & Son." My junkin' forays blossomed to include other counties. Before long, I was rooting around in cellars and attics on the other side of the Northern Cascades, the Olympic Mountains, and eventually over the Rockies. The whole bloomin' country was now unsafe from my full-blown, full-out, take-no-prisoners, antique raids as I charged about the hinterlands, demanding to dig around in some old geezer's out-buildings full of what I knew was the coolest crap ever, just waiting to be unearthed. If you tried it nowadays, you're apt to be met with, "Naw, we've already got that up on Ebay. We got elebenhunnert dollars for the last one."

But, in the early seventies the whole country was a bowl of cherries, and don't be fooled: even then, no matter where I went, I ran into plenty of people that knew more about antiques and their worth than I did, or do now, for that matter. But that didn't stop me. I'd learn from my mistakes, stick to what I *did* know, and forge ahead. My ever-widening circles coincided with my ever-increasing knowledge gained from further travels and experiences while rampaging about the countryside, attempting to rape and pillage those who knew less than I did. It wasn't easy. Sometimes I had to travel a fair distance to find someone more ignorant than me. More than one stubborn old fart told me to keep on traveling—straight on into hell. And so I would. I can safely say that I've been to hell and back several times.

And that's got me to where I am today. Today I know just enough about a great many categories of antiques, genres, periods, styles, and forms, countries of origin and the related fair market value of all of the above, that I qualify for a few free frequent-flier first-class roundtrip tickets to hell and back. I know just enough about just enough stuff, that I'm constantly in trouble over something. Usually it's because I thought I knew more than I actually do. You'd think I'd learn. My wife is almost always the first person to clue me in on my intelligence void; daily, and in regard to a wide variety of genres and categories. She's happy to point out my obvious lack of knowledge in how to operate a microwave, hot water knob, steering wheel, and turn signal or toothbrush, to name only a tiny portion of things I know much less about than I only a moment before thought I did. She also sends me on regular trips off into hell, where I'm obligated to find my own way back. Or not.

Back when I was still in the infancy of my antiques career, though, when I was still fascinated with what I thought I knew, and was willing to apply my recently-absorbed newfound, deep-seated wisdom about antiques into a practical means of thereby acquiring for myself wealth, I hit the road. Occasionally, the road hit back.

The small town of Ritzville, Washington, just an hour or so west of Spokane, and hours east of my home base and my small antique store, held the path of asphalt that chose to slam me around. Often. Truth be told, almost every time I tried to skitter past Ritzville, hopefully unnoticed by the sleeping beast that must have been dwelling just below the highway asphalt, a just waiting, giant imaginary hand would reach up out from under Interstate 90 and nonchalantly whack me into the ditch. Or the median. Or into the clutches of a greedy gaptoothed grinning garage mechanic. Ritzville had a magnetic vortex about it, not unlike the hungry mudpuddles that had so regularly fed on me as a child.

Feverishly, and with a nice vanload of kitchen queens, round oak tables, pressback chairs and hotel dressers scored from second-hand stores and flophouses in Spokane, I'd try to sneak past. Soon, with a steaming radiator and a blown head gasket—at one a.m.—I'd coast up to a dark garage to sleep, and wait for my regular and ritualistic Ritzville road repairs to commence.

Returning from North Dakota with a Chevy one-ton van full of goodies, while towing a loaded, single-axle trailer with only one tire and six inches of snow on the ground isn't an imagined scene in my memory. Dragging the meteoritical glowing memory of a naked and squared-off, ground-down wheel hub for miles on I-90 in the middle of a frozen night is something not forgotten. Although below freezing, the pavement was dry and sparks still flew in all directions and vividly illuminated the white night world outside. And just so you know, semitruck drivers get all pissed off and honk at you as they roar past; many flash their lights at you, as if you didn't know you were dragging an erupting Mt. Vesuvius down the road in the dead of night. In the dead of winter.

But if I stopped, I'd freeze to death. If I left my trailer full of oak secretary desks and oak dressers by the side of the road, it would be empty when I returned. Nothing left to do, I figured, but to drag my one-wheeled spark-spewing *extreeeemely* loud trailer the rest of the way to Ritzville, where they could empty my wallet. The length of sparsely traveled interstate that I scraped and drug my melted hub along escapes me now, but I think the tire came off about halfway between Spokane and Ritzville. If you want to know exactly how far it was, you'll hafta go measure the groove down I-90 yourself. Around twenty-five miles, I'd guess. After being constantly assailed by quirky circumstances or whatever the cosmic phenomena were that magically cropped up to seize up my engine's cylinders, wheel bearings, cooling systems, or trailer axles, I tried to outmaneuver and outwit Ritzville. That caused all hell to break loose; actually this next time it was my empty *trailer* that broke loose.

It was a new trailer; new to me, anyway, and I was in a hurry to go to junkin' in Montana. It was summer. Midweek and midday. I was alone and in a mad dash to get past Ritzville, the town without pity, with an empty van towing the empty fourteen-foot-long flatbed trailer. Roaring quickly past in the feeble hope that the giant hand of roadside woe wasn't aware that I was there, in broad daylight and doing eighty-five, I made the mistake of checking my rearview mirror. If I hadn't done that, I would never have known that my trailer had come loose and was somersaulting down the freeway and flipping end-over-end in the dry median. Naturally, my next mistake was to stop.

The dust cloud my frisky trailer had raised during its acrobatic interlude only briefly alarmed a couple of motorists that had been fortunate enough to watch the show. Relieved to be alive, they roared past while I rolled my gymnastic two-wheeler up to the van's trailer hitch for re-attachment. How it is that the trailer landed on its feet, unharmed, impressed me. But the gray-haired, fifty-something Washington State Patrolman that roared up and screeched to a halt was not impressed. So I asked him if he'd seen the whole thing, thinking he couldn't help but be impressed. After all, the tongue of the trailer had gouged up big chunks of eastbound Interstate asphalt, and there'd been several airborne full flips—sideways and lengthways— but he wasn't having any of it, even though I told him that it was a stellar performance of roadside carnage few people get to see.

"No, son, I didn't see it. I didn't have to. I was five miles east of here, but I knew all hell had broken loose. The dust cloud you raised could probably be seen clear from South Dakota. I thought it was a train wreck or herd of stampeding cattle." I liked this "Stater." He talked like we were in an old Western. I liked him up 'til when he inspected the big garfs in the asphalt, took my driver's license information, and told me the Washington State Department of Highways was gonna bill me for the holes in the highway.

I thought about asking him what he thought of that twenty-rive mile stretch directly on the other side of I-90 from where we stood. The twenty-five mile section that had a groove all the way down the right-hand lane. But I didn't.

For months after that junkin' trip, I dreaded the arrival of a big fat road repair bill that never came. The anguish and dread I suffered, expecting to see a Department of Highway restitution tally equal to the cost of financing the entire U.S. Olympics Gymnastics entourage scraped a few years off the end of my life, but those are the crappy years anyway.

And that wasn't the last time the town of Ritzville carved off pieces of my vehicles, my wallet or me. Even now, when boarding a plane at Seattle-Tacoma International Airport, I'll ask the flight crew to tell the pilot to avoid flying over Ritzville. That there's this giant invisible, sucking vortex that's probably caused by the earth's crust being too thin at that spot, which allowed Earth's magnetic field to escape too rapidly, which cause big metallic things, like cars and trucks and trailers and planes, too, mostly likely, and probably anybody with a metal plate in his head—to end up in the ditch.

13

Slideshow

We used to "do Brimfield" every May and September. We quit doing the July shows because of the heat.

Brimfield, Mass., hosts one of the largest and wildest pop-up antique markets a person can handle. On both sides, acres deep, on Highway 20, a few miles from Sturbridge. One traffic light. Goes on for over two miles. We loaded up many semi-loads of 40' trailers over time. Cheryl and I were "camped out" at night under our truck behind the "Treasure Chest Café" as usual. The mosquitos there are used to feasting on *us* and we didn't want to deprive them.

We had bought a load of stuff, a 20' "U-Haul" load, from a strange old cat in Worcester, Mass; the junky load was *old* but it was all in such bad shape we called it "furniture from hell." That way we didn't have to be ashamed of it. And you can sell anything at Brimfield—for the right price. Whatever cash we generated we converted into better pieces to send West. And that's somewhat of a version of how most people do it; arbitrage, I think it's called.   I   purposely misspelled a "Furniture from Hell" sign with a couple of "F's" and "N's" backwards. And no, nobody *fought over* this crap, but it drew them in because of the clever advertising. Some folks just want to prove you're wrong. Sort of "Ya know, I betcha this idiot here doesn't even *know* what he's got!" (And *that* is another major Brimfield mental driver—looking for the "sleepers"—and trust me we *ALL* suffer from that one; one of the biggest reasons we're there.) So they spent so much energy trying to convince themselves they're smarter than me, eventually they give up and buy a three-legged chair or a small dresser with one drawer missing from us and leave, dragging it across the dead grass. I'd holler, "Next!!" They were on their way home to fix it up and make a bundle. Ever try to come up with a matching chair leg or build a new-old drawer? Yeah, good luck on that.

Cheryl and I had made the mistake of over time, meeting and fraternizing with a dealer couple across Highway 20 who were from *Slapover*, Arkansas. They were funny and we were fun loving. But we were all *very* busy and overworked, as well as underprivileged; spend a week there and you'll know what I mean.

While there at Brimfield we didn't see a lot of one another that week—just as well. I've always referred to Brimfield as a "concentration camp without fences." Though I realize that's a stupid thing to say. [Yep. ED.] Their names were John Anderson and Pam, I believe. Staying there is not for the faint of heart. But we always made the best of it; you have to. You signed up for it.

Many, many things happen during the usually *nine* days I would spend there and when it's over you are shot. You are fatigued. But guess what? The human psyche is weird. Once it's over, you're so relieved, you just might want to quietly (or maybe not quietly) celebrate. You find some new inner juice.

Everyone is gone from our lot at the "Treasure Chest." We are done, but waiting for our truck driver to show up much later, around midnight Sunday to pick up our load. Along with our 20' U-Haul, I had my little Mazda pickup, both of which we would drive back to drop off the UHaul.

It was reasonably deserted and quiet in our neighborhood, most dealers on our side of 20 had packed up once the heavy rainstorm started. It rains *here*, where we live, but these sudden storms that crop up back East? Holy cow.

The first time I ever drove in Upstate New York, we were heading toward "the City" on I95 when one of these storms broke, and it was biblical. We passed hundreds and hundreds of cars, trucks and buses which had pulled over to the shoulder while this monsoon raged on. *ALMOST* the *only* cars on the thruway were wearing plates from Washington, Oregon or British Columbia!

On one side of the Treasure Chest's building itself was a long string of now empty "rentatents," white, which were connected together and open inside with no inner walls; outer walls only. This long white worm was on a nice slope down to Highway 20.

Cheryl and I ducked in the doorway up the top end of the slope to witness the cascading river which was rolling on down the clear "Visqueen" floor inside. Daylight was all but gone and the dark clouds overhead hastened evening. The rains still came.

I don't know whose idea it was, or if we just looked at each other and said the obvious: "Slip and slide!" I angled my little, and now nicely washed, pickup, with headlights on, pointing down the length of the canvas tent. We hadn't had a shower for a while, and the nice warm rain bath was a real treat.

Sometimes one of us would make it, buck naked, down to the bottom, a hundred feet or so, to smack into the canvas wall at the bottom. But mostly we were end over teakettle or flat on our back with feet in the air. Cheryl mostly mastered it by sliding sideways, surfer style (these dang California kids). This went on for two hours, while I also had my radio on. Every once in a while, a "Beach Boys" song would be delivered, just for us.

The next morning, before leaving, we went across the street to say goodbye to the folks we knew over there. Noticing that most of the folks in their one very large open-sided event tent had not done much packing out the night before, I asked.

"John, you guys are usually cleared out by now. Did all that weather last night hold you up?" I also noticed most of their trucks and vans backed into position for loading out. They were all busy doing that now.

"Well, yeah, Alan. We were slowed up by that storm, but most of us just plain gave up once it got dark; we decided to spend another night."

"You guys had lights over here."

"It wasn't that; we just couldn't get anything done over here. We couldn't concentrate."

"Why's that?"

"That would be your fault. You and Cheryl." When he proceeds to explain to us why they were distracted we understood. It hadn't occurred to us what the running, slipping, sliding, colliding, and falling nude picture show would look like from where they were, magnificently "projected" onto the tissue thin canvas screen. Not that that would have stopped us. Evidently they were enjoying the free backlit live naked puppet show so much, they fired up their barbeques and cookers, opened their coolers, popped popcorn and partied.

* * * * * *

Not long after, a year or two later, I was working my "booths" at the "Portland Antique Expo" in Oregon when someone sneaks up behind me and pinches my butt—hard. I spun around to see John from Slapover with a big grin on his face. Antique dealers are well-known to travel.

When I got home from that show, I told Cheryl what John had done. She laughed and said, "Do you know how many times he pinched *my* ass in *Brimfield?*"

"...Umm . . No. You *told* me all those bruises were from the slip-and-slide." All I know is that if *I* grab her ass *I* get slapped. But if you're a good-looking young guy from "Slapover" it gets overlooked.

14

I SEE NAKED PEOPLE

I realize your opinion of me couldn't get much lower than it is right now, but I'll keep trying; so here goes: I'm a nudist.

I always thought I was—I never liked clothes—but when I grew up that type of evil was not encouraged, far as I knew; but then I didn't know much about anything else either. I have the report cards and testimonials from friends to prove it. [That isn't true. He didn't keep the report cards, and he doesn't have any friends. ED.] So I didn't have the courage or opportunity to act on my inclinations. Until one day about ten years ago I was listening to my local KNKX N.P.R. radio station. The honey-throated Robin Lloyd comes on and she—the D.J.—says, quite erotically, "Well, if any of you listeners are going hiking in any of our national parks today, be prepared to see naked people. Today is the summer solstice and nobody will stop you."

WHAT!!!

I was scheduled to run the shop that day and when I got the news on the radio I was stuck in the kitchen doing work my wife should have been doing. So that was that. But just wait till next year! OOOYAH.

One year later we were ready to go. By we, I mean me, Jamie—a young blonde bartender at my local bar, Nicole—a server, Dave Robertson—the town drunk, and a dude named Alex.

We have a nice park here, close by over on "Dash Point" in Tacoma; the park carries the name "Salt Water Park" with nice hills to climb. Serene. It was a wonderful and liberating experience; we had a great time. [First of all, they got arrested because it was a state park, not a national park. Alex was a dog and Nicole kept her clothes on. Jamie had to stay up in the woods getting interrogated, while Nicole, her dog, and the two naked idiots got sent down to the parking lot after being told to go pick up litter. ED.] So we were ready to do a lot more of that.

Jamie, who by now was a sworn-in nudist, like me, located a local nude resort in Shelton, a fifty-minute drive away, called "Arcadia," after an ancient Greek culture without clothes but with lotsa wine, grapes and sunshine. (All the beaches in the Greek Islands are clothing optional. I go as often as I can.) So we started going there once or twice a year. My heavenly-bodied young wife won't go to any of these places—she says she has "nothing to wear." Yep, you can go ahead and work on that one all you want. And I wish you luck. And it was during one of my visits to "Arcadia" alone, sitting in the pool relaxing in the sunshine, when a young couple I had met there a year before were talking about the Portland, Oregon "naked bike ride." Their names were Dennis and Janie and it turns out I had watched Janie grow up on Kinwood Road in Lacey, Washington—same age as my oldest son—small world.

Then they started talking about Sauvie's Island in Portland, on the mighty Columbia. I'd heard about the nude beach down there but never had plans to go—too far; but, "Tell me more about this bike ride with TEN THOUSAND naked people?"

So they did. Then Janie says, "That's always on a Saturday; the next day you should go to Sauvie's Island."

After a little more information gathering, which included the knowledge the bike ride was only three weeks away, I made my decision. Then I asked for more information on the Island.

"Gate six," she says, and Dennis confirmed it. "Gate six." Because, they told me, the other gates down to the water are all for normal people unfettered with debased aptitude and attitude towards having their nether regions revealed to the heavens. Gate Six.

I don't think anyone can truly envision 10,000 naked people, with or without wheels, not really. And I shall make no attempt to describe it here.

Well, maybe just a little bit. It is a sea of pulsating carnality jiggling, bobbing, bouncing and throbbing in front of, and all around you. And that's just the women.

Saturday, at the ride. The "ride" itself doesn't start until just before DARK; the preceding six or seven hours are invested in getting everything "tuned up," the amplifiers, acrobats, yoga sessions, body painters, clowns (lotsa naked clowns), snake charmers, bartenders, dispute resolutionists, Kamasutra instructionists and women trying to figure out where their husbands went. And areola readers (that's where I come in). I kept an eye out for a person or two to corroborate "gate number six" being the correct one for the following day's frolic on the Island. I found more than a few *very evenly tanned* personnel who each one said, "Gate number six." I went to sleep that night confident in the knowledge that I had not been *lied to* about where the nude beach was! Yes, it has happened before, "Hey, Alan, go pee on that wire. The electricity is off; it's okay." Off I drifted in peaceful slumber, visions of [Censored. ED.] dancing in my head.

Sunday morning June 28th—cooler, cloudy but beautiful. Coffee, breakfast and then a serenely utopian ride through hydrangea farms as well as other floral farms over actual country roads. Later, I came to the levee and saw concrete steps leading up to and over it. I looked for any numbered "gate" type signs. Seeing none, I asked a carful of folks unloading their picnic gear and other stuff how we know which gate is which.

They pointed at the concrete access and told me, "It's stenciled right there—number one." Oh. Cool. Only five more to go.

Every few hundred yards there'd be another. Four, five, six! Here we are. It's a quarter after ten and cloudy, so I didn't expect a ton of local nudists for awhile, and I was right, knowing intuitively that most all of them that had been involved in yesterday's bacchanalia were resting their sunburned genitalia and would be there later. When I crested the levee and surveyed the beach and river (did I tell you that the bike ride is also a pub crawl? It isn't over until two or three in the morning). I wasn't surprised to see maybe only eight or ten people present, none naked, yet.

I was disappointed at all the litter—lots of it—SOLO cups, broken beer bottles, cigarette butts. Last night's kegger, maybe. So, because I've nobody to talk to, look at (or away from) or annoy, I thought I would get good ol' gate number six spiffed up. I got a huge black "Husky" trash bag, the body-sized ones—think "Dexter"— from the van, along with a couple cold ones. (No, not bodies; beers.) The reason I was sad and disappointed to see the litter all over the place was that Janie and Dennis and others in the pool that day had told me how proud they were that they kept "their" beach spotless. So I went to work.

For an hour or so I picked it up, the beach litter, then took a break standing in the cool water near an orange bikini that never once put down her phone. It was hot, the weather AND the bikini.

People are gathering, still no takers, not on the, you know, the naked front. When I crossed up and over to deliver half-a-ton of other people's party trash to my van and grab another bag and refreshment, an SUV, driven by an obvious grandma type lady was offloading a LARGE cooler full of enough stuff for her, a couple teenage weaklings, and grade-schoolers. At least she was TRYING to. I said LARGE cooler, right? I offered to help—she was grateful—kids were useless. Keep in mind, though, it's still early—I'm the only naked person there so far. Kids all ran down to the river and did what they're supposed to do, run away from a naked man. Gramma offered me a sandwich. I declined, said I've got work to do. She seemed disappointed.

I went down to the water near the orange bikini—she did nothing but take "selfies" the entire time I was there—and I stood knee deep in the river, cooling off and ready to fill another trash bag. I finished my beer and started off onto the half of beach and litter I hadn't covered. Now it's getting hotter.

At 1:15 in the afternoon, I have picked the beach spotless and I'm nursing a cold one while again cooling in the Columbia, when a nice Hispanic gentleman comes trotting down to river's edge, near the orange bikini and me with my sack of garbage, and huffs out, "Senoruhmister-uh-sir, this beach 'familia.'"

Now I've been to enough nude beaches to know that, yes, many if not most, are kid friendly. It was cool in Maui to see little kids and TEENAGERS of all ages surfing with NONE of the shackles my generation grew up with.

And that is what I told him, "It's not unusual to see kids at nude beaches." The girl in the orange bikini stopped taking selfies, rolled over with her back to us and began jiggling. Choking on a corn chip, I figured.

"No. No. No. These is not a nude beach."

"WHAT!?!" I hollered. That bikini appeared to be loosening itself from all the spasms the girl was undergoing while choking. I was ready for a Heimlich maneuver, but first: "Yes! It is! I was told by ten or more people that the nude beach is "GATE NUMBER SIX!!" I was not buying into his bullshit.

"Si, Si, Si. But it is not these gate six. Is 'nuther gate number six—one, maybe two miles more." And he points upriver.

"What! There's TWO gate SIXES??" That girl doesn't have much longer—I can hear her fighting for her breath; I better untie that bikini. "You're telling me that the nude beach is miles away from here?"

"Si." And he was gone. I was soon to follow. I stood there nervously crushing my nearly FULL can of beer, paralyzed while scanning the, by now scores, of people of THIS gate six beach.

They were all smiling—as though they'd seen enough.

I stuffed my can into the big sack of their garbage and began to drag it up the sand when the bikini rolled back over—face smeared with tears and mascara—she musta got that corn chip down—and she purrs in a sultry voice, "Goodbye—and THANK YOU for cleaning up our beach." Big smile.

Being too speechless to utter anything other than "Anytime," I left, dragging my second heavy sack of Sauvie's souvenirs. (I wasn't smart enough to say, "The least you can do is come with me.") Gramma and a few other women waved goodbye as I drug my sorry sack up to the steps.

I was about a half mile away when it dawned on me, she wasn't taking "selfies" at all—she was videoing ME. FOR THREE HOURS!

MY gate six beach is also known as "Collins" Beach. A nice walk through the woods to the sandy beach later, there it was, with naked people everywhere. And I can guarantee you that the best laugh they had that day was when I told a circle of maybe eight or so what I had just done! I watched as the story was relayed up and down the river. I heard the reverberations of laughter.

There wasn't a speck of litter anywhere.

15

THINK, MAN, THINK!

While it may be true that men are from Mars, I have my doubts as to whether women originated from Venus. Or, if they did, the women I have known must not have remained on the planet rumored for its love and tenderness for very long before they broke camp and took up residence here on earth.

I say this because of the torment they love to put us poor men through. And, from what little I know of it, from personal experience anyway, few of the attributes and compassionate qualities of the Venusians are exhibited for any great length of time by any of the women with which I've been in circumstance, or maybe I just bring out the worst in them. I do realize that, other than lifting heavy stuff for our wives, *begging for sex* is the *main reason* that we men were put upon this earth in the first place, and what would an earthly relationship be if not for *that* most natural, healthy and time-consuming lifetime endeavor?

Being subsequently and repeatedly turned down, ignored, told to go fix her a sandwich, rub her feet, or to "just get the hell away" from her, it's an important building block in the very foundation of interplanetary bondage. That's the arrangement, and for the most part, all men accept it, and we plan our days and lives accordingly, with ill towards no one; we cheerfully accept the fact that we've come this far for the explicit purpose of being little more than exploited.

The true anguish comes in other less satisfying and more frequent forms. Just as one example: I've heard of loving couples who've spent years together in what some might term relative harmony; then, simply because they can't agree on the *colors* of paint with which to decorate the walls of the rooms of the house they're finally able to buy, end up in divorce. Begging the question: what *in hell* were the *guys* in these situations thinking? They should have learned, years before, that this is how these lovely creatures supposedly from that planet Venus, feed. They feed on our mindlessness. Having our own actual opinions, attempting to *reason*, worse yet, arguing or refusing to repaint the same wall for the *seventy-sixteenth* time does nothing more than interrupt, and then accelerate, their feeding. These men forgot a simple basic: we don't know what we're talking about! Never talk back; she's gaining nourishment in knowing you are willing to be miserable for her. But, if you balk or chafe under the strain and she becomes aware of it, you have done little more than interrupt her as she peacefully grazes away. Now you're really gonna suffer. Her voice becomes increasingly shrill and piercing as you keep making more, yet more trips to the paint store. "This is NOT teal! Teal is BLUE! Not GREEN! And this is NOT a TRUE oyster white! Have YOU ever seen an oyster THIS color?" Reminding her that you're from Iowa, and that you've never actually seen a real oyster will do nothing more than cause her to dive in for another snack.

Though that was simply one petty example, it demonstrates what most men have eventually learned; at least the men that possess even the smallest amount of personal remedial survival technique. It also serves to demonstrate the degree of subserviency to which most of us men are willing to submit ourselves in the slim hope of a warm meal and a roll in the hay; although not necessarily in that order; ALL Venusian expatriates are aware of this and capitalize on it. Any intelligent, red-eyed, mouth-breathing, knuckle-dragging male whose

DNA can be traced back to that planet having the same coloration as his corneas will also concur. And, while I'm busy ranting on the subject, let me give the best advice EVER to any and all men wishing to survive interplanetary cohabitation: NEVER, under any circumstances, BE RIGHT! If, for some reason, you have found yourself in a situation where you've actually *won an argument*, as unlikely as that sounds, you'd better check out Uranus, and if there's anything left of yours when she's done with it, book the next shuttle. The only way to survive a catastrophe, such as accidently winning an argument, is to *immediately* begin apologizing profusely, and at the speed of light. If you're quick, and convincing enough, maybe, just maybe, she'll allow you to maintain residency on this planet, where you'll enjoy the privilege of further serving her. There will be a probationary period of time, however, during which you will *not* be allowed the luxury of groveling for sex.

All of which brings me to my actual point. Our garden. Actually, it's our roof garden. We are urban dwellers, living behind and above our three-story downtown Tacoma antiques shop, with what I'd like to think is a rather cozy garden on our roof, that I've created and nurtured over the last twenty-five years or so.

Just recently, I've been informed by my darling diaphanous divine enchantress, while doling out to me my daily directives, as well as my meds, that I'm no longer allowed in the garden. Unless of course, there's some huge containers and giant trees to move around to where she likes them. Otherwise, I'm banished from the garden which, the better part of three decades ago, with the aid of two dump trucks full of dirt and gravel, four more trucks loaded with trees, bamboos and exotic plants, shrubs, barrels, tubs, containers, railroad ties and old split cedar rails, as well as an entire lumberyard full of new cedar for decks and fencing, and with the assistance of a small army of winos, crackheads, and my own kids (back when they were still dumb enough to occasionally work for me) I installed what many people consider an inner-city rooftop garden to rival that of Nebuchadnezzar's back in ancient Babylon. Except mine doesn't hang. And I did it all when the building department wasn't looking. They did eventually notice and then spent the next four-and-a-half years trying to hang *me*.

The reason I've been cast out of Eden? Aphrodite's exact proclamation was that I "don't know what I'm doing," a term that she normally saves for our brief, but I've always thought satisfying, sexual encounters.

She's right, of course. I am indeed horticulturally challenged. I wouldn't know a delphinium from a Dalmatian—I do know, however, that once you plant Dalmatians in your garden, they take over and you *cannot* get rid of them; their roots seem to go everywhere; and they'll choke the living daylights out of everything else. But my crimes against nature I now find out include murder. Every single plant, tree, flower, and ladybug that has croaked in the last twenty-five years, did so because I "murdered" it. It's because, I now learn, I "don't even know how to water them." Although I've somehow kept ninety-nine percent of them alive through my inferior watering capabilities, I've now been relieved of that chore. Oh, and *every* single weed in *every* single planter is there because, in her exact words, I "planted it," evidently on purpose, and just to piss her off.

The latest wedge of discordant divisionary planetary misalignment, however, is all over earth. Not the planet itself. I'm speaking about dirt. In case you're wondering how I got all of the truckloads of trees, lumber, tubs, rocks, and most earth onto my rooftop, it was accomplished with the help of a huge boom-truck. I rented a large flatbed truck with a giant hydraulic extension crane. Since then, I've added several more tons of soil, one one-hundred pound bag at a time, by carrying them on my narrow and pathetically sloped shoulders up an extension ladder; the only hydraulics involved being supplied by my knees. Both of which are already quite sore from—yes, you guessed it—begging for sex. But back to the dirt. Or, more specifically, back to our roots. And to be even more specific, the roots of my pet weeds, and the precious dirt that clings to them—the dirt that my wife, in her supreme celestial wisdom, refuses to shake out from the clumps of roots whenever she goes about killing off my favorite weed patch by uprooting them and hurling them off the roof into the lower midheavens where they land, sometimes harmlessly, on the busy sidewalk far below. My uprooted and freshly-slaughtered weeds take with them on each toss an average of twenty pounds of my hard work, in the form of nutrient-filled, vintage, fertile topsoil.

Some days, while she's busy killing off one of my finest half-acre crops of quack grass at the speed of a commercial potato combine in high gear, I'm on the other side of the building, crawling up a tall ladder with a sack of soil, regularly purchased from our very pleasant, always happy to see me, local dirt bagger, otherwise known as the Home Depot Garden Department. The following is a brief synopsis of the "reason" (and I use the word every so loosely) that I've poured tons of blood, sweat, tears and money into purchasing *extra* dirt:

Me: "Why in hell are you throwing all that dirt off the roof?"

She, who once ruled an entire continent on her home planet of Venus: "It's full of weeds, dumbass."

Me: "But the weed's roots are clinging to mountains of perfectly good topsoil."

She who rules: "So what? And it's *not* any good anymore; it's worthless; it's tainted."

Me: "With what?"

She: "Well, *weed roots*, for one thing. Haven't you learned *anything?* Good lord, you are a moron!"

Now, it is at precisely this point where I have a serious choice to make—do I attempt to explain to her that dirt is dirt, and that I'm getting too old to drag dirt bags up a three-story ladder, and that she could shake or hose all of my sweat-soaked hard-earned soil back into the otherwise quite thriving eco-system that I somehow conceived, created, and have in my unintelligent blithering male stupor, maintained all these years—or, do I say something clever and sarcastic; something she may actually understand, but that will also greatly enrage her because of the fact that through the sarcasm she may sift the slim possibility that I could have a point. So I say something like, "You know what? You're *right*, honey; *I just read* something about exactly that! All the farmers across America have begun removing *all of the dirt* off their land, once they see weeds start sprouting. Then they *truck in* acres of new dirt, from the closest *certified* dirt farmer, *one bag* at a time!"

She who feeds on the soft tissue of those from other, weaker planets is thinking: "Hmmm. I'm beginning to feel a little bit hungry; wonder what's lying around I could gnaw on…"

He who should have known better than to mouth off to a creature that is not only universally superior to him in every way—except, possibly, direction finding—realizes that she hasn't fed on his anterior parts for an hour or so, raises his eyes heavenward, searching the afternoon sky for an early glimpse of the red planet, where he knows there is peace and tranquility, whereas once it had been known for discord and war, there is none, mainly because there's *no women there*, there's nothing left to FIGHT OVER or ABOUT! Suddenly, innately, his will to live kicks in, and he coos, "Wow, you look *good* in those overalls; have you been losing weight *again*? Let me go make you a grilled cheese sandwich. Hey, I'll betcher toes hurt from all that weeding. How about a foot rub?"

<h1 style="text-align:center">16</h1>

THREE WEEKS ON THE ROAD
ACT ONE

The following story concludes in Ritzville, Washington, at the Perkins Cake and Steak restaurant on Interstate 90. (You, dear reader, will suffer much before seeing that conclusion. However, you won't suffer much as we did back then. And it won't take three weeks, either— unless you are a real slow reader.) Danny Woollett and myself are only five hours away from returning home after being three weeks on the road. Sitting there in a booth, I'm eating my apple pie and ice cream, while Danny's reading a cheap paperback. Everything is just fine.   Three weeks earlier, when we left Lacey, Washington, to fill my twenty-foot truck and twentyfour-foot trailer with a fine load of antiques from Buffalo and Jamestown, New York, as well as everywhere and anywhere in between, everything was fine then, too. The three weeks and thirty-eight-hundred-mile meandering odyssey in between was the part that wasn't so fine.

My Chevrolet two-ton box truck with hydraulic lift-gate ran fine. It had been deaccessioned from the recently defunct ONE-WAY-RENTALS NATIONAL truck fleet and was in good shape—only five years on the road. My newly-acquired tandem-axle trailer was also slightly used; barely broken-in actually, being as how it was only a couple of years old. That would soon change. In the next three weeks that aluminum-covered trailer would age dramatically. So would we.

Within the last month or so, after re-acquiring both truck and trailer from my Walnut, Iowa, "partner," Olin Chapman, Danny and I in that time had readied the rigs for departure. My "partnership" arrangement with Olin had consisted of me providing the cash and truck necessary for him to "junk" in the Nebraska-Iowa area and then deliver the goods to my monthly auctions at the Thurston County Fairgrounds in Lacey. We'd split the "profits." Except, after a while, there wasn't any. So, I now had the truck and trailer back in my care. We left Lacey around eight in the morning heading east, over the Cascade Range. I cringed when we cruised past Ritzville, Washington, approaching Spokane, and soon the Idaho border. Ritzville, for once, let me slip through unscathed—probably because Danny was driving. With Ritzville behind us, I scrunched down for a nap. The dry eastern Washington climate and summer noonday sun overhead required that the windows be at least partially open. Danny had napped earlier when I stopped for gas in Ellensburg, where I checked the truck's body fluids. Although I knew my truck didn't burn oil, I thought it odd that the dipstick read two quarts low. Danny snored away while I added two quarts and off we went. Somewhere just on the other side of Spokane, maybe Coeur D-Alene, Idaho, Danny got hungry and evidently the *truck got thirsty*. I tried to remain asleep while he checked under the hood. Soon he was shifting gears and we were heading into the Montana foothills. Because we'd almost always drive all night on these excursions, we'd also always try to stock up on sleep. And Danny was like me. We both could sleep anywhere. I could hear Danny rattling plastic food wrappers and guzzling from his halfgallon milk container.

A hundred-and-fifty or two-hundred miles later it was my turn. Danny disappeared in search of the service station's restroom while I plugged the gas nozzle into the truck's filler neck. Opening and climbing under the hood in the afternoon Montana summer heat gently fried my sleepy eyeballs. I plucked the simmering dipstick from its oily orifice. *What the hell? We're low on oil again!* I dumped in two more quarts and Danny reappeared with more road food. It seemed to be getting hotter out while I bore east, and Danny dealt with his eats. Before long he was asleep again, with his chest covered in Cheetos.

Negotiating hills, even in an empty truck of this size doesn't make for good gas mileage; especially if there is a trailer involved. We stopped again, Danny gassed up while I went inside, this time foraging for snacks and soda pop; it was hotter'n hell outside and we were all thirsty. I bought us more future dental misery in the form of candy bars and two cokes; we hit the hot Montana highway.

We'd just finished our candy and pop and were peacefully soaring along at about seventy in the searing heat when the curtain rose on—Act One.

Smoke and flames began billowing out from under the truck's cowling and hood. Danny jammed on the brakes and pulled onto the shoulder. I was standing on the running board with the passenger door open, waiting for the truck to slow enough that I could jump off and run around to open the hood. I held onto the doorjamb with my left hand, my right shoulder against the door itself and my right hand held our fire extinguisher—which was of course, a half full (or half empty, if you like—have it your way) square half-gallon of warm milk.

I hit the gravel running and by the time I was in front of the smoldering grill in position to unlatch the hood, Danny had scrunched the truck to a stop. I quickly set the carton of Darigold milk down in the gravel next to my feet in order the facilitate the use of both my hands, which was necessary to handle the heavy hot hood that was heaving horrific noxious huffs of black smoke and orange flames through the space between the hood and fenders. I could hear crackling and crisping coming from under the cowling, sounding similar to a deep fryer.

At the same moment I threw the hood open, Danny had run around the front of the truck to join me, he being a fireman and all. And that's when he kicked over our fire extinguisher. I bent down to snatch up the milk carton just in time to see the last couple of glugs gurgle into the gravel and into my sneakers. I moaned in resignation, stomped on the carton and straightened myself upright to watch the bonfire—which was now inexplicably out…. !

The fire hadn't damaged anything. It seemed to have contained itself to the top of the engine block in the ravine of the big V-8, inside the vee itself. And it was over with. The paint in that area was non-existent now and the insulation under the hood was coal-colored, but the spark-plug wires, carburetor and other thingamajigs were fine. We looked at each other, shrugged our shoulders and climbed back inside. We started the engine up and watched as it idled. Everything was fine. Off we went.

Curiously enough, we were able to drive for another seven or eight hours—approximately two more tanks of gas—before the truck's engine decided it was time to initiate a flamethrower again. Only this time it was the middle of the night, and we didn't have the contents of a Darigold fire extinguisher to kick over and pour into my by now very nasty-smelling sneakers. Bypassing motorists couldn't see the smoke because of the inky Montana night, but the flames were visible throughout half the Bitterroot Mountains. More semis and more horn blowing. And then the fire was out again. Again, no explanation why it was out or why it had started. As soon as we saw that everything was fine, we left the side of the road in full confidence that we'd make it to New York; regardless of how many times we caught our truck on fire, or why.

Somewhere around Billings, Montana, and the South Dakota state line, Danny and I compared notes and were able to pinpoint the problem. The problem as it turned out originated with the dipstick! Both dipsticks: the oil dipstick that was not the correct equipment needed to obtain an accurate crankcase containment of engine oil in my truck, because it was from *some other* vehicle and was too damn SHORT to register oil! AND the stupid-ass dipstick "partner" of mine that had stuck it in there. So, *each and every time* Danny or I was either asleep or in the bathroom, the other of us—the driver—diligently checked the oil and subsequently *added two quarts* to an engine that didn't burn *or need* any more oil. Our engine was drowning in extra engine oil. At some point—whenever it became especially heated or overworked, such as when pulling a long hill for example, some of the extra oil began boiling out the filler cap and onto the engine block—where it eventually ignited; then it would continue to burn until it fried itself dry.

Knowing that the source of our spontaneously combustive eruptions of heart-pounding, downshifting, brake-stomping panic attacks was actually a chain-smoking financially vacuous quasi-partner sipping his endless cup of coffee down at the town café in Walnut, Iowa, was more annoying than thinking something was seriously wrong with my engine! I wanted to go to Iowa and kill him! (As time would prove—had I done that very thing I would have saved myself thousands of dollars.)

On the other hand, over the next few days, whenever my truck decided to spit up a halfquart or so of boiling oil onto itself and then light it on fire and belch black smoke for a while, it was no longer a mystery, so it was easier to ignore. Easier for us anyway—Danny and me. It never got easier for the passing motorists. Smoke and fire originating from moving vehicles gets people into a mood all its own. If we made the decision to stop and lift the hood, the worst thing that happened was the downtime. Time was wasted watching and waiting for a fire that would soon burn itself out anyway—while we stood there, hood up, nonchalantly eating a sandwich and calmly watching the sun set over the Utah or Wyoming badlands, the semi-drivers that we'd passed at the last rest stop, truck stop, or on the last steep uphill grade, blew by us—horns wailing. After the fire died out, we'd try to make up for the lost time. Each time my empty rig passed a big rig on a steep hill the driver stared us down with a look of what appeared to be mixed disbelief, disgust, irritation, and something that resembled pity—but not quite. My horn didn't work. Well, it did work; it's just that it sounded more like an angry bee trapped in a jar.

So after awhile, whenever we caught fire, we just kept driving. No downtime. Most of the smoke went off to the sides of our truck's windshield and therefore didn't interfere with our ability to see or drive. This proved to be a lot more entertaining for us than running around in circles, screaming and kicking over milk cartons. From where we sat it was hard to tell if driving while on fire—compared to being stopped whenever we were aflame—was more or less entertaining to anyone we passed, because we couldn't see too well out anything other than our windshield. Our vision was greatly obscured by a thick black even blanket that hung—and seemingly flapped in the wind—alongside the truck cab side windows. Our hearing, however, was not obscured; horns were still blaring. I'm not sure even today what the connection is between smoke and horn honking; but there is one. Soon the overactive oil pump that disengaged the extra oil onto the overheated engine block released enough that the seventy mile-an-hour fire tired, and it once again grew relatively quiet along Interstate 90. We did have to listen to and answer some stupid questions, though, while standing over the urinals of several western state truck rest stops.

The question was first asked shortly after our initial fire, and if I'm not mistaken was asked by one of the many CONSOLIDATED FREIGHTWAYS drivers—*corn flakes* they were called—on the road because of the big "C.F." logo: "Where you boys headed?"

Now, both my vehicles—truck and trailer—had current Washington license plates on them. So from where we had left was obvious, but when I told him where we were going, he looked amazed. And doubtful. Then, when I told him that we hoped to return, not only with the same truck and trailer but with both of them loaded up with antiques, he grew incredulous, somewhat disdainful and mildly annoyed that I had accidently just peed on his boots. One or two differing versions of the same conversation were had for the first two or three days, as Danny and I pointed the blackened grill and hood of my two-ton Chevrolet toward the rising sun.

After that, nobody bothered asking us much of anything regarding our destination. Ever.

17

Three Weeks on the Road
Act Two

By the time we'd driven all day and night for a couple of days, and as our eyeballs swirled around in the sandy sockets, grinding noisily away at what some onlookers might've mistaken for alertness, we were somewhere in Wyoming. Where I don't know.

I do know that we were in the middle of what would be our seventh—and last—engine compartment fire. The engine had finally purged itself of all of its unwanted viscosity; the last of it was burning away as peacefully as a billowing Viking funeral boat on its way to deliver the deceased to Thor or Valhalla. Or whatever it is on the far shores of the Great Divide. Danny and myself, with our eyes the same color of dying embers lying at the base of a spent funeral pyre just stared straight ahead, and catatonically awaited the eventual flameout of our fiery chariot, when there suddenly seemed to be more honking and blaring than normal outside the driver's door window.

Weakly, I rolled my window down to be sure. As the last of the deep-fried oil on the engine's vee simmered itself into oblivion, the black smoke turned blue, a sure sign that the fire up front was dying. When the stream of smoke thinned more yet, I was able to see the faces in the car next to me. They were frantically screaming, honking and waving at us as I drove. With the pedal still to the metal, I politely waved to them, nodding my head in my now customary fashion and smiling, as if to say, "Yes, we're on fire. I know. We're always on fire. It's okay." "No! Behind you! Your trailer!" Not exactly what I expected to hear.

Now assuming our trailer had caught a glob of molten flaming gear oil or some other pyroclastic chunk of fiery debris and was somehow afire, I took my foot off the gas and attempted to focus my glowing red-coal eyes into my mirror and down the side of the truck into the near-distant geographical past.

In the mirror I saw, not fire, but a familiar replay of sorts, from what some folks might take to be an old Western. Off into the sagebrush there could be seen either a cattle stampede—or an unfolding train wreck of some kind. One thing was for sure; all hell was once again breakin' loose behind me. In the middle of all the dust and swirling dirt, uprooted rocks and uptorn sagebrush, I caught a glimpse of the twenty-two-foot-long runaway aluminum-covered wagon that was once connected to my truck.

A convoy of three or four semi-trucks with their trailers still connected zoomed on past, politely pulling into the left lane as they did so, airhorns blasting, while I stopped my still slightly smoldering truck on the right-hand shoulder. I heard their horns—in concert— fade into the distance ahead of us. We walked cautiously back to survey the train stampede. With the reddish Wyoming dust settling, we saw that our chucked wagon was still upright and sound, appearing as if it was a sullen and angry bull amidst the stand of brush that had slowed it, happy, though, in its newfound freedom to be peacefully grazing away in a newly discovered pasture. Defiantly, it seemed to stare up at us as if to snort, "You ain't seen nothin' yet—come on and get me."

After extracting the now benign hollow trailer from the meadow of Wyoming sagebrush where it only briefly grazed, we hooked it by its muzzle once again to the hitch of my truck. As we shifted gears away from the small open rodeo arena behind us, Danny and I had a brief conversation over the ever-so-slim possibility that there could be a repeat performance. We quickly agreed that the problem lay not in the hitch, which was only slightly mismatched in ball-size to the coupling, nor in the fact that we didn't have a *real* safety chain like normal-wussy people would have; the problem was that there wasn't enough *tongue weight* in front of the trailer's axles, so the tongue was bouncing up and down too much. And that was also causing our nylon rope, a.k.a. safety chain—to wear out, hence, the resulting sagebrush stampede. We agreed to fix that when and if we remembered to.

Of course, within the next tank-and-a-half of gas we forgot, and before long we were able to watch as a twilight dusk of another lovely Wyoming sunset framed the dark silhouette of a bucking and snorting trailer stampeding a swath through sage and scrub-brush, passing us on our right as it did so. We stopped and simply secured it by snuggling it up with more nylon safety ski-rope. Somewhere in that stretch I swore I'd buy a nice heavy cookstove or something to stick up front in the trailer to offset the erratic slamming that our hitch was suffering. I soon forgot to do that, too. Three times the Wyoming wilds got to see a huge silver-covered rampaging trailer stamp and snarl its way through the chapparal—and desert-brush while rolling over prairie dog villages in search of freedom. Three times we subdued the wild beast and snugged it back onto the back of my big green and white lead beast.

The logo of the now long-gone One Way truck rental people was still painted on the sides of my truck—three large cartoon elephant figures—joined together by their trunks and tails—single file. One large papa-type elephant was in front; hooked up to and followed by a mama sized pachyderm, baby derm behind. All three of them were smiling. The name of the company had wisely been painted over or sanded off—or something—I don't remember what, but the happy little elephant family was allowed to remain together, hitched up to one another, forever. Completely the *opposite* of my truck and that damn trailer. As I walked the length of the truck's box to climb back in behind the steering wheel, I reached up and slapped the baby elephant in the face.

"YeeeeAAAAAOooom!" went the eighteen wheels of a passing Kenworth, "FRRT"—"FRRT" went the two short blasts from his air horn after he had.

Over the last couple of days the frequent and familiar sound of an air horn passing us by had seemed to change somewhat. The first time that we'd caught on fire, the loud lone intrusive blasts seemed only to signal irritation and a clear judgmental negativity on the part of the horn blaster. It had almost sounded like a firm admonition on the part of *real* truckers that we'd just better not mess up *their* territory—*their* highway—by abandoning any ugly burning hulks on their horizon.

Now, two days later and after we'd been on fire seven times and had seen our trailer break free to romp and roam all over the Wyoming landscape four or five times, the blasts were shortened bursts. They didn't sound angry anymore; two or three more *short* blasts. The kind that as kids we used to get passing trucks to emit for us—for entertainment—by holding one fist up in the air and jerking downward twice on an imaginary handle or something, which would somehow universally evoke a couple friendly toots from the driver. (Who knows what that gesture would evoke from most maniacal semi drivers we have on our highways now.) I opened up my right fist; it was slick and oily—just like my hair—from slapping that elephant.

There was grit mixed with the oil as well and it felt just like what seemed to be in my eyes. When Danny wasn't looking, I wiped the elephant grease off my palm onto the underside of his already filthy pillow.

We were almost out of Wyoming. Now it was South Dakota's turn.

Our continual Interstate infliction of ourselves and our equipment upon the innocent plant and animal life of South Dakota wasn't too remarkable, compared to the chaos we'd served up over the last few hundred miles. For the next several states we were hardly ever the main roadside attraction. We had to go back and search for our trailer only once. It had made its final and futile bid for freedom somewhere around Santa Fe, North Dakota, galloping freely across a barren sand pasture that closely resembled the very recently transmitted pictures of the Martian landscape. Each place we had stopped for gas or food, or maybe a brief sleep, the front page or every newspaper boasted big pictures of Mars. People all over Wyoming and the Dakotas were ogling these nasty pictures of rocks and an endless barren wasteland of gravel and sand—*exactly* what was right outside their window—if they'd just put their paper down and look! But if you made the huge mistake of talking to them about how maybe they should pack up and move their wrinkly selves and their wrinkled kids to someplace with plant life, water and warm-blooded living creatures, they'd start goin' on about how they lived in "Gawd's Country." I told them that if that's the case, Mars must be heaven itself—and if that's true—how bad can hell be?

After once again rounding up a grazing trailer and tying the coupling together, then ritualistically slapping a loud smeary handprint—across the face of a grinning elephant, this time the mama elephant—we bought some heavy chain and U-bolts. We'd grown tired of tracking migrating and waywardly stubborn rolling stock over the Martian landscape. *"N thet wer the last round-up for ol' silver—we chained him down reeel gud. After thet, he warn't goin' nowhar no more!"*

Extra loops of heavy chain, once it dribbles down onto asphalt moving underneath the hitch and coupling at sixty or seventy miles-per-hour, makes a beautifully distracting light show at night. Lively sprinkles of sprightly sparks dance in the blackness, alerting sleeping drivers that they should maybe wake up and pay attention. Possibly even speed up and get closer for a good look at what all the fireworks and celebration is about. Then, once they see that it's nothing more than some loose safety chain harmlessly humping up and down on the highway, they can panic and pull up next to the snoring driver, Hannibal, who is driving his herd of elephants over the Continental Divide and into the interior of Mongolia or Mars or Minnesota—he can't remember which.

Then, after upsetting young Hannibal over a few measly sparks, the previously panicked motorist or trucker is told to shut up and go back to sleep and to mind his own business. And that's just about when the trailer tongue came off the hitch and then applied itself to the pavement. Now we really had some sparks. The dangling bouncing chain held the trailer by its snout, not allowing the trailer to leave formation. By the time I stopped, the coupling was red hot; therefore we had to wait a while to recouple it. We used the down time to take a link or two out of the chain's slack and thereby reduce the quality of the fireworks, Interstate entertainment, and future panic attacks from slack-jawed sleepy-eyed drivers—many of Norwegian descent.

Danny finished tightening the U-bolt on the slightly shortened safety chain. "Think that's enough?"

"Oooh yah-shoor-yabetcha-yaa, don'tcha know? Now let's go find some yummy *loote*fisk for breakfast."

"What's lutefisk?"

"You don't want to know."

18

Three Weeks on the Road
Act Three

Whichever states came next as we marched eastward, I'm unable to recall now. This particular road trip was one of scores I made over a period of many years and is possibly the most memorable. But it's been about twenty-five years since my last cross-country rampage, so my geographical recollection of what states we next laid waste to is somewhat blurry. Illinois and then Wisconsin. Is Chicago a state? I know we went through New Mexico right after Minnesota. And I think Cuba was right in there somewhere. We had started out with a road atlas. Danny had used up most of the eastern state pages for toilet paper. I'd used others, mostly the southern states, for wiping elephant grease and as "napkins" while driving and dining at seventy miles-an-hour. I saved the map of Washington State in case I needed a clue to jar my memory of where I was from in the event of amnesia. Or severe road dementia, which already was evidently settling in.

But I do know that we never again "lost" the trailer; not in the Montana-Wyoming definition of the word. Once in Pennsylvania and two times in—I think it was Guatemala—or a place that sounds a lot like that—it came "loose" and swayed around quite a bit, attracting some attention and creating a small amount of mild alarm.

A buncha loud sparks flew and we caused one hitchhiker to change direction and run across Interstate 90, where he began thumbing for a ride back the way he'd come.

Eventually we made our way to Jamestown, New York, and bought a nice loada junk from my friend Dave Nord. From there on up to Buffalo and Clarence, New York, to deal with all the Jeff Wiesburgs, Joel Birnbaums, Max Sloans and Dan Cutinis I could find. Buying cool stuff from Bernie Kirchner on Old Salt Road, and cheap—but profitable—cool stuff at the Ransom Road Auction Barn, and Clarence, New York, is a fading memory of my gloriously distant past of a long career doing what I loved. Wading around neck-deep in antique shops and auction barns, willing to wait for something to fall through the cracks—something I thought I could market three thousand miles away at my shop or auction. The thrill of *not* knowing what might surface made it exciting. It was indeed Indiana Jones every day for me—back then.

And there was no time for dawdling. I had babies to feed back home; so did Danny. After two full weeks of shops, barns, sheds, sales and country auctions, as well as scant sleep, few baths, and pinched pennies, we left for home. Truck and trailer were both packed to the rafters, and I was satisfied. Danny was grateful to separate from people that talked funny and that it—our trip—should soon be over.

Because the trailer was loaded—well loaded up near the front—there was never again to be a problem with separation anxiety between the two vehicles. We were confident of that. Because of the excellent packing procedures I employed, there wasn't enough air space inside the truck or trailer for a termite to breathe. It was all about payload. There's no profit in shipping New York air three thousand miles. I've always tried to buy things that break down, disassemble or fit into or around something else. So we weighed in heavy. And that might have become part of the new looming problem.

Creaking and groaning through the eastern states on our western return trip was an uneventful and relaxing change and we made good time. But what those eastern people call "mountains," people from the Rockies downright laugh at. What people from the Rockies call "mountains," people that are used to the Cascades scoff at. The steeper the terrain became, the heavier we seemed to become. I think it has something to do with physics—and by the time this trip would be over, I'd need one.

Whatever my—only slightly used—trailer had weighed empty when I first bought it, it got considerably lighter as we had traveled east. And *the trailer itself* was becoming slightly lighter yet, now that we were on our return trip. The reason was, again, physics. Not that I actually know anything about the laws of physics; I know less about physics than I do about geography. However, I am aware of the many laws against littering that most states level against sloppy motorists. We'll get to that soon.

When I first inspected my "new" trailer, I did notice the few holes around the heads of a handful of the hefty aluminum screws that anchored the aluminum sheet metal to the box frame. Just insignificant sorta-small-roundish holes around the screw heads themselves. The screws weren't loose, but the metal was. Just enough to flex a tiny bit in these areas. I remember asking if maybe they—the manufacturers—should've put nice big rubber washers under those screw heads so that I wouldn't have these teeny holes in my nearly-new utility trailer.

"Squirt some caulking in there—that'll fix it up." Sound advice from the guy who's selling the trailer. "That's as bad as it's ever gonna get anyways—them little specks you call 'holes'." With a typical used car salesman's scoffing snicker. "You wanna see some holes—come on over to my house—I'll show you my roof. Say, ain't you a roofer?"

"No. Just squirt some caulking in there—that'll fix'r up."

This is the physics part: when wind is moving at, say, seventy miles an hour down the flat sides and roof of a cheaply-made, very thin-gauged aluminum box, it grows fingernails. It's a simple fact of physics. Wind, also, having little else to do, is always looking for small imperfections to pick at with its nice new invisible fingernails. By the time Danny and I had stopped at Ellensburg, Washington, on the first toe of the first leg of our journey eastward, my tiny round "specks" were not only multiplying, they were now egg-shaped. By the time we'd introduced the truck to external combustion during our inaugural roadside Montana milkcarton kickoff, the egg-shaped holes had begun hatching cute little vee-shaped notches. By the time we'd lassoed our bucking Brahma back onto the butt-end of my blackbelching smoldering truck, somewhat just past Butte, I noticed that the notches had grown. I noticed then, also, the curious little alumi-curls rolled up and shuddering just behind each elongating wedge-notch—caused from the wind scratching away at my trailer's imperfections. Each of the once tiny little tears had magnified into a nasty flap of irritation. Much like the nasty painful flaps of skin that dangled from my already cracked and chapped lips. Each time I realized that my tinfoil trailer was worsening, and whenever doing the baby elephant walk back to the cab, I'd take it out on a cartoon elephant. I had a whole herd of 'em—three on each side—and I think there were two more, faded and mud-covered, on the overhead roll-up door at the back of the truck. But I left them alone, not because they were out of reach, as were the two papa-bull-grinning elephants on each side of the truck. The back pair was too filthy and too far gone to discipline.

Watching my oversized sardine can rolls grow thicker as more wind scratched and clawed away at my shredding trailer was much less entertaining to me and my elephants than it appeared to all the Bekins, American Van Lines, "Corn Flakes," and hundreds of other big-rig drivers that watched my trailer's slow demise. They enjoyed watching us unravel. "What'sat trailer o-yours made of—gum wrappers? Har-har-har!" With my teeth, I pulled on a shred of dry skin that hung from my lower lip, making it worse, which caused me to yelp in pain as I zipped up and flushed the truck stop's urinal with my foot.

By the time we were halfway through Dakota—which one, I don't know—if you ask a Dakota native which one you're in, they'll always say, "The *only* one."—my rolled up sardine can lid wedges were two and three feet long and had by then unrolled due to the wind's nimble fingers. So then I had a series of aluminum pennants fluttering, and growing, in the wind, which nicely signaled our eastern charge.

Night brought out the best we had to offer those who had the good fortune to follow us east. Between the several times that my truck tried to burn us alive with boiling oil—which lit up the night sky beautifully—along with the grinding abrasive halts my trailer's coupling made—which also sparked much interest because it looked like a traveling steel mill had just tipped a giant ladle of splattering molten metal soup all over the darkened Interstate 90 corridor—we threw in this bonus attraction: long skinny silver ribbons of metal were tearing down the length of my circus trailer's roof and sides, shimmering and streaming behind us while illuminated by moonlight or headlights, they flashed and fluttered, mesmerizing all who dared to creep up and follow us on our eastern pilgrimage—and later, when we were on our way back again on our western pilgrimage as well.

And if that wasn't entertainment enough: intermittently one of our slivers of silver would tear loose and sail off into the tailwind behind us. In my mirror I'd see the writhing roll spinning and flashing in moonlight, appearing as if it was a coil of contained lightning caught inside a tornado. The following motorists saw it, too. Headlights erratically jerked left and right, dodging the scary flashing luminous spring-loaded coil of foil that flitted this way and that, until it either went over or past or under them. Looking back on it, I guess this would be considered littering.

Over the total of seven thousand or so miles that me, Danny and our herd of elephants traveled while towing our sometimes-connected circus wagon waving brilliant silver pennants, we were able to deposit small metallic bits of it in every state we appeared. Sorta like the Lone Ranger and Tonto. A silver bullet here, a silver bullet there. Whatever damage we did to the environment by littering, however, we more than made up for in the lives we saved along the way; also like the Lone Ranger and Tonto. Many was the driver who, just as he was falling asleep at the wheel, was caused to slam on his brakes and only nearly die of fright because a flashing curly wad of heavy tinfoil slapped him across the windshield.

So here we are, loaded to the gills with furniture, lamps, stoves, stained glass windows and fancy doors, trunks, boxes, slot machines, barrels, tins and bins and who-knows-what. On our way home. The steady climb toward the Continental Divide begins. Less than half of my trailer's skin had peeled away by now, not enough to lighten our load significantly; barely enough to even make mention. The slow uphill climbs, even short ones, are noticeably more laborious for the lumbering well-oiled Chevy, and it never once complains (not on this trip anyway). Going down long steep grades I slip it out of gear and let it idle while coasting up to eighty or eighty-five miles an hour; giving the radiator and gas mileage a boost while, at the same time, affording the engine a short rest. The accelerated gravitational higher speed realerts the itchy fingers of the wind resistance which re-alights onto my trailer's imperfections and with a nimble grip furiously fiddles and yanks away at its tatters of fluttering tinfoil, tearing off and indiscriminately tossing thin shreds of trailer shrapnel at the terrified drivers behind us. But, thinking of it as littering never crossed our minds. Littering is what we nearly did on our way while crossing Montana. The second time. We almost littered-up Montana real good.

Not to mention the fires we started—again.

19

THREE WEEKS ON THE ROAD
ACT FOUR

Hannibal, Tonto and with Silver, our standard bearer, still tethered and bringing up the rear, made it okay up the Rockies and through all the states that only look like Mars. The happy herd of elephants, although still smiling deceptively, was tiring from the many uphill battles. And Hannibal, while negotiating some of the more perilous terrain and during some of his less patient moments, had slapped the livin' shit out of the smaller elephants for one reason or another. But it was through the stern stewardship on Hannibal's part that the motley awkward crew and caravan had been captained back across the Martian Alps in readiness to now reinvade Montana. Although the United States of Mars and the correspondingly treacherous mountains of the red planet were indeed behind us, with the truck-load of maniacally grinning pachyderms, the tricky "Big Sky" state still lay before them. Not to mention—*the town without pity*—Ritzville, Washington.

Our many banners still bravely waved—unless we went down-hill too fast which made the wind tear them off and throw them at innocent eighteen-wheelers. Otherwise, there were our silver pennants stiffly crinkling away, proudly announcing the impending return of the victorious and intrepid road warriors. We were now only three states—three green states—away from our safe and celebratory arrival home, loaded with untold riches and spoils from exotic faraway lands like Titusville, Pittsfield, and Oil City, Pennsylvania. Oak rolltop desks from Buffalo, New York, waiting to be refinished, Brunswick slate pool tables waiting to be rebuilt, curved glass china cabinets that needed new glass. And tons of other yummy projects that involved the use of methyl-ethyl-ketone, my apparent chosen drug of choice, *paint and varnish remover*! Many are the incomplete sentences that I failed to finish bec....

We hadn't had an engine fire or lost a trailer for...oh, I dunno, a total of maybe two thousand miles? The last time our trailer even came disconnected, but not lost, was on our way east into Pennsylvania. After that we'd bought and stuffed a few pieces of furniture into the front of it to weigh it down. Which worked fine; everything was fine—yeah, I know—a sure sign.

At Billings, Montana, and which to be truthful, geologically and topographically still seemed to retain some traces of the newly universally popular characteristics of Mars, we stopped for gas. There was a noticeably steady wind blowing in directly from Mars—southwest—and I had clocked it at around one hundred-sixteen miles an hour. My still quite youthful jowels and eyelids wobbled and flapped about as I pumped decomposed dead mammoths, mastodons, dinosaurs and liquified fossilized leafy vegetables of *true* antiquity up out of the Billings reservoir and into the bellies of my eternally cheerful herd of insatiably thirsty slaphappy elephants.

Leaning at *exactly* forty-five degrees into the continual wind while pumping my gas, I asked the guy on the other side of the pumps who is also leaning into the wind at the same angle, and who'd already told me that he was a Billings native, "Does the wind always blow like this around here?"

To which he answered, "What wind?"

I looked up at my once shiny but somewhat oily trailer, now half-skinned and with its many dark and long horizontally lateral streaks down it; exposing all sorts of rocking chair legs, oak dresser drawers and corners of trunks full of other folks' long-since dissolved pasts. Dead people's stuff. A boneyard of normal people's private, boring, mundane, and simple histories were still partially concealed, yet soon to be for sale again. And I love it. I loved the unanimity of humanity as well as the anonymity of oldness about it. I loved it all.

* * * * * *

Gassed up and gone. Headed across the longitudinally situated remainder of Montana. Everything's fine, still. How many more stops we made that night I can't say; somewhere in the neighborhood of two or three—one stop every one-hundred-fifty miles or so.

Butte, Montana, was our next anticipated pullover for fossil fuel. I was grateful that it would be the middle of the night when we'd hit Butte, and not during normal business hours. Otherwise I'd be obligated to have to stop in at "Tony the Trader's" place. Where I'd be verbally abused by Tony for two hours or so and still end up leaving his junk store empty-handed; I'm tellin' ya, the antique business has seen some strange cookies. With Tony, as soon as you expressed interest in an item in his store, and he had some good ones, it instantly became "not-for-sale." Essentially his plan was to only sell you stuff that you wouldn't buy. I *always* left his place pissed off and empty-handed. He was in that same spot, with the same stuff for decades; and people call *me* crazy. "Tony the Trader" wasn't much for trading, either. He finally croaked some years back, and as far as I know, he *still* has all of his junk.

Fatigue, although it was mixed with relief—or at least partial relief—because from all appearances it looked as though we might actually make it home, was perpetually grinding away at our eye sockets. I rolled the square corners of what was left of my ground-down eyes around on the crunchy grit inside their grindy caverns—attempting to focus into the driver's mirror.

The dim flickering headlights behind me had been chasing us for some time now, but weren't attempting to pass. My dim flickering eyesight had only caught glimpses of whoever was behind us; the reason being, whoever it was, was practically on top of us. Nearly riding poor old Silver as he did so. I glanced repeatedly into the truck's right side-view mirror in several attempts to figure out what kind of a vehicle it was that rode our ass. His lights never shone into my right-side mirror; only occasionally did his left headlight seem to catch my left mirror.

From this, I wearily concluded it wasn't an eighteen-wheeler. It must be a passenger vehicle, and it must be one with only one headlight—because, the right one was evidently burned out, and most likely it was an older six-volt vehicle—probably an old farmer's pickup, something built before 1955; this latter conclusion being drawn because of the dimness of the beam's intensity. Or—that it possibly had a bad generator, which also would explain the flickering yellow dimness.

Or *maybe*, a single apocalyptic, anonymous horseman, carrying the flickering torch of damnation, was pursuing us! Maybe we had just driven through and over ancient Crow or Blackfoot burial grounds. *It was midnight* and we had no doubt rolled noisily across the grave of a sleeping brave who was, on behalf of his entire nation, now behind us, ready to pounce and extract savage satisfaction for our breaking the ritual silence of sacred eternal consecration!

Or—*maybe* the trailer was on fire.

EE-YAAHHHIIIEEE!!

"Danny! The trailer's on fire!!"

Tonto, who was dead asleep, groggily opened one of his enormous red eyes and instantly broke camp from his momentary semi-residency inside his private happy hunting ground, and snapped alive, thrashing around and flutter-kicking himself upright in the seat, he had his door open and was riding sidesaddle before I could bring the wagon train to a halt.

Danny, because he still retained a love for either firefighting or fire itself, naturally arrived at the scene before me, but without even so much as a half-carton of sour milk to kick over into my shoe.

Only a second later I'd run to the back of the trailer to join him. I, however, arrived fully equipped—with two bottles of warm beer. That had been the extent of our firefighting ordnance capabilities throughout the entire trip, once we'd failed our original Montana milk run.

Sure enough, an invisible ghost warrior had shot pore ol' Silver in the left flank with a flaming arrow or something, and it was cracklin' and snappin' away like bacon in a skillet. I quickly handed Tonto, the fire chief, a bottle of "Rainier Beer" firewater and I twisted off the cap on the other one.

Shaking and then squirting my extinguisher onto the flames and into the crack that appeared to be the source, I saw that Tonto was guzzling on his stubby. "Pour it in here, you ignorant heathen," I hollered. He grunted, then joined me as I emptied the balance of liquid into the joint where the trailer's wooden frame wheel-well connected to the chassis and metal frame. The flames died while the wood continued to hiss for a minute or so. Dust and grit swirled into our faces when a pony-trailered Atlas Van Lines blew past. Three short horn blasts dissipated into the Montana night as the semi disappeared over the hill ahead of us. In the near black, I put my hand on the tire closest to me. It wasn't right. I squatted down on my knees to find that it was completely flat; the rubber had already broken its bead from the rim. It had gone flat some time ago. Reaching back further, placing my hand on the companion tire, the tire that occupied the tandem axle, which was now independently carrying the whole load on the left side, I quickly found it to be hotter than hell; as in *almost* ready to catch fire itself. "This was a friction fire!" I hollered.

We weren't far from Butte by this time, so we figured if we kept our speed low, hugged the right shoulder to lessen the weight over the left wheel, and took our time, we'd make it to the full-service station that sat just on the west side of town. They were always open and that's where we'd planned to stop anyhow.

I don't remember now, but I think it was a big Texaco station. Big by Montana standards, back then anyway. I do know that the station sported a giant orange tomcat that was big by anybody's standards. He slept all day in a cardboard box on top of the sales counter next to a sign that read, "Leave me alone! If I'm asleep *do not* pet me." And that's because he was up all night, out raising hell. I know, because I had a horrible experience with him one night while on another cross-country trip by myself. I don't have time now, but the short story is: I ended up standing outside the back of my truck at three a.m., naked, and in two feet of snow because of that damn cat.

And on another trip yet, I had ignored those written instructions and made the further mistake of petting him. It wasn't a mistake so much because of the claw marks he left on the *back* of my hand. It was the grimy, gritty oil residue his fur left on the *palm* of my hand. He was the nastiest cat I ever met. After petting him, my hand had the same coating on it that it would have each time I'd discipline one of my elephants.

After being passed by rumbling scores of growling eighteen-wheeled big rolling boxes, we rolled under the brighter lights of Butte's best big beast-in-a-box and were able to ascertain what the problem was. Apparently, the same person who had engineered the application of heavy-duty Reynolds Wrap aluminum foil siding onto my trailer had also been allowed to oversee the suspension system.

The spring shackles that sat over each of the tandem axles had been cleverly constructed in such a fashion that if one tire went flat—or missing—the shackle above the other wheel automatically *collapsed*. In fact, it actually *reversed* itself in its configuration. No longer in the shape of an *upturned* bowl, but now a *downturned* bowl-shape, with the wooden wheel well resting on top of the other tire: *rubber-friction-wood-equals = fire.*

After the Texaco tire department sold me a new one-hundred-twenty-five-dollar heavyduty tire and installed it, the suspension shackle was again buckled back up and into its much more familiar over-the-rainbow appearance. The way that shackles should look. Standardly engineered leaf springs pushing the weight up off the axles and wheels, instead of the reverse—buckling themselves and pulling the load down onto a sizzling, simmering single tire.

The nice red-haired young man with the remarkably bad complexion—from his appearance he had been born and raised in that gas station and probably had been sired or at the very least, reared and nursed by that grimy orange tomcat—smiles and waves at us as we roll off and away. Butte is now behind us. It's a Friday night. It's almost two a.m.; Danny is all tired out from dealing with tire fires and putting them out and putting new tires on. He scrunches back down in his spot to sleep while I shift our way up the Interstate 90 on-ramp and drift onto the highway. No headlights or taillights in sight, either direction.

The more vigilant operators of eighteen-wheelers while on a long haul will diligently avoid metropolitan areas on Sunday or around closin' time. Saloon "closin'" time. Now I'm more than aware that people no longer drink to excess in Montana, nor here in Washington State where *I* reside. Society has been busily and consistently improving itself over the last few decades, to the point where we are now. Back in the late seventies things were different. Traffic, in any case, for this or that reason was reasonably light.

And that's why I could easily see the dim flickering light of someone following me.

We'd only traveled four or five miles and here we were, apparently with another murderous sleep-deprived pyromaniac of a dead savage on our heels. I felt like I was in one of those old Sinbad movies. The ones with the sword-wielding skeletons that just keep *com-*

ing and *coming*. I mean, for the love of God, how many tires does a person have to continually ignite in order to pass through the state of Montana?

"Danny? I think we're on fire again." Calmly I eased off the gas and kicked it into neutral.

"Uh-huh."

"I wish I was kidding."

"Well, *piss* on it!"

"I'm plannin' on it—do you have to go?"

"NO!"

By the time I pulled over, stopped, and went to the rear of our convoy of the accursed, the flickering firelight was fading. By the time Danny showed up after concluding I wasn't kidding, the fire'd gone out. The glowing embers of wood grain were still glimmering in the blackness, so we knew I hadn't been hallucinating. And the sweet smell of a very near campfire seemed to waft about us, so there was no arguing.

Confounded by *why* we'd caught fire *again*, I reached under the smoky wheel well for my second time that night.

My tire, *that same wheel* wasn't flat—it was gone.

"That pimply-faced little bastard didn't tighten down our lug nuts!" I screamed into the Big Montana sky. Danny began wailing incoherently.

"I'm gonna go find that greasy damned kid and kill him—then I'll chop him up and feed him to that mangy cat!" jumping into the cab, right after I punched a baby elephant in the mouth; good and hard.

"It just never ends, does it?" Danny rhetorically mumbles, slamming the door behind him.

Now I am not about to drive the necessary—and legal—several miles in the wrong direction—towards home—to double back and dissect a certain terminally acned tire jockey into cat food, so I began my U-turn maneuver. Cursing.

Taking advantage of the light traffic, and that maybe whatever Montana cops or Butte police might be anywhere thereabouts had already stopped a drunk driver three blocks away from his last saloon and was therefore busy elsewhere, I cranked the wheel hard to the left. Into what appeared to be a slight dip in the otherwise flat and grassy medium that lay in front of me, where my headlights shot across Interstate 90's eastbound lanes. It's summer—it's Montana—I know for a fact the median is solid ground—not mushy.

Remarkably deceptive things can take place under the stars. Many's the life-altering circumstances that capriciousness, lack of vigilance, carelessness, horniness, or perhaps a thirsty passion for vengeance has been spawned under the light of the moon. This night the moon deceived me in my passionate rage to go and kill the young pecker-headed Mister Clearasil.

The median wasn't nearly as flat as it had appeared in the moonlight. Or in my headlights. It was shaped a lot like the reverse-buckled upside-down-rainbow leaf springs on the left side of the tattered trailer of toast behind me. It was a narrow canyon.

So I stepped on the gas, just to make sure we'd make it down the short embankment and up the other, shorter side.

The overall thirty feet or so length of my truck was longer than the gently curved ditch was wide. As the front bumper dug into the gravelly bank of the far side of the median, the bottom of the hydraulic liftgate dug into the bank of the near side behind us. All six of the truck's useless wheels were now suspended—as should have been my driver's license at that point—and we hung there, dangling all six of our whirling feet. The beams from my headlights were barely seen through the sweet Montana grass upon which the grill that my elephant truck now peacefully grazed. Danny sighed deeply, locked his door, fluffed up his filthy pillow and farted.

Then it dawned on me! The smoldering trailer of eternal hellfire was situated sideways while parked directly across the dark westbound lanes of the freeway! I briefly envisioned a Coors or Olympia beer truck plowing into a big shredded square aluminum—unlit from the side square canful of antiques. Thereby driving up the median price of my remaining inventory—I decided it wasn't worth it. We needed to get out of that median. Fast. We needed a large tow truck, now! Although at this point, a beer truck would've been nice, too.

In the distance I saw the headlights and running lights of a big rig rolling east. I knew he'd have a CB radio and would, if I could get him to stop, make the call for a tow truck. I bailed out and fell four feet into the bottom of the dry grassy canal. Scrambling up the hill and over the top I began waving him down as his "jake brakes" chatter-growled away at the rapidly shortening distance between us. He came to a complete stop, barely illuminated from the side by the lights of what still shone from my grass munching nearly submerged headlamps.

His airbrakes hissed loudly as I mounted the passenger side footplate and opened the door of his Peterbilt. His left hand still on the wheel, I watched as he activated with his other hand, the thumb-button on his CB handset. After the call had been made for the biggest tow truck in Butte, I thanked him for stopping and asked him if he'd drop me off a couple miles closer to town; so that I could begin searching for my new tire and wheel rim.

Happy to oblige and equally happy to abandon the scene of what should, at any moment, become a roadside atrocity, we left, leaving Danny to flag down the thundering hordes of two a.m. saloon evacuees swarming their way west on Interstate 90. As we drove off, the nice man asked me, "Are those *elephants* right there, on the side of your truck?"

When I attempted my one-word answer in the affirmative, I was drowned out by all the overlapping conversation that suddenly crackled and garbled out from the CB speaker box fastened above his dashboard. He quickly turned it off, nodding his head in the relative silence while making the next two or three gear changes. Soon, we were about halfway between the Texaco station and the perpendicularly stationary traveling elephant rodeo behind us. That's where I hoped to find my newly-purchased unfastened tire. He stopped—I jumped out.

As he drove away, I crossed back over the median to begin my needle-in-a-haystack hunt for my wayward wheel, noticing as I did so, how much flatter the grass median was in the spot where I made the crossing on foot. Much more so than where my truck sat, wedged into two hillsides, feet dangling in the dark and waiting for an obliviated cowboy in a pickup truck to obliterate the obtusely positioned trailer that was attached to it. The trailer's coupling was also hopelessly buried in the gravel; there had been no chance of Danny and I disconnecting the loaded trailer.

As the eastbound tractor-trailer and its quiet driver drove into the distance, I also noted that he hadn't blown his air horn. One of the very few semis in nearly three weeks that hadn't.

Not only did I fail to find my tire in that stretch of highway before the tow truck and I both arrived back at the scene, Danny and I couldn't find it afterwards, either. We'd looked almost everywhere in between—in the dark—with no luck. We would spend a couple hours early the following morning with the same results.

Luckily for the pockmarked kid who had put a pox on my already quite cursed trailer, he was off work by the time the tow-truck dropped us off. Maybe they'd just hidden him out back, amongst the mountain of frazzled, bald, and dead tire casings; where he'd probably been conceived, hatched, or spawned in the first place. Although my initial rage had subsided somewhat, Danny's had not. He was growing more short-tempered, rather than less. We spent the last half of the night sorta sleeping—but not exactly. An all-night gas station on a Friday night isn't always a restful stopover spot.

In the bright light of a Montana summer sunrise, and after we had resumed our search and failed, we had to wait for a wrecking yard to open in order to find a matching wheel to fit onto my trailer's oddball naked hub. The gray-haired old geezer with the itchy red beard was happy that he had customers waiting for him when he came to open up his yard.

As it turned out, my new trailer had been engineered at the tin-foil factory to allow me the luxury of one more—and final—surprise. The wheel's lug bolt configuration held the singular pattern of—are you ready for this?—a 1954 *NASH RAMBLER*! What in livin' hell would a late seventies tandom axle utility vehicle be doing made with 1954 Rambler components?!? But it was indeed. And it was indeed my lucky day—because they actually had one. 'Course, 'cause it was rare, it cost a little more. After paying for it I noticed how it was the same color and looked a lot like my old one. Good, I thought. I wouldn't want my trailer to have wheel rims in differing colors. What would people think?

The daytime manager of the gas station could replace a *defective* tire, he told me; but not a *missing* one—the reason that it was missing managed to elude him, no matter how I explained it to him. He was, however, willing to cut me a "hell of a deal" on a used—"brand new"—tire. And they'd mount it onto my rare '54 Rambler wheel for free. Why, he'd even oversee the nut-tightening phase of the operation himself. I made sure to look at the tire first. It *was* still a new tire; almost. Still had those funny little rubber nipples in some spots.—in fact, it looked a lot like my old one—the one I'd owned for a total of maybe thirteen miles before it went wandering around in the Montana mountains, bathing in moonlight and emancipation. The big stinky orange tomcat vigorously stretched in his cardboard box-bed and I could have sworn I heard him chuckle while I paid for my second tire.

The fourth guy, the older one feeding the cat, was scratching at his infested scroungy beard, and he looked a lot like the guy from the wrecking yard that sold me my "rare" 1954 Nash Rambler rim; the one that matched my other ones.

As we passed, that sorry-assed flea-ridden cat looked right at me.

As we creaked, growled, and rolled our way down the gritty and beer can strewn tarmac, preparing for takeoff from the Texaco for the second time, I glanced in the window of the smoke-filled café next door to the gas station and noticed the cluster of guys sitting at a booth, drinking coffee and feeding that gnarly cat. I couldn't say for sure, but I thought at least three of 'em had red hair, same color as the rancid tomcat.

20

Three Weeks On The Road
Act Five—The Curtain Falls

The Bitterroot Mountains of Montana, little more than yesterday's bitter memory; the foothills of the Cascades—and home—lay before us. Five more hours, and after three weeks on the road—which is only a figure of speech because in our case, half the time we were in the ditch—it would be over. We'd been back in our very own Washington State for well over an hour.

The tally of roadside events, if they could be referred to in those terms, reads as follows: a total of seven times our truck itself had been on fire, while the half-stripped-bare air-conditioned trailer only erupted into flames twice. On the other hand, the trailer had come loose from the truck on seven different occasions and in nearly as many states. Only four, maybe five times, however, did we actually have to go look for it. The other times, it had remained attached by the sparkling safety chain while the trailer's tongue drug along the highway and illuminated the night skies. Other pieces of the trailer were scattered all over the upper half of the American part of the North American continent—and still are, most likely. While Danny sat in the booth across from me, reading his trashy paperback, I was busy finishing my warm apple pie with vanilla ice cream.

Danny didn't want dessert. The Perkin's Pancake House was reasonably busy, it being situated just off Interstate 90 and highly visible to motorists and truck drivers traveling west or east. There were several big rigs in the spacious parking lot, including two or three of the then ubiquitous Consolidated Freightways tractor-trailers.

A tall, well-built middle-aged gentleman wearing a new-looking straw-colored Stetson or Resistol cowboy hat, a crisply-pressed checkered blue-and-white short-sleeve shirt, faded but clean blue jeans and brightly-polished cowboy boots walked towards us, picking his teeth as he did so. Expressionless, he stopped at our table, removed his toothpick, and pushed his hat slightly back, exposing on his forehead the thin red band where the hat had sat, and spoke. Slowly.

"Well," with a note of resignation in his voice—a hint of you're-gonna-find-out-anywayssooner-or-later, type of tone, "…it's only fair, that you boys know…that you've cost *a lotta* people…*a lotta* money."

Danny and I looked at each other, then quickly craned our necks to see if either of our perpetually self-combustive vehicles had spread flames to any of the real trucks and trailers that neighbored them. Seeing no evidence of pandemonium or pyroplasm, we turned back to the toothpicker. I noticed the heavy gold rings that he wore; Black Hills.

"*But,*" he began again, still slowly and this time with eyebrows raised…"it's only fair…that you boys know…you've *made* a lotta people…a lotta money." Well, that sounds positive, I thought, and how do we get our hands on our cut? And what in hell is this guy talkin' about in the first place?

If I remember correctly, neither Danny nor I spoke. I mean, think about it—what would *you* say? We just sat there and blinked, in silence, waiting for something that resembled the riffling, scuffling sound of another shoe getting ready to drop. Maybe one with a foot in it—one that might kick this slow-talkin' cowboy's aptitude for dinner conversation into a higher gear; preferably one that made some sense. Not knowing what types of questions to ask—or maybe because we were just plain afraid to, out of fear of what the answers might be, we said nothing. We were two midnight jungle lemurs staring into a flashlight. I leaned to the left and once again quickly glanced out the window, just to make sure; if we were on fire, it didn't appear to be spreading fast enough to get too excited about.

"You two boys and those chariots of fire of yours…are known about all over America. You didn't know that, did you?" Finally! He was talking at a near normal pace. One that didn't allow my mind to wander…much. Instantly, I started denying anything bad that might've happened anywhere south of Interstate 90; like Texas or Nova Scotia. Still with lemuring eyes blinking into the harsh lights of what was beginning to sound like a nationwide accusation of some sort, my mouth automatically began babbling something about innocence through ignorance and how we prob'ly didn't even do it, anyway, whatever it was. I looked at Danny and into his big round innocent eyes. He was nodding in obvious concurrence. Defense rested.   The furrowed brow that the tall listener standing before us wore now told me that I'd probably talked way to fast and way too defensively for him. So I started over. He held up his hand, as if he'd heard enough.

"I'm just telling you young men that you're famous. Especially in Las Vegas. And you *have been* for the last three weeks. It *was* three weeks ago you left Washington State—right?"

"…Yah." Why would he know that?

"Then, the first thing you did, once you crossed the Idaho panhandle, was to catch your truck on fire in Montana, right?" Although he was getting spooky, at least his conversational cadence had caught up with what could be considered normal in its clip.

"…Yeah, that's about right—but we've been on fire lotsa times. Especially in Montana. In fact, night before last…"

"You were on fire a few more times, I know. I was in Seattle at the time, pickin' up a load for Cleveland, the one I've got sittin' out there right now. The last time you were on fire you were also sittin'

crossways over Interstate 90 and it was in the middle of the night."
Now he *was* scarin' me.

"So how'd you know about what was going on with us when we were clear across the mountains, and in Montana?"

"That's what I'm trying to tell you boys—*everybody* knows, every long-haul big rig operator in the U.S.—especially the ones who *gamble*—have been tracking you for the last three weeks!" I looked at Danny. When I did, I'm sure I saw signs of overloaded circuits crackling and little tiny neuro-switchboards fizzing away while the acrid smell of burning wires curled about inside the void this conversation was creating behind his dulling eyes.

"You have heard of Las Vegas?" Now he was getting condescending. So I acted as dumb as we evidently appeared to be—to him, anyway.

"Yeah, hey, Elvis made a movie there—*didn't he*, Danny?"

"Elvis whoooo?" Danny robotically answered back while blankly staring into the distance, which was no further than the empty off-white wall above the booth bench where I sat. The look in his eyes told me he had broken down and was lost somewhere maybe just south of Gary, Indiana.

"Have you heard of the Las Vegas gameboards? The ones *off the grid*? The ones not meant for the general public-type gamblers? The ones that the real players bet on? The betboards that have all sorts of oddball stuff going on? The ones that can go on for a long time and the odds can change every day—or every hour—and nobody knows anything about it except for the high rollers and side-betters that are following whatever it is that everybody's betting on?"

"Nnnoo."

"Have you ever heard of Cannonball Run? Ever see that movie?"

"Mmmmaybe."

"Well, it's like that. At least it was in your case. Except you were the only ones in the run. You were running against yourselves. And the odds were *way* in favor of your losing. At least that's what I thought, so you cost me a bucketful of money. You cost almost everyone that I know, money."

And he said it in a voice of painful quiet surrender, as if he was almost proud of it. But it still didn't make enough sense to me to carry on a two-sided conversation about it. So I let him carry the load.

"And you didn't know anything about it—that's what made it interesting. It all started when you-all broke down for the first time in Montana."

I held up a forefinger, "We never broke down."

"That's right—I'm sorry, the first time you burnt your truck down—you attracted a lot of attention then. So when you told somebody that you were goin' all the way to New York with those two rigs, someone called it in. Pretty soon you were up on the boards, with heavy odds that you wouldn't make it to New York at all, and if you did, it'd be without one or both of those units. The betting was structured the same way, with the odds changing every time you had one of your—mishaps.

"Ooookay…?" Danny and I are exchanging glances, things are kinda coming into focus.

"So after all the fires you had and the trouble you had with your trailer comin' off all the time…you do know that they make trailer balls in different sizes, right?"

Two lemurs looked at each other and blinked. "They do?"

"Yep. You might want to consider finding one that fits your hitch if you plan on keepin' what's left of that trailer you got out there. You know what: I've seen some real bad plane wrecks that looked better than your trailer."

"Me, too." Well, I'd seen *pictures* of plane wrecks. And he was right.

"So when you guys made it to New York, bets were paid off and that part of it was over with. There'd been a lot of people involved— but *nothing* like the money that was on the boards when you *left* New

York and headed back for Washington State! That's when you lit *everything* up!"

I at first assumed he was talking about our frequent nocturnal luminescences all along Interstate 90; I then recalculated that he was probably still speaking in reference to Las Vegas.

"At one point, the odds against you making it back to here— with both rigs—was something like a hundred-and-forty to one. You've been on every CB frequency in America nonstop with every bookie from coast-to-coast taking long odds on your making it back to here, and *I* never talked to one person that bet in your favor. So I think it was the high rollers in Vegas itself—and the bookies—that you made rich. I, for one, still can't believe you made it. From what I heard, you boys were a helluva spectacle. Every time you pulled over to put out a fire or dig something outa the ditch, the airwaves and the gameboards came alive."

"Are people after us—for something? Like, we don't owe anybody anything for…?"

"No, no, no," he interrupted; "You're not in any trouble with anybody. No one blames you guys for anything. Wull, not that I know of anyways. I'm just lettin' you know, now that it's over with. That's all. Hey, I have to head on out; you boys need to take care— like that's gonna happen"—(under his breath).

I looked down at my melted puddle of vanilla ice cream for a moment or so. When I looked back up and out the window, I saw him flick his toothpick in the general direction of my truck and trailer. I continued to watch as he climbed into a Consolidated Freightways rig and fire up the diesel. Danny and I looked at each other and began laughing.

So, that was why all the truck drivers in America had quit asking us stupid questions. That was why they hadn't even attempted to converse with us once we'd caught fire the first time. That's why they never stopped to help us—something that, in the 50's they used to do. That's why they were always honking at us. That was why that truck driver I flagged down just west of Butte was so quiet. Why he nodded his head knowingly and why he'd shut off his CB as soon as it began crackling with overlapping conversations, all the CB garble was about us! And they'd known from the beginning that we didn't have a CB.

They'd all worked in a nationwide orchestration to keep us in the dark. We weren't supposed to know anything about it. I guess they figured if we knew—we'd bet, too—and I guess that would've messed everything up. 'Cause most of the time we probably wouldn't bet against any likelihood of us getting ourselves home in one piece. (No, that's a lie; I would never doubt our abilities.)

* * * * * *

Driving off of that Texaco station's parking lot, past that smoky café when leaving Butte for the last time, I remain haunted by what I may have seen—in the window.

The shadowy cluster of men sitting together with that giant filthy orange tomcat looked familiar. And all four of them wore the same dark blue grease-packed coveralls. In fact, they each looked genetically somewhat like the other three.

One guy, I knew for sure, was the gas station manager who'd just sold me my "second" tire. I also recognized the tow-truck driver from the previous night. I'm almost sure the third guy was the "missing" red-haired pimple-ridden nutless wonder that had installed my "first" tire the night before. I remember him getting interrupted while mounting it, by the CB in the office suddenly crackling away and him rushing to quickly turn down the volume....

21

MISCHIEF FRAMED BY DECREE

That was as close as I ever came to Las Vegas stardom. Being the cheap source of somebody else's expensive entertainment while providing an extensive roadside distraction for the entire nation's consortium of truck drivers. And, at the same time delivering the theatrical spectacle of the summer; we were the ultimate road movie! And of all the—what sounded like—millions of dollars in bets that had changed hands, not one of the gambling ratbastards that had won, flipped us a tip.

I've never been much of a gambler. Being in the antique and, especially, the auction business, any desire I may have had to gamble was drained out of me long ago. The antique and auction game is gambling enough. Normally a good gamble, I might add.

But I've always loved slot machines. Antique slot machines— mechanical ones specifically. I've no interest in the electronic "antique" machines. I don't know how to work on 'em. Although I've never been gifted with superior mechanical inclinations, I've enjoyed finding and repairing antique slots to the point I self-learned the repairmanship part of it. Pinball machines and jukeboxes? Now, that's a different story.

Because of the higher-tech nature of old pinballs, and worse, jukeboxes, I've always hated them. Not true—I love'm—they hate me. Each time I purchased either, over the last thirty-five years, in perfect working order, mind you, it would immediately cease to function as soon as its ownership was transferred to me. In that very second.

"There ya go. She's all yer's; and she's a beaut. Best one I ever seen," jamming my money into his pocket and patting the glistening Wurlitzer model #1015 on its perfectly varnished mahogany dome top.

As he drives away I hear something that sounds like an infant's sneeze: a tiny little wheeze-cough-gurgle. I bend down to see if the colorful bubbleator is still gently blowing little bubbles into the rainbow of liquid. Not only has it apparently developed a hairball; I could see blue smoke rising from the back of the now silent beast.—And that's that. It never works again. Not while I own it. As soon as I sell it, at a significant loss, of course, it resumes functioning just like the day it left the factory.

It was a thirty-nine-cent capacitor.

Having no capacity of my own for capacitors, diodes, relays, schematics, and particularly electrocution, I chose, years ago, to avoid gambling with anything electronic. Even flashlights scare me. I've had some close calls, just while using a simple flashlight.

So I stuck to the old mechanized one-armed bandits. And I got into plenty enough trouble with those—one, in particular. And it wasn't even mine; all I did was fix it for a guy, and the next thing I know, I'm headed for the electric chair.—Well, maybe not the chair; but me, the machine, the sledgehammer, Elliot Ness (Olympia Police Chief Chester Brewer) all wound up on the front page of the State Capitol's newspaper.

It was a 1946 aluminum "Pace" nickel machine. I'd cleaned and repaired it, oiled it, fixed the springs and fiddled with the payout slides until it ran smoothly and elegantly. Larry Tunison, the actual owner of the tabletop model, single-appendage game of chance, had agreed to allow me to display the bandit, for sale, in my small antique store. After it was off the disabled list.

There it sat, on my store counter, in all its proud tawdry elegance, beckoning its future would-be owner into purchase negotiations. Guys especially. One guy in particular. That guy, as it turned out, was Police Chief Brewer. Only he didn't negotiate; he just sent in a couple of detectives and they confiscated it. Negotiations were over. Saddened by the clean spot its absence left on my otherwise evenly dusty counter, I called Larry and told him of our recent violation at the hands of Olympia's finest.

Fit-to-be-tied, although not blaming me for being unaware that *ownership* of an antique slot machine was technically just as illegal as *placing them in operation in* Washington State; even though it was nothing more than inventory. He was willing to kiss it goodbye—reluctantly of course. Knowing the old adage about not fighting city hall, we simply wrote it off.

A couple of weeks later, a customer of mine that loved any and all of the old coinoperated machines I'd had over the last couple of years, stopped in, looking sheepish. He'd purchased, among other things, two or three cool peanut and gum machines, and a nice little "Pok-o-reel" trade stimulator a few months back and had been saving money to buy a full-sized one-armed bandit from me. He had indeed previously salivated all over the Nickel "Pace" before its confiscation.

He was sheepish because he was, of all things, one of the two detectives who had confiscated it. He told me again how he had nothing to do with it, and how terrible he felt. I believed him totally, as I had the day that they left with it in the trunk of an unmarked police car; he had truly felt horrible about it. He couldn't even look at me, staring at his shoes while I had argued with the senior detective. He just shook his head. I thought he was gonna cry. I felt worse for him than I did for Larry and myself.

He was still ashamed as well as visibly embarrassed over it and knew that, in principle, it had been a miscarriage of judicial enforcement. Relative to that very thing was why he was there, again; although off-duty and not in any official capacity. What he was about to tell me—he made me promise—"didn't come from him."

Knowing that neither Larry nor I had made any motley futile plans of contesting the confiscation, because the letter of the law clearly defined the (obsolete) illegality of what was nothing more than a mechanical ornament. It was to us at that point, water under the bridge. When my customer/police officer, recently-turned-detective/friend covertly informed me of the planned eventual destination of the mechanical wonder, I no longer wondered. I no longer wondered why Brewer would go out of his way to snatch such a harmless device out of an antique shop.—After when it was soon to be forgotten about—it was slated for situation in Brewer's basement; his own "recreation" room. Well, wonder of wonders.

Having seen somewhere in my past, some version of this movie, I indeed did prepare to take on city hall; knowing full well we'd lose, but that was going to be the point. If we did nothing, it was destined to become part of the Chief of Police's personal estate. If we pressed the issue into court and "into the light of day," as those of us that are only half-naïve might call it, at least he'd have to destroy it; because that's what "the law" required. Anything, we figured, just so that bastard couldn't have it; which was the only reason he legally stole it from us in the first place, from what I could ascertain.

After explaining in Thurston County Superior Court that we were there to petition for the destruction of what was, legally, nothing less than contraband, the wisdom of Judge Hewitt Henry prevailed: kill the innocuously evil device; sledgehammer it all to hell on the back steps of the city building—tomorrow at two o'clock, in full view of the bereaved; just as we had petitioned. Small victory, to be sure, but nothing more could be hoped for.

The full-color picture encompassing a half-front page of the Daily Olympian didn't catch Brewer's best angle. He was a little on the portly side and by the time he—not an underling—had smashed the legally evil corruptive contraption into oblivion, his face was beet red, and he was perspiring profusely. Watching him grub around in the rubble for the handful of nickels that had been inside the machine was a somewhat fulfilling moment. I had videotaped the whole execution with a borrowed camcorder, because KOMO news TV said they'd love to do a story on it, but the camcorder hadn't worked properly—or I didn't know how to run the damned thing correctly.

Other than dispatching the five-cent mechanical wonder into that big casino in the sky, the *real story*, the story of *why* it was bludgeoned to death in the first place, was also obliviated by the Daily Olympian, although fully aware that I had pressed the court for immediate execution, as well as why I wanted to be present as witness when it took place, they treated the *real* story with little accuracy or informancy in their dispatch, journalistically speaking. I was to have, as the years were to roll on, many other similar lessons. (We all know what is suggested by "unavailable for comment..." The fact that you've been begging the publication for an interview so that the truth can be told, and you don't hear from them, or miss the call, until you're enroute to another state or country on business, and they call two hours before their print deadline, such as the Maine Antique Digest once did to me, escapes all readers. They remain oblivious. *Two hours* before deadline, mind you, and the Maine Antique Digest, the "Antique Dealer and Collector's Bible" is a MONTHLY journal!

During the next Washington State legislation, myself, among several other purveyors of the old slot machines, took it upon ourselves to spearhead a humble but effective grass-roots campaign to lobby for a statute change. After making several supplicative phone calls to Lt. Governor John Cherbourg and when legislation finally adjourned, any one-armed bandit manufactured before January 1, 1949, was now a collector's item. And legal.

Because of the stir brought on by the slaughter of the innocent slot, phone calls started coming in from Eagles Clubs, V.F.W. posts and other organizations that had squirreled away scores of the three-wheeled whirling works of wonder. Instead of disposing of them, decades before, as they were supposed to—legally—they had locked them away, boarded them up or installed false walls to conceal them. In hopes that someday they'd—legally—be able to again employ their talents in money raising for whichever club the machines had long languished. After reading that "Elliott Ness" Brewer was pillaging the countryside for gambling contraband, the organizations that were secretly aware that they had some, exercised due diligence by making the decision to purge themselves of them. By calling me, and other antique dealers. From the attic of the Tacoma Gun Club, the basement of the Olympia Country Club, and secret rooms within fraternal organizations came Mills, Jennings, Paces, Cailles and Watlings. In singles, pairs, threes and sometimes rows that had occupied an entire wall.

How I would love to relive those days of crime and corruption.

22

SEABECK

We took all five of our kids camping near Bremerton years back, all ages between five and thirteen. I had a big "Duallie" (four wheels in the back) crew cab pickup truck with the sliding type door on the side. We slept in that while the kids had the big tent to themselves. Summertime, of course, and the popular Seabeck heavily treed campground is full. All the "where's my golden arm?" stories and other spooky ones told while we watched the fire die out and the little darlings (smelly, noisy things, aren't they?) were installed into their cozy tent. I kept the truck's sliding door open because of the heat. The whole campground has grown quiet and peaceful.

* * * * * * *

How is it that peace never lasts? Just look at the world today; we're over six months at this writing into Putin's invasion of peaceful Ukraine; *millions* and millions of people's lives *ruined* all in order to feed *one criminally insane* creep's rancid ego. I'm sorry.

* * * * * * *

Maybe two hours of camp comfort sleep later, I hear a large dog barking in the nearby distance; then a second one. I lie there and listen as they knock over a metal trash can and argue about it. Now it's quiet so I drift off again, but not for long.

Another metal trash can bites the dust somewhere else along with some barking, but not too much. "These mutts are making the rounds," I thought to myself, and I dozed off again. Later, I was to hear them raid another one or two cans, but not too near me.

It was very quiet in the wee hours when I heard some slight rustling around in the area near our campfire perimeter. Then I could discern some "snarfulling" close to my open door, so I sat up.

I love dogs, and Labradors are one of my very favorites; so now I'm looking down out from my truck at a black lab (the best) as he snarfulls his way past me to the open tent door where he stops, with his head inside. I crept out and stood quietly behind him.

He needed to be taught a lesson. I was going to teach him to stay home and mind his own business, to let people sleep. I hate being awakened for no reason, like school, employment, housefires, etc. I once tried to start a fight with the entire "Buffalo Bills" football team because they woke me up while partying on my porch. (Please refer to my first book, "*All the Ways I Found to Hurt Myself—The Bills.*" Just let me sleep.

I stood behind him and brought my bare right leg all the way back to swift kick this noisy nosey hungry garbage monger clear into the next landfill when my eyes told my locked and loaded leg this might be a bad idea. "This is a *giant* dog!" I told myself. "He's a monster!" Another smaller portion of my brain spoke up and said, "This is *not* a dog—you idiot. This is a black bear!" Suddenly I did not want to teach him *anything* by kicking his gonads and him into the tent. My right leg was quickly lowered so that *both* legs could propel me back into our truck. When I slam rolled that door loudly shut, he wheeled around with an angry grunt and took off running. I think I woke up the entire campground; dogs were barking everywhere. I could hear people all over cussing in their tents. My kids slept through it.

But they wouldn't have—not if I had kicked that big-assed stud muffin in the chestnuts. That would have awakened at least the ones he stepped, or rolled or fell onto; who would have hollered, which would have woke up the others. In any case, that bear I'm *sure* would have instinctually taken the insult I nearly delivered coupled with my screeching, thrashing kids as an attack that equaled life or death, a visceral "fight or flight." Under those circumstances I'm also sure he would have fought. My kids woulda lost.

It was *that* close! I was grateful I did have good night vision. And all five kids.

* * * * *

EPILOGUE:

I actually met this bear a second time. We didn't recognize each other until we were introduced, and he didn't remember me; he was in no condition.

I was selling "Jacuzzi" bathtubs, thermal windows and shower stalls at a lot I rented in Bremerton, corner of "Pioneer" and "Kitsap Way" about six months after our camping trip. A scroungy guy in a black dirty old pickup pulls in "looking for a shower." I told him there was a truck stop a few miles that way where he could get cleaned up. He squinted his eyes at me and told me he wasn't looking to take a bath—he wanted to *buy* a fiberglass or acrylic shower.

So I sold this grubby dude a 3'x3' shower for $125. He puts down the loud tailgate which was broken, when he says, "We'll just lay it over my buddy here. I did *not* like the sound of that so I set my end down to take a look. And there lies a dead bear. "Whoa! Where'd you get this big boy?"

Obviously proud and happy that I had asked, this nearly toothless hillbilly tells me how whoever is in charge of Seabeck Campground—Washington State Parks, I think—hired him to eradicate this black bear that was bad for business, making messes and terrorizing campers. "I know this bear!" I began, then I told him *my* story. The look he gave me when I told him how I was gonna teach this bear a "lesson" told me he didn't believe a word of it. He'd listened to a lot of tall tales and he had that, "know one when I hear one" kinda look.

23

CAMPING WITH CHERYL

We have always had an old classic convertible of one make or another, but the ones we enjoyed to camp with in particular would be one of our late '60's Cadillacs and mostly our '68—the green one. The one that was always on fire.

Cheryl and I learned over time and more than one old "Caddy," they run *very* hot, and because of that, are prone to "pre-ignition," carbon buildup and backfiring after you shut it off. Sometimes they just keep running for a while and shoot flames out from the manifold. It's always a big hit with onlookers, especially at night. People peek out their windows to see who's getting shot and why is that car on fire. But they sure were nice to drive.

She and I went camping in the Mossyrock State Campground and were told to go up onto the nice grassy area next to the thick dark woods. No tent, just bare bones camping. We laid out our stuff and unrolled our sleeping bags and scooted in to study the stars. I wasn't exactly thrilled to be right *next* to the untamed forest. While camping a different time Cheryl and our sister-in-law, Vicki, *had* run into a bear, a large cinnamon bear, here near Mossyrock Dam. But I was tired so I went to sleep believing I would probably get eaten by a bear; I thought fifty percent, maybe. "G'night, honey, I love you and it was nice knowing you."

"Mmumfgm."

Maybe one hour after I had gone to the land of deep sleep lying on my back after stargazing, I realized I was *BEING EATEN!* My *FACE* was being eaten! Noisily! Slurping and huffing! A giant black bear was actually *TASTING* my face! All over! Hot steamy bad breath! I started screaming and tried to fight him off! That, momentarily at least, seemed to hurt his feelings and he backed off, but when I sat up, he came at me again. He wasn't done devouring my face.

I was being eaten by the *most affectionate* black lab on this earth! You woulda thought he was *my* dog and I'd just returned home from the war! My wife was about to die laughing. "Oh, big brave Alan got his face all slobbered up by a little puppy dog? Did him wet da bed? Maybe you should brush your teeth and wash your face before you go to bed. You prob'ly smell just like his dog dish."

I heard somebody elsewhere in the campground call for his slobbery tongue thrashing love hound. He skedaddled. My wife kept laughing. I cuddled up behind her and used her long curly hair to dry my face. "Whaddya doin'?"

"Nothin'."

* * * * * *

It was in that same Caddy on a different camping trip when we had just left Wallace Kellogg, Idaho area when something odd happened on a nice summery Sunday afternoon. We had the convertible top down, sailing east on I-90.

We tried to stop in Wallace when we could, to visit the little ice cream shop in town. They had *the best* licorice, in those two or three-gallon tubs. This day they only had maybe a quart or two left in the tub; I've always tried to buy in bulk, so we made a deal—I bought it all—and we hit the road.

Cheryl drove and I fed her ice cream from the bottom of our big cardboard bucket. I of course fed myself, too. She's a pretty dainty little diner so I gave her smaller, neater spoonsful so as to not get her and her hair all licoricy. Me? I didn't care too much about the wind blowing licorice dribbles all over my face—I mean, you never know, I just might meet up tonight with a nice black lab that would just love to wash it all off in my sleep. Or a grizzly.

We did finish it off and I could barely move, so I climbed over the seat to take a nap on the sunny back seat. I don't know how long I was able to sleep off my ice cream overdose when I realized Cheryl was annoyed about something, and it wasn't me for a change, so I didn't care. I tried to go back to sleep. I could "see" the treetops of the Great Northern Cascade Mountains whizzing by through my closed and partially comatose eyelids when I registered Cheryl's slightly erratic gas pedal. "What are you doing?" I asked, eyes still closed.

"I got a couple fools in an orange G.T.O. that're buggin' me."

Apparently they would pull up next to us and stay there, so they could check her out. Then they'd pass us and slow down. Then she would pass them, only for them to repeat. "I think they want me to stop and give'm blowjobs." "Well, I don't blame them for that," I thought quietly.

My bladder was talking to me anyway, so I asked, "Where are they now?"

"Right behind us. Real close."

I sprang up, feet on the back seat, knees braced on the seat back and apart, unzipped and let 'er fly. Yellow piss was goin' all over a beautifully restored '67 orange G.T.O. and my face looked like I'd been eating coal dust. Wide-eyed, they drifted way back, not to be seen again.

24

MEESE

As long as we're swapping wildlife stories, here's another parenthetical pair. But first, I'd like to clear something up that's irrannoyed me, ever since I was in grade school.

If plural of "goose" is "geese," why on God's green earth is the plural of "moose" not "meese"? This isn't rocket surgery *or* brain science; it's *common sense,* right? I mean what do we have to do to get this changed—an act of Congress? Oh, wait, that would be the wrong people to approach; most of them don't even speak the same language; think "Tower of Babel." I withdraw the motion; besides, they have much more important things to do that they're not doing.

I had shipped a 40-foot-long container of antiques up to Anchorage and had sponsored my own sale and auction at the armory on "Seward" Avenue, and was driving an older "rentadent" station wagon. I was driving down "Muldoon" early one morning to open my sale. Approaching a rather long curve, I noticed an older full-size pickup emerging from around that curve towards me; typical oncoming light traffic, except his headlights were blinking erratically. "That dude has a 'short' in his headlights," I told myself, and I monitored his taillights in my sideview mirror as he disappeared behind me. "If he doesn't get that fixed he's liable to catch fire," I mumbled to myself, then I looked ahead, almost too late.

I saw two boxcars, each with four spindly, knobby and lanky legs coming right at me, sideways. I had been going fifty m.p.h. when I hit the brakes. My tires were screeching as I slid up to the belly of boxcar #2, within inches of that cow moose's kneecaps. Neither cow even so much as blinked. My hood ornament was level, and inches away, from her belly button. And they stood there.

She slowly turned her huge head to look at me. I was given a distinct "Just *what* do you think you're *doing?*" look from her. Along with, "You *know* the rules up here." Indeed I did. The rules had been explained to me by my friend, Al Patterson, in whose house I was staying, years before: "You can beat your wife, you can beat your kids, you can beat your dog. But *don't* hurt our moose!" And Al was an attorney, familiar with Alaska law, so I had no interest in decreasing the City of Anchorage's moose herd—which consists of 800— down to 799. They slowly moseyed off and away from their own private crosswalk. Which is *anywhere* they are. My station wagon would have taken out all four of those stick legs. She would have sheared off the top half of the car and *both* of us would be dead. Glad I had good brakes on the old "rent-a-dent."

That guy in the pickup was *WARNING* oncoming drivers that there were *moose in the road.* But nobody had explained this to this "Cheechako."

* * * * *

On our way to "Thunder Bay, Ontario," driving a 24-foot "U-Haul" truck around midnight a few years back was another *very* scary moose encounter in which I was fearful not just for the big bull, but also for my wife.

Maybe twelve o'clock at night with *no* traffic, way up North, getting close to Canada, off Lake Michigan, a lot of up and down short hills and a full moon. I actually hesitate to say the moon was full—which it was, simply because for *some* reason—99.9% of the time we see *a moon* in any movie or TV series...the moon. Is. *Always.*

Full! Why? Does that make it a better production? Or do they only film *that* scene one night a month? Oh, I can see it on the set now, "Okay, cut! That was no good. Uh-oh. The moon just changed. It's not quite full anymore—okay, clear the set—keep your costumes on and come back in a month. At dark sharp." I mean, it's just stupid. Do they think their ratings are gonna plummet because they showed us a crescent moon or a half moon once in a while? Are the censors to blame for this? Is there something titillating about a partial moon? Partial nudity (or full) okay, but *no* partial moon? Who knows what our youth of today will be triggered to do after witnessing that shameful scene? I betcha they can find it on the almighty internet, though, *full moon.* I'd like to give'm all a full moon. Where was I? Oh, yeah, thundering my truck at 65 m.p.h. to Thunder Bay, to pay for the new transmission a local shop installed in my broke-down and abandoned pickup truck that my friend Bill had left there for me.

We were gaining speed on a good downhill grade, *maybe* 70, when we spooked an enormous *rack* from the brush on our right. It was connected to and running with an elephant of a bull moose! He made the moose *I've* seen look like donkeys!

The best thing for lots of critters' safety at night when on the road is your *horn* because they often mistake your headlights for safety. So I laid on my horn while loudly downshifting—this was a good old five-speed clutch. *And* I was braking. He never did get in front of us, for which we are all grateful, but soon the point came that our speeds *matched* which was the next crucial moment in what *could* go wrong.

He was *full* speed, and I am trying to slow on a steep hill, with a full load. That moose rack covered and "clacked" on Cheryl's half of the windshield. He was panicked, swaying that five-foot rack from side to side. He and I both were veering left towards the ditch and a long rock wall. I was *still* passing him slightly and please know, this whole thing only lasted a few seconds—but tell that to your sphincter—my fear at this point was his humongous swaying rack would easily shatter Cheryl's door window—along with her beautiful face.

Seemed like forever, but he drifted back, and soon we had passed that gentle monster of his own paradise. I saw him in the moonlight thunder off the roadside and down into the land of few loud metallic interlopers, safe for now. I'll have to ask Cheryl what we did next. I think we stopped the truck and…I don't remember…went and peed probably. And hugged. Well, never mind that, she just came home from visiting her mom in California, to *remind* me what happened next. Good timing, Honey.

Once we'd passed him, apparently we did *not* stop, we just kept going, laughing hysterically.

Cheryl just now told me we didn't need to because we'd already "crapped our pants."

She, of course, was more worried about that magnificent animal, as was I, but *I* was *more* fearful for her; they are *powerful.*

How many women can say they were close enough to French kiss a bull moose? At forty miles an hour?

25

Mom Was Right

Three days ago, we detained a criminal; and it did not go smoothly because he didn't want detention. This guy had been a problem here on Broadway for over a year. At least that is how long he has been threatening to kill *me*. Short story:

In front of six or seven of us on the sunny sidewalk, he assaulted a three-year-old—then was ready to fight one of the women there when I got involved. High water pressure in the nose, mouth, and eyes he did *not* like. When he charged me, I went low for a waist tackle. He didn't like that idea either. I *was* driving him backwards, though, but at some point our eyes met when I saw him readying a nice fat "haymaker" roundhouse swing. Halfway around, I ducked and it landed on my wife's left jaw. That's when I took him down. With one problem: my arms were wrapped around his legs so I donated a *lot* of skin to the city sidewalk, as well as hemoglobin. He's going to be gone awhile.

The E.M.T. showed up and dressed my wounds, including a couple truckloads of gauze in the process. Within one day the gauze congealed into the exposed fascia of my arms. It took me four-and-a-half hours to separate the fabric from all the exposed meat. *Then* I went to Urgent Care. When they asked what happened, I explained and added, "Four hundred pounds landed on these arms, his two hundred and mine."

The following is an interruption—think "infomercial."

My mom had been a nurse and she'd told me when I was maybe twelve years old, "If you want to catch staph infection, go to the hospital; that's where most people get it." "Why would I want that? I just wanna catch fish. And I don't want infected ones. Aren't hospitals supposed to be safe?"

"Yeah, *too* safe—they drown everything in alcohol and kill off all your natural "bugs," so staph moves into your wound."

I had filed that one and for the rest of my life felt squeamishly uneasy whenever I or someone else swabbed me down with alcohol. So there I am at Urgent Care talking to my very capable Dr. Stephanie.

"I inhaled an entire quart of rubbing alcohol prying that gauze outta my 'garfs' for fourand-a-half hours." Proud that I'd done it antiseptically sound. "That stuff burns like hell, too." She was pretty and I wanted her to know how tough I was. "We don't use alcohol anymore, or hydrogen peroxide either. They both kill off all the *good* germs."

"You're talking about *staph infection,* aren't you? What *do* you use?"

Above her mask, her forehead and eyebrows went up to form about twenty horizontal lines, as she nodded in silent concurrence. "We use warm tap water. It's safer."

* * * * *

So my mom knew way back then.

* * * * *

I had a kitten right around when I was ten, maybe nine. A little black and white number who slept at my armpit every night—we were good buddies. He'd follow me around like a puppy, and I thought that was the coolest thing ever, that he took me to be the most important person in his little world. Not yet knowing what dismal sadness and grief would come of it. You know how little kids just take off running for no reason sometimes? That's what I did—from our back door and heading up the trail toward the woods to drive some stolen nails into my four-story tree fort. My little armpit cuddler didn't want to be left behind and soon caught up and passed me.

I was full stride and mid-air when he came full stop from a dead run as cats can. My right heel came down onto the top of his tiny head. Instinctively collapsing my right knee to take all the weight I could off him, I folded into a limp pile around him, and scooped him up. He seemed distressed but looked okay; he wasn't.

By the end of the second day of my tiny buddy not eating or drinking because of a broken-and frozen in place-lower jaw, the obvious was approaching. Obvious to my folks, anyway. My kitty and I were in denial. All he wanted was to crawl on me, curl up and purr. I just hoped he would heal up and get better. Every once in awhile he would look up to see if I was still there holding him, staring into my eyes and purring again. He seemed so happy. He was dying.

"Son, he's starving to death." From my dad.

"Maybe his jaw will be better tomorrow," I tried to reason. And that is when my mom offered up some of the strangest bit of voodoo of all times to my young hopeful ears. (In fact, that's still true today, because it has never been corroborated by anyone I have encountered.) "Alan, when a cat is *going to die*, they will get a diagonal line going through their left eye."

By the time I was fifteen or so, I *knew* my mom could rattle off some nonsense not worth listening to, like all fifteen-year-olds, but at this young age I still paid attention. I looked at my dad who was looking at her with a "Where in the *hell* did *that* come from?" gaze on his brow.

I came home from school on the fourth day, picked up my friend and went to my room. He was purring his open-mouthed little head off as he stood on my stomach, sniffing my face and hair, nuzzling my cheek and looking lovingly into my eyes.

That's when I saw the streak running from top right to bottom left of his left eye—clear as a bell. Circumstances had diagonally cancelled my kitty. All hope also now cancelled, I knew what I had to do. Passing our woodpile, I found a suitable club for my young hand and, both of us trembling, him from hunger and thirst and me from fear and grief, carried my little package of devotion up the trail to our doom.

I set him down on his thin shaky small legs and stood up, bawling my eyes out and raised my club as he raised his wobbly little head to look at me for the last time. I told him how sorry I was to do this terrible thing that must be done. I gave him one last tearful look.   That's when I learned how spineless I was. Oh, I hit him hard enough, but I could *not* keep my eyes open for the "hit" I needed— that *he* needed. I'd missed his head. Again. Same thing, partial only. I just couldn't do it right because I couldn't watch. It is sad to say that it took the *eighth* blow to make this barely even alive small creature for *my* comfort lie silent and still. I had botched it. I tried to do the merciful thing but had turned it into a bludgeoning. My poor small empath.

I buried him there, threw the club and drug the shovel home, loudly watering our trail of tears as I did so. I stayed outside 'til dark, blubbering away my sorrows partly for him but mostly for myself realizing how self-centered I am.

* * * * * *

My mother had been right about that one, too, because I *saw that line* plain as day. I wish I hadn't …but something had to be done. Too bad it was me that tried to do it. My dad had offered, but I declined, saying, no, he's my kitty, I'll do it. Believing I was man enough. The poor thing.

26

Transformers

October tenth, 1962. It was a dark and VERY stormy night.

"Typhoon Frieda" or the "Columbus Day Storm" hit us hard here in the Northwest. We're not used to the kind of abuse we got that night.

Electricity was the first to go. But everybody ended up with lots more firewood than they had the day before. Trees came down by the truckload; big Douglas firs, three-four feet thick, uprooted. Many across people's houses, cars, garages and relatives. Smaller trees just broke off and sailed across the road. And it didn't let up.

The rather large grove of older "second-growth" fir trees across Kinwood Road sounded much like nearby Fort Lewis when their firing range was going full blast. A small grenade here, another one there, then machine gun *"BAP! BAP! BAP! BAP!"* When the falling tree snaps off all the larger and smaller limbs of its neighbors on its way earthward, to yet another mortarlike "KA-WHUMP!" when landing.

I was a little over seventeen years old so I thought this was the coolest thing since firecrackers. And girls. I was to sustain serious injury from both in the years to come. I've never been much worried about things that explode, mainly because I couldn't afford to buy them. However, I've always been afraid of women. And I would later learn they too can sometimes explode; especially the ones with pretty red hair. I've actually always been afraid of *anyone* deemed smarter than me, which includes pretty much *all* women, quiet people and people that don't procreate. But I wasn't afraid of falling trees or tree limbs from above—the loggers call them "widow makers."

So nobody in our house was surprised when I announced my intentions at around eight o'clock that I was going to go up to "Jimmy's" house to see how things were going in their dark home.

"Yer gonna get *killed* out there."

"Mom, I'm taking the trail, not the road. There's no trees all the way up to his road, just bushes."

"That wind is going to blow your skinny ass all the way to Oregon!" from my dad.

"Well, that's cool! 'Cause I've never even been outta this county. Which way is Oregon?"

"It's the same way the wind's blowing, dumb-ass!"

The cat woke up from on top of the sleeping dog that he always slept on, and both followed me to the door. I assumed they wanted "out." When I opened it their eyes got real big and they became afraid; neither one of them cared for all the roaring and shrieking that the wind was doing. The dog whined and crawled back behind our woodstove. The cat stayed there staring into the noisy black abyss. I think he saw something out there that he didn't like at all, because he took to that "fight or flight" stance cats have—full alert, tensed, ready to leap and run—in whatever direction necessary. I think it might've been a herd of elk rolling around in the typhoon on their way to Oregon. Lucky bastards.

"*Will you close that damn door!*"

"Dad, the kitty wants out."

"Well, then, take him with you, and get the hell outta here! Hope ya both like Portland!" "Isn't Portland in Maine?" Proud that I actually passed a class. "C'mon, kitty, you want *out?*" He looked up at me, and seemed to say—"Do I *look* that *stupid* to you?" And headed back to the fire. Off I went, into the wind.

And it was warm, balmy even, no lights anywhere. The world seemed immersed into an impossibly over amplified bowl of "Rice Krispies." "*Snap!! Crackle!! Pop!!*" all around me with an occasional long tortured "*Grooooan!*" of a falling, about to crash land, fifty-foot-tall stack of green firewood.

The trail emptied into a maybe two-acre field of brown grass, black tonight as was all. Where the tall blowing dead vegetation ended, the gravel and small dirt road to Jimmy's home joined. In three or four more strides I would turn right. Then it happened.

My brain—my very being—my consciousness "imploded!" and I was out cold. For how long I had no way of knowing, probably around half an hour judging by our plastic green "Westclox" that hung on our wall when I made it back. I did not go see Jimmy. My head felt like it was in a vise.

When I had lain there on my back with barely the energy to open my eyes, I realized I *was* dead and I was okay with that, I guess. I accepted the fact and knew I couldn't do anything about it. I was, however, concerned about *where* I ended up; I had heard stories about the possibilities. I lay there for a while watching the millions of fiery sparkles cascading down onto me. "That's a good sign," I thought. But on the other hand, isn't fire a clue that I might've ended up in…wait a minute, I'm *not* dead! I sat up and scrutinized the sky, still shimmering sparks.

The fog lifted and as cranial things cleared up somewhat, it dawned on me that the power pole I lay right next to had exploded. The burning huge transformer *directly* above me had gone to hell and it did its level best to take me with it. I'd had enough.

I rose on wobbly legs and hobbled home. The loud fiery concussion—that I *do not* really remember—had blown me off my feet and rendered me unconscious. I curled up behind the stove, on the floor with my wimpy dog and cat.

About the same time I had been nearly sent to some kinda happy hunting ground there was a nice lady named Joann Smith, laboring away with a sea nymph two states away. The Daughters of Titan, or some say Neptune, are said to frolic in our seas and rivers worldwide; these tiny "oceanicas" are sprinkled mostly in our oceans and larger waterways and apparently they are susceptible to severe wind changes because this night, October tenth, 1962, the winds of "Typhoon Frieda" blew one small sea sprite out of the Pacific Ocean and into my life.

At the same time the anvil of "Thor" was sending electric charges from the heavens to eradicate one lower form of life on earth—mine—Cheryl Yvonne Smith was born. My future bride. The one with the *most beautiful smile* I have ever seen. Long legs and gorgeous curly red hair. It was the best of nights, it was the worst of nights.

I'm pretty sure that concussion didn't help my grades for the next year and a half, and they were already bad enough.

27

THE CLAW MACHINE

The "Fun Circus" was a large popular hangout for all the pinball enthusiasts in the area. On Pacific Avenue and 13th, here in downtown Tacoma, in the six-story beautiful and historical "Luzon" brick building. It's gone now, just like most of the great old Victorian structures that all of our West Coast cities, in the seventies, and even now, we couldn't wait to tear down and build something truly ugly. Portland, Oregon, being an exception. Seattle has completely sold out; it's one big Nike, Planet Hollywood, Cheese Factory, Starbucks and Amazon. Seattle no longer has the "soul" it once had. But I'm old.

Doug Bassett, another local antique dealer, told me about a cool old oak "claw machine" that was moldering away in the basement. Doug was *not* one to get his hands dirty. Or his feet wet. Or risk over-working *any* muscle group whatsoever. I would be the one to do all the above.

The 1933 Art Deco "Chicago Coin" claw machine was owned by "Randy," the proprietor of the Fun Circus, above the muddy base-ment. It was to be a simple enough deal—three-way split— Randy, the owner, Doug, who did nothing and still does, and some strong, dumb and simple brute named Alan to haul it out, clean it up *and* market it.

On a warm and sunny summer morning long ago, I loaded up one of my extension ladders, some heavy-duty 1" thick rope and my right-hand guy at the time, John Swales.

The Luzon building's access to the basement was outside, hidden from pedestrian view because of the steep incline of 13th Street. It was a 4'x4' hole in the vertical wall that supported the sidewalk, facing the street, with the building itself at my back. We removed the panel and were hit by a rush of hot steamy/stale dank air and a heavy scent of mud. It was to me reminiscent of all the swampy lakes' edges I had stomped around on as a kid; smelled like home to me. Of course, musclebound John, who was rather finicky about nearly everything, especially his hair, didn't like it.

"I'm not goin' down there—it's dark."

"Our eyes will adjust once we get outta this sunshine. Help me get the ladder around these corners."

"It's dirty."

We did struggle to "bend," so to speak, that ladder through and down to the soggy earthen floor, about twelve feet. It was very tight, but we scraped and angled it around and forced it down. I made my descent. I'm already sweaty, but now I'm standing in two inches of muddy soup water in a low budget steam bath. And I have my very own light show.

In fact, what I saw then, I had only seen in movies.

There was in the corner a bare wire. A *live* bare wire, and it was hanging down from the floor above me, about twenty feet away. And it was *swinging!* There was, of course, no wind down here, but it was pendulous. It was its very own *perpetual motion device.* After it had swung over and contacted something metallic sticking out from the brick wall—an old pipe perhaps—with a loud sparkly **kauvooot!** And a bright shower of sparks would fly in every direction; then it would swing back the other direction, only to return a few seconds later for another loud, brilliant contact, like clockwork. Repeat. Like I said, only in the movies do you see this—you are never going to witness this in real life, right? Yet, there it was, in full bloom. John got bored up on top and bravely climbed down. He was halfway there when he witnessed my special effects.

"What the hell was that?"

"What's what?"

"That noise, and where'd that flash of light come from?"

"I dunno, I didn't see anything." As I sloshed my way through all sorts of junk toward the six-foot-tall three-foot-square arcade device.

"There it was again" And it's comin' from over there!" He's still on the ladder. "I can't get this thing out alone. I need some help here." He climbs down two more rungs and then:

"Gahhh! There it is! Is that electricity!?! What was that?! Are you trying to scare me!?! Aheeeyah! There it goes again! Is this one of your damn tricks?"

"Will you stop fooling around and help me?" He finally makes his way down and realizes his feet are now wet.

"Hey! I'm standing in water! Is this *raw sewage*? Yeeow! There it is again! How are you doing this to me?" One foot back on the ladder.

"I told you your eyes would adjust, getcher ass over here. Did you bring the rope?"

"What rope? Eeyah! Dammit! There it is! It never stops! Alan, that there's **electricity**!

And I'm standing in *some kinda* water! I'm pretty sure I read somewhere how you..."

"Here, I'll lean the top over to you, I'll take the bottom. I wouldn't want you to get your hands dirty. And don't drop it when that thing goes off again."

"Yeeeah! I've only seen stuff like that in the movies. This doesn't happen in real life, does **it?**"

"Leave it right here by the ladder. *I'll* go get the damn rope." Knowing full well that if he went he'd keep going. The Greyhound bus station was right across the street. John was macho like that. The real fun was about to begin.

After getting some good loops and knots around and under the nickel machine I let John ascend from the Valley of Hinnom, Gehenna, the Valley of Death, to the top of the ladder, with rope in hand. He finally stopped screaming every twenty seconds. He felt safe up there, sucking in all the nice healthy exhaust from the hundreds of cars barreling up 13th Street, inches from his face.

We hoisted it, sliding its back panel up along the ladder to the point where I could get my back under the bottom of it, so I could ascend the ladder backwards, "Atlas" style. Mud is now dripping all over me. I could also feel some tiny incisions from the metallic trim, its bottom on my now bare skin. We'd taken our shirts off a while ago.

It was *all* we could do to get to the top, and it was getting heavier by the minute. John and I were both pouring from our pores. We started angling it through the corners and out the access hole, to freedom.

The eight-to-sixteen-foot extension ladder that I stood on had barely made it through.

After one hell of a valiant effort it became clear that the six-foot arcade of antiquity would *not*. It was too wide. We were done.

"Alan, I can't hold on much longer."

"I know. Neither can I. I'm going back down." I was still in the roofing trade part of the time, so my legs were in great shape from packing hundreds of bundles of roofing material up ladders. At this moment, however, my thighs *were done*. I had no choice. I *had* to depend on whatever I had left in the tank to get back down to the bottom—the machine would crush me if I failed. I could see that one in the papers: *Antique Dealer Flattened by his Antiques!*

"Just take as much weight off me as you can!"

"I…Ammm!"

And now it was time to cuss a lot and recover. John came down the ladder to where the claw monster leaned on the ladder. He sat on the rung with his feet on the article of our defeat. We panted in our private electrified steamy mud bath for a while. Then it hit me! (Not the machine. It wasn't *that* clever; it would be decades before we'd invent machines that would fight back. I went outside to get a newspaper the other morning and got run over by a "hologram!") My friend, Rex Bennett, had a tattoo business upstairs in a small shop off from the noisy "Fun Circus." *And* he had a *trapdoor* under an oriental rug in it. Something *else* you only see in movies, right? I only knew about the trapdoor because that's how I was shown where the claw machine was before I agreed to "the deal."

I was in no mood for formalities or niceties or requisitions of any kind. "We're gonna go this way. Grab the bottom."

"What? Which way? *That* way? It's even darker over *there!*"

"Shut up and lift!" We did indeed head into the far dark corner, where I knew there were stairs.

"Eeew! What did I just step on? Was that a skull? That was nasty! Are there rats down here? What is *that* smell?"

"Just follow me, and don't drop it again!" I found the dark stairs and started up.

"Where are we going? It's even darker up *there.*"

When we got near the top, I felt my head touch the underside of Rex's secret passageway to Mudville.

"Just keep coming," I told John, as I gradually pushed up on the hinged door with the top of my head. I felt the carpet slide down and off the door. Then, when the wooden door was vertical, I flicked my head back slightly and heard the door hit the floor.

"What in **hell** is going on?!?!" I recognized Rex's voice. His back had been to us, and he was tattooing some poor guy. He stopped to face us. "*Alan!* Is that you? What the hell *happened* to you?"

The sweat in my eyes was evidently mixed with not only mud, but blood. This machine *had* fought back.

"You look like shit! Get outta here! I thought I'd seen it all in my day. Well, I've seen everything now. Crawlin' up outa the sewer in the middle of the day, in the middle of my shop, in the middle of my tatt...." His voice trailed away behind us as we moved closer to the exit and my van.

"**Sewer**!?!" Did I hear that old guy say *sewer*?! I *knew* it! Do you know how many diseases we just swam around in **down there**?!?"

"You ready for some lunch and a couple cold ones?"

"Sure! But I'll have to go fix my hair."

28

TACOMA WASHINGTON AREA TWO DOLLAR BILL

The following is *not my* story;
this is a recent interview with a normally
very quiet and private character:
"TWO DOLLAR BILL."

Me: "Thanx for meeting with me, Bill, I know you've been busy."
"Yeah. Doin' what I do is exhausting; you should come with me sometime. You may not know it, but it's hard bein' me."
"Maybe so. But can you tell me some stories; I've heard about you and I know you have some great ones?"
"You mean just pick some from over the years? Like random?"
"From what I've heard they're *all* pretty random. Judging from what people have said after running into you at the bottom of a freeway offramp—at the stoplight."
"Buddy, are they ever."

Now, before Two Dollar Bill begins, please let me elaborate by "setting the stage" as it were: his stages *are* freeway offramps with a stoplight, where Bill—looking quite raggedy, possibly homeless and haggard, unshaven and donning dirty jeans and shirt, while also sporting a neon green faded baseball cap with the name "Bill" ON the bill, includes his auburn-colored braided ponytail trailing out from behind and down the middle of his filthy shirt back.

Two Dollar Bill's tattered old cardboard placard which hangs by a copper wire around his neck reads:

NEED HELP?
HOPELESS weirdo WANTS to
ASSIST IN SOME SMALL WAY
Even a couple bucks helps, right?

In order to understand when motorists "read" his placard, you have to realize people really don't read—not much—not in this situation. Bill told me he watches people's eyes when they pull up and stop, doing their best to not make eye contact with his.

But what they DO see is, the twenty to forty TWO-DOLLAR BILLS he has fanned out like tail feathers on a male peacock in his gnarly old left hand. Brand spanking crisp two-dollar bills—they DO see these—even though they are actively and furtively doing their level nervous best to NOT LOOK. They look. They squint. Then they squint at the cardboard sign on Bill's chest. Just long enough to NOT read the fine print.

Now, I think, if you are like me, you might agree that a two-dollar bill IS an odd currency, not regarding denomination, but visually; EVERYBODY takes another glance or two, askance, at one. "Is that a twenty—a fifty—or what?" Because we don't see lots of them in circulation, yet here's this scroungy dude with a huge handful of them and one LONE two-dollar unit in his grubby RIGHT hand, supplication fashion, hands upturned in a pleading fashion. Needy, as if asking for mercy. A lowly slave before Pharoah. Genuflecting. Groveling.

"What? What is it you want, and get away from my car," is what Bill said he got a lot. To which he would very softly and plaintively answer, "Nothing. I just want YOU to have THIS." At which point he would carefully thrust out his right hand, the one with the lone two-dollar bill in it close to the driver, where he or she could actually scrutinize it, all the others still fanned out—left hand.

And that's the moment when it all changed. That's the very moment that I understood Two Dollar Bill was trying to GIVE THEM money! And that's when the party started.

After his demonstration to me of what he was up to, I began to understand what he was doing to these poor unsuspecting and unprepared innocent motorists of all ages and stripes. "I call these things I do—'experiments into the theory of unpredictability.'—they DO NOT see it coming. They don't know how to respond. It's sort of my own private study in human reactions and sociology. And you wouldn't believe some of the stories."

"That's why I'm here, Bill. Did you study Sociology in college?"

"Hell, no. I hated every minute of school—why would I go to college?"

"Fair enough. Is "Bill" your real name and can you tell me some stories?"

"No—it's not my real name; I don't want people to know who I am. And yes—I'll tell you some examples—how much paper and how much time do you have?"

After telling me that he only occupies his spot on the offramp intersection for a maximum 15 to 20 minutes, because that's when a cop or a journalist might show up, he informs me that a lot can go down in those few minutes—IF people roll down their windows— he begins: "Some people just glare—most people's mouths are open while they're trying to figure out WHAT my angle IS; I mean that IS how we're all programmed now, right? 'This guy MUST be working some kinda scam. NOBODY that looks like he does is gonna be standing in the rain handing out money…right?' And that's when the light turns green And people start honking; off they all go—with that same look on all their faces—asking others in their car—'What in hell was THAT all about?' A few take a picture as they accelerate.

"I can almost smell the crossed up and overheated wires in their brains crackling and fizzling. The people that interact with me get it the worst; if they ask me what I'm doing, then I get to look them in the eye while pushing this money gently into their reach. All they have to do is take it while I PLEAD with them to do so. Some of them can't handle it. THEY CALL THE COPS."

"One time, a few years ago, before the cops showed up, a couple guys drove up in a pickup, window down, and asked me the usual question, 'WHAT are you doin'?' After telling the driver while trying my damndest to give him my two bucks, he says, 'I don't have any change but we just bought a dozen doughnuts, here take one,' pushing the boxful my direction."

"I don't want your change OR your doughnut; I just want you to take THIS!"

" 'OK, I will—but not until you take a doughnut!' So I took the doughnut and he the twodollar bill. Off they went. After a few confused but ecstatic 'customers' and some annoyed ones along with all others that render me invisible, a state patrolman comes walking up to me—the lady who I was talking to quickly rolled up her window. The cop says (what else?):"

"' So we got a couple of calls; what're you DOIN'?"

"The doughnut I had reluctantly taken earlier, I had placed on top of the ten-inch square wooden guardrail post behind me and before I answered him, I pointed at my doughnut and with a deadpan look at the officer said, 'Don't touch my doughnut.'

"He looked longingly at my fluffy treat and declared, 'I don't wantcher doughnut. TELL me whatcher DOING!'

"Well, the best way to explain is: I'll just let you watch. By this time fresh cars had assembled. I approached the first one, money outstretched in both hands, two cars, no takers. Third car snatches the bill from my right hand and quickly rolls up the window, getting his left wrist squished by his own right forefinger on the power window button—the two-dollar treasure goes blowing up the line of cars behind him, onto Interstate 5. After a few more no takers—they were watching the cop—they don't want any part of whatever it was that I was doing wrong, he goes, 'So you're GIVING money away?!?' 'Yep.' I watched HIM trying to connect neurons to other neurons, convincing himself that I must be doing SOMETHING illegal. I could tell he wasn't having any luck, so I helped him out.

" 'There's NO LAW against giving away money. I checked.' I saw a sudden flash of brilliance light up in his eyes, and, 'Hey there, Mr. Bill' (he had heard me tell a driver when asked who I was, 'Two Dollar Bill,' I guess he thought it was my last name). 'Can I see your I.D.?' Now he felt like he was getting' somewhere.

"I handed it to him and went back to work while he walked away, whistling, towards his patrol car, satisfied he was gonna get me for something, ya know? Child support or failure-toappear or jumping bail or indecent exposure or whatever."

"How long was he gone and what happened next? Did he make you stop?" "About fifteen minutes. He walks up to me, watches me for about sixer seven more minutes, then hands me my I.D. and says, 'well,' he called me by my real first name and stammers—'Just… just…JUST DON'T GET HURT!' Then he was gone, glad to be rid of me. That's the day I learned to not stay in one spot for too long, get outta there before they start rollin' up."

"Was that the only time the police harassed you?"

"Oh, no. They get real pissed. It wasn't long after that time— that was at 320th and I-5—that a cop nailed me down at Highway 18 and I-5 exit and he was real mean."

"I'm here for stories, Bill, and thanks."

"No problem. So I'd just gotten there and this 'stater' comes slidin' up in the gravel—almost hit me, JUMPS out and hollers, 'You can't beg for money HERE!'

"So, I'm scared, and I said 'I'm NOT! I'm giving money AWAY!'

" 'No, yer n…,' he says, and that pause coupled with all the money I fanned out in my hands, told me everything I needed to know—he'd heard all about Two Dollar Bill beforehand. So now he goes, 'Well—ya can't do that here, either—go down there, somewhere else, ya can't do it HERE.' 'Cause I guess this was HIS turf. Ya know?"

"How about examples that didn't involve law enforcement, how people react?" "No, that, so far, was almost the last time the cops came around—but there's a million other stories about NOR-MAL people; like the time the lady in the new Mercedes rolls up, rolls down her window, and tries to give me twenty bucks!"

"Did you take it?"

"NO! I politely declined, while holding my hands, full of money out towards her.

"Then she goes, 'Well, WHAT DO you want?'

" 'Nothin', I just want YOU to have THIS.' And I hand her a brand new two-dollar bill. She wads up her twenty, throws it on the floor of her Mercedes and starts bawling! I mean, she was havin' a breakdown! The light went green—'Thank you! Thank you! Thank you!' she hollers as she drives away, still bawling her eyes out.

"Then there was another time over on 272nd and I-5 North that an older pickup truck pulls up with a buncha stuff in the back, two people. The woman was driving and both looked like hell. She says, 'we don't have any money.' Quietly, while staring straight ahead.

" 'Well, if you take this, you will have,' as I handed it to her. She took it, looked at it, then me, and asked, 'Who ARE you?' 'Two Dollar Bill,' as I pointed at the bill of my hat where it says BILL.

" 'Our house just burned down! We just drove away from it five minutes ago; we lost everything! This is all we could save!' as she jabs her thumb over her left shoulder, SHE starts cryin'.

" 'You're the first person we've talked to since; and you GAVE US this! Bill! THIS MEANS everything's gonna be OKAY!!'

"Now she's REALLY crying. 'God bless you, Bill! I'll remember this for the rest of my life—I'll never spend it!' through her tears, as they drive onto 272nd."

"Do you make all the women cry?"

"No, only those two, so far; I've seen a few others well up a little—because they're so surprised, I guess. Because it's so random; they don't see it comin'. That's why I enjoy doin' this to people— all the differing reactions—it's so cool to watch people's brains start twitching around in their head; I mean, what would you do?"

My own brain twitched at this query; I knew what he meant. If I had no idea about Bill's oddball "project" here, I don't know what I'd do—I really don't. So I just shook my head. I think I heard a rattling sound.

"Ya see what I mean? Folks can't FIND this anywhere in their mental roll-o-dex." (I already noted that Bill was no "spring chicken.") "It's sorta like 'Candid Camera,' but the light turns green and that's that. I get to mess with 'em even more sometimes."

"For instance?"

"Car pulls up—I'm at THE PORT OF TACOMA Road and I-5—guy has three screeching little kids jumping around in the car which has so much snot and whatnot I couldn't see through the windows. He takes the two bucks—eyes wide—and asks me, 'What do you want me to DO with it, Two Dollar Bill? Do you want me to go get you SOME FOOD?' Kids are squallorin' like hell. 'What should I DO with this?' he asks again.

'Well, in your case I'd think about gettin' a vasectomy. Hey, you got a green light.' And he was gone. So he got some free money—good advice—a great experience and a free insult. My cost? Two bucks."

"True in that case, Bill—the two bucks, I mean, but you give away a TON of other two dollars with not much of a story to go with them, right?"

"Not really. It's HARD to get people to take them. You wouldn't believe how much cajoling I have to do to get them to take one. Almost NOBODY does! Except for the time I donned my Santa costume and did it on Christmas Day; I WON'T be doin' that again. They all just snatched them outta my hand as they sped by, not even a 'thank you.' No, it's not easy to tell people 'It's okay, this is a gift—something you'll talk about later' sort of thing, just NOT at Christmas time, people want ALL THEY CAN GET that time of year, JEESH!"

"Okay, more of the other abstract interactions; sounds like you have a lot of them, please indulge, please divulge, because I can tell you enjoy telling these anecdotes." "That's why I DO IT! So that I can relay to others HOW WEIRD we are as a society! Happy to share these short vignettes with, you know, normal people who probably never witnessed and enjoyed seeing OTHER NORMAL people sitting in their vehicles, brains aflame with disconnect. While I'm BEGGING them to take money."

"You mentioned 'insults.' Any more like the vasectomy guy?"

"Yeah, there's others—I can't think of too ma—oh, here's another one: dude pulls up and doesn't want the two dollars but finally takes it because I'm getting ready to break down in fake tears, then HE says, 'What should I do with it?' which is a stupid thing to ask me because I'll come up with SOMETHING. I had already noticed what HORRIBLE teeth he had. So quite naturally I said, 'I'd go straight to the dentist!' Then somebody honked. If they had a filthy car and they ask that, I tell 'em, 'Go wash your car,' or 'get a dog that doesn't bite,' then while driving away I hear 'em holler, 'He never bit anyone BEFORE.' I mean some of them act like I just gave them some magic beans or somethin', like they're gonna go home and plant them and end up with a giant cow or whatever."

"Beanstalk. It was giant beanstalk."

"Oh, yeah. Well whatever."

"Do any of them get really annoyed? Besides the ones that call the cops?"

"Oh, not too many. Here's the deal—first of all there are a lot of them that will NOT look.

They sit there, blankly, not turning their head; some look like they're praying."

"What are they praying for?"

"They're praying for that infernal light to turn green!! So that they can get the hell away from my whimpering ass!"

"You don't ever feel in danger? Nobody has threatened you?"

"I've not gotten that, yet, I mean so far. I've had lots of negative, but not violent stuff. Most everybody—well all that TAKE the money—are tickled pink, some over the top. The trick is to GET them to take it—oh, that's what I started to say—here's the deal: MOST people DO NOT want to be messed with! They don't like leaving their own safe little thought bubble and deal with some geezer standing in the ditch. The fact I'm trying to give them money is like me scraping away at their brain—fingernails on a blackboard, 'DANGER, WILL, ROBINSON—DOES, NOT, COMPUTE!' type response. Once in a while I get some hot-tempered squawker that spews me some vitriol and meaningless vituperations. But violence? Never."

"You talk funny."

"It's fun to watch soccer moms with a buncha kids in the car—Mom looks away as soon as she sees the money, obviously she's been boondoggled before and won't look back; won't face me. The kids—wide-eyed—are all yelling, 'Take the money! Take the money!' These moms, they all drive away screaming at the kids something about taking candy from strangers. 'Mom, that wasn't candy, that was MONEY!'

"Then there's the ones that stop—they're looking straight ahead, haven't seen the money I'm presenting towards their window—and they have a passenger who's watched me and apparently understands. So they start arguing. The driver's window is still up, of course, and I can hear the wife/passenger tell him to take the money. 'Roll down the window and take the damn two dollars!' He starts yellin' at her and I can hear them fighting all the way through the intersection."

"So your little sociology experiment is just to see how many happy families you can split up? Because I think I'm starting to see a pattern here."

"No. No. No. Well, maybe. I mean, if that's all it takes—one two-dollar bill—they weren't gonna last long anyways. But if it was ME that caused it…that would be kinda cool, ya know? Wait a minute! Are you messin' with ME?"

"I don't think so. I thought I was asking the questions."

"Hey, I've had a few people trying to give some spare change, some coins, you know?

Couple quarters, some pennies, nickels, or whatever; three or four coins; and they WOULD NOT take the two-dollar bill unless and until I took the coins! Then they were happy—the transaction had SOME sense of normality to it—the smoke of cerebral discord and discombobulation stopped seeping out of their ears. They were satisfied that I hadn't somehow tricked them. And that has happened several times. Then they leave me standing there, confused as all get out."

"But most of your victims or customers or whatever you call them are appreciative, though, right?"

"Absolutely! It's like the thrill of the week or month or year for some, you know? I mean from the way they act—I dunno—maybe it WAS. I mean, we don't know what they're going through—what's going on in their pathetic little lives. Maybe that small two-dollar interaction brought one or two of 'em offa suicide, right?"

"Yeah. Or drove them to it."

"Y'know, there was one car with a couple in it, just like the one I told you about; he wouldn't take my money and she lit into him; they'd turned right onto Orellia Road when I heard the car backfire, I thought, I couldn't hear any more bickering, but I could see them swerving towards Kent Canyon. Then a crash."

"Sooo…what happened?"

"SeaTac police said it was a murder/suicide and that the guy got it backwards; when he was here in front of me and ignoring me, he didn't look too bright—and that's what she was tryin' to tell him;

I heard the word 'dumbass' a couple times. Do you think I might have caused **it?**"

"I don't know, Bill, would you like to believe it was you?"

"Hmmm…"

"Bill, you seem to have a multi-faceted personality; have YOU ever thought about suicide?"

"I don't know. SHOULD I?"

"Any more cheerful anecdotes?"

"I mean, I guess I never really thought about suicide for myself; it was always something somebody else did—like buyin' a Rolls Royce or something. It's mostly something only rich people do. It's their business; I've always believed in the 'live and let live' approach, ya know?"

"I do now. You mentioned the media. Have they given you any grief or anything?" "Not really. They HAVE tried. That's why I keep moving. That, AND I have to lay off for awhile; because they call or text their radio or TV station. I leave before they get there. Also, if I do it too often, word AND pictures go all over spaceface or wastepage or whatever you people call it. 'Cause I see some people up the line of cars, leaning out the windows, hollering 'Hi! Two Dollar Bill! Hi!' phone in hand. So I lay off for a few months; or I go farther afield, like Lacey, Auburn, Interstate 90 or wherever. But so far so good." "Why are you afraid of the media? Have you done other stuff you don't want the general public to know about?"

"Wull…yes, but that's not the real reason. It's just that what I do as 'Two Dollar Bill' HAS to stay anonymous, under the mainstream—you know—the WIRE; that's the word I was looking for. This whole performance art two-dollar deal can't work if this is known by everyone in the whole state! I mean, I can see it now: cars pull up and they all mumble, 'Hey, Bill, how ya doin'? Is yer knee any better? How's the kids? Thanks fer the two bucks, we really count on 'em you know—that's how we make our car payments. Well, see ya tomorrow. Not exactly the same thing is it? Yeah, the last thing I need is the media…and the police."

"Well, Bill, thank you for talking with me. Sounds like you have a lot of fun. Like that first cop said, ''Don't get hurt!'"

"Oh, I just remembered one you might like, and this one's a hoot. I-5 and 272nd again, northbound. SUV comes up to the light, both windows down on my side, four youngish African American guys in it. Driver takes the two dollars with a big smile and says, 'What about my passengers?' I said, 'Sorry—only one two-dollar bill per vehicle—hey! Now, yer ALL FIDDYCENTS! And the five of us LAUGHED AND LAUGHED. I could still hear them laffin' two blocks away, goin' down 272nd.'"

29

Marines!

Okay, this is another one that has no humor in it as far as I can see, and it took over a month to heal. This, when it happened, my wife and I did not find too funny. I doubt if you will either, but you might; depends on your level of sadism.

We recently were on a vacation cruise to Mexico and while ashore in the lovely port city of Mazatlán, doing the typical tourist trek around town, were wrapping up our excursion. After passing through customs into the Nice Mercado before boarding our ship, our small group of six or so stopped for a cold one at the little outside cantina, "The Green Bar."

The general area was rather busy, with loud music playing, so the gals, my wife Cheryl included, went up to the small pergola to dance. I was looking for a chair, with not much luck.

An African American gentleman next to where I stood was massaging his wife's foot when I interrupted them: "Sir," I said, "I want you to know that I DO NOT have a foot fetish but I'm very good at what you're doing there—I'm Swedish and my daughter is a massage therapist." To which they both enthusiastically agreed to let me take over. They, like us, had hoofed it all over Mazatlan and she looked exhausted, and very grateful for my offer. Her husband, even more so. He left to get a beer.

Thirty seconds into it, I was bent down, over her foot, when–KRRACK!—felt like a baseball bat hit me on my head! I heard some-body yell, "GET AWAY FROM THOSE PEOPLE!" I stood up to see a man around my age snaking through people, chairs and tables to disappear. He'd clubbed me with a beer bottle!

"There's one for the books," I said to the couple I was assisting, while rubbing my skull. And I resumed, after finishing my first beer and ordering another.

Soon, the same thing happened again. "I told you not to touch THOSE PEOPLE!!" And off he goes, he'd sucker punched me with a beer bottle on the same spot! Again! I thought about chasing him down but decided to once again let it go. I mean everybody was trying to relax and enjoy themselves, so I made light of it, but by now we knew what he meant. So I picked up where I left off.

This time he came at me from a different direction, seeking a new line of attack; some people just don't give up when they've got a job to do. And once again all my defenses were down; what are the chances, you know? A billion to one or so, I figure. And there I was laboring away over a nice hot sweaty buncha toes and instep when WHANGG!!! A third airstrike lands solidly on the other side of my bruised and throbbing cranium! My left temple.

This one I'm not gonna take sitting down (although I just had). And once again, he'd hollered, "DON'T TOUCH THOSE PEO-PLE!!" I was right on him—or them—because I was seeing double, when he hit the brakes.

My buddy, "Bad Tom" (yes, we sometimes cruise with friends we've met along the way, including a "good" Tom and a "bad" Tom. Truth is, neither one is very good. One is just worse than the other one) had seen enough of this from across the terrace of tables and rehydrating tourists. He'd jumped up (you should see this guy jump) and cut off beer bottle bonsai at the pass. I grabbed this guy by his shoulder and wheeled him around 180 degrees (not "Bad Tom," he would be too hard to wheel around—the other one).

This is when he decided to fight. He dropped his empty bottle of beer and nailed Tom, right after Tom had said, "Why are you hitting my friend with beer bottles?" indignantly but politely (he's like that).

I took great enjoyment in watching this ex-Marine's right hands (both of them—remember I'm seeing double) bounce off Bad Tom's midsection. From the way it looked he might've broken both right wrists when he ninjaed on that springboard, the way he started massaging them.

THEN ninja bottle boy spins around with his back to us, throws all of his arms up in the air, and starts hollering, "Marines!! Marines!!" with a "come hither" gesticulation. Repeatedly, "Marines!!"

Tom and I looked at each other. I could tell from the look in all four of Tom's eyes he'd reached the same conclusion I had: that this guy had left his sanity in the past some time back. I was done rubbing feet, chasing him, and pondering his past. The Marines never arrived. Neither did the Cavalry.

A handsome young man with a machine gun strapped onto his shoulder did show up, while I sat with a mini block of ice on each side of my head.

He politely asked what had happened—I told him, and he asked a couple other people what they'd seen. And that was the end of that. (He may have been a Marine, but I think those guys are Mexican Navy.)

That's when my lovely Irish-Italian (Sicilian) wife glided down from the very loud dance floor. She wanted to know (1) could we take the handsome young machine gun dude home with us, and (2) what was it she was overhearing on the dance floor that involved *me*? She had assumed I'd either groped somebody (which was partially true) or I had been "streaking" again.

After I gave her a quick synopsis—you know—a guy hit me three times over the head with a beer bottle, and then he hurt his hand hitting Tom's stomach…

"WHAT!!?! He hit TOM? Where is this guy? I'm gonna kill him!!" as she jumps to her feet.

I pointed towards the small Mercado's exit and where the tractor-jitney choo-choo FISHER PRICE-type trains were, to take cruisers back to their ships. Off she went, although I was begging her not to. I should've pointed her the other direction, towards the water; I wonder what she would've done then. Probably gone in the water and then beg for mouth-to-mouth from that machine gun kid, or a chest massage maybe. (I know she likes that, when handsome firemen straddle her and massage her upper torso—I've seen it. "Yeah, she's breathin' better now!" The day that happened, when she opened her eyes, I heard her say, "Am I in heaven?")

I will, from the best of my recollections relate what happened next, to my lovely knightess of a wife; from what she told me. (Remember, you've been warned.)

When she got to the jitney cars, there he was, sitting with his wife in one, waiting. Cheryl climbed up and seated herself behind him and said, "Mister, I'd like to know why you did that to my husband back there!?!"

The guy jumps to his feet, wheels around and dives over the seats onto her. He's punching at her and landing some, while she's matching him punch for punch, although she's pinned and on the bottom (she grew up with four older brothers). Cheryl was trying to work her right leg up to his torso to throw him off. Losing some of his leverage to get a good punch, he goes for her throat—and her eyes—one hand squeezes her throat while the other hand claws away at her right eyeball. She's still pounding away at him while his wife, behind him, is yelling, "Earl! Earl! Stop it!" and yanking at his jacket.

Eventually, Cheryl got her foot high enough for purchase to kick this bastard off her and out of the open car onto the asphalt. (I don't know where the wife ended up.)

As Cheryl tried to get upright and put herself back together best she could , while blinded and nearly chocked to death, they disappeared. She stumbled back into the mercado in that condition, half hysterical, trying to tell what had just happened. She was violently shaking.

A couple of the women in "our" group and a nurse lady that we had met—from a different ship—whisked her into the ladies' room close by.

Cheryl's "aviator Ray Bans" is what saved her sight. They were broken and gone, but he had gotten past them at some point and his fingernail had sliced her soft contact into two halves, so that also had helped to contribute to the salvation of her cornea. The nurse lady was able to extricate the contact.

The bruises were immediate and myriad. On the throat, face, arms, back, ribs and stomach of my bride. Small abrasions on her knuckles. Next few days she hurt all over.

 By the time they'd made it out of the ladies' room, I could hardly open my mouth; the third beer bottle, the one that hit me in the temple area, just above my left ear, had begun to interfere with my jaw opening or closing. For the next three days I could only eat VERY FLAT food.

Nobody saw him again. We think that once the onshore authorities had relayed the story of the attacks to the ship's security, he may have had "instructions" to stay in his stateroom for the remainder of the voyage.

All I know for sure though? Them there "PACIFICO" beer bottles are HARDER THAN HELL!

30

GOOD CITIZEN

You know those local community-conscious meetings that good citizens are encouraged to attend? I used to attend most of them here in Tacoma. Not anymore. And everyone's grateful.

The Pierce County Health Department put out a call-to-arms citywide for property and business owners to show up. They said there were two pressing topics that needed discussing. Nine a.m. Wednesday morning, City Hall, tons of people there, all good people, civicminded redblooded progressive conservatives, patriots all, and concerned about our immediate future. And two cops. And me. Whenever the cops see me, we both flinch. They stood the whole time this meeting went on, in front of all of us, all wary-like, expecting a big fistfight or something. One eye on the donut shop on the corner.

Amanda from the Health Department led the charge. The first topic on the table was our local drug addicts and the souvenirs they leave on the sidewalks and planters when they fall out of their arms. A few people ranted on about how bad they had it where they were. "My tires looked like pincushions when I came home from Wal-Mart." "My dog hasn't been outta the house for three months. Now he's got a bladder infection, and so do I." I thought to myself, "You probably shouldn't be sharing a needle with your drug-addled dog."

On and on it went until Amanda announced that "they" had a solution: start up the needle exchange—again—down on Commerce Street near my front entrance.

I think Amanda and others of her ilk were sorta new to Tacoma because a few of us let them know how bad it *had* been a few years back and how much work it was to get rid of them, almost. That had the cops nodding in agreement. Earlier they were nodding off. Amanda was adamant. Gonna be the best thing ever for Tacoma, bluebirds and rainbows, unicorns and serenading sasquatches. Eventually I'd heard enough. I raised my hand. "It took us twenty years to get rid of most all of them, this is nothing compared to what it **was** like. Why would we invite them back?" She immediately goes back to unicorn dust and sparkle-donkeys. I raised my hand again.

"Amanda, what part of town do you live in?" Oh, the North End? Good, our oldest and most exclusive part of town.

"How about we make you this offer—for the first six months we put that there needle exchange on the street right in front of *your* house? After that we'll take it."

Everybody turned back around to see what Amanda's reaction would be to that deal.

Her reaction? "Well, that brings us to our second topic for discussion today, prostitutes. What do you folks think of our prostitute problem here in Tacoma?"

And yes, you probably already guessed it, up goes my hand for the final time that day. And it was the only one up, so she had to call on me. I heard some guy a few seats away mutter quietly, "They're ugly." Just when Amanda thought she was through with me, she goes, with an exasperated sigh, "Yes. Please, go ahead."

"Well, I think they're too expensive!" A *very* loud collective gasp and then half the room erupted in laughter. The two cops I could see visibly shaking, faces red with tightly closed mouths, choking on invisible donuts. Then it all died down. I guess I figured I still had the floor, so I said:

"And two of 'em still owe me change."

31

Newly Acquired Information

Back when I did a fair amount of public speaking, in one form or another, I got invited to speak at our local Rotary club.

They had intended to throw me a curveball, I think, but I worked it out and all went well. I say curveball because it was a sensitive subject. I believe they assumed I'd make an ass of myself as usual; however, I did my homework, and it went okay.

The subject was on marital bliss and sexual harmony in the bedroom. Well, it could be in the kitchen or on the—well, *I don't care* where you do it! I knew they didn't think I would rise to the challenge, but I did. I did all the research and I even boned up on the all the latest fads, not that this group of old geezers could handle those.

I didn't share with my wife the nature of the topic they had given me. I get enough grief from her as it is. I didn't need any revisions or alterations. I was scratching her back the other night—it always itches right after I shave it—and she's goin', "No, left, no, other left, yeah right—why'd ya move? Go back—up, no, up, no, too far! Go down, not that far!" That's when I made the mistake of saying, "Honey, your back didn't' come with a roadmap."

"Wouldn't matter, you never were any good at following directions."

When she did ask me what my talk was about I kinda blurted out "Boating Safety— safety on the water." I had only sank two boats when I was a kid, but I grew up around all of our lakes in Thurston County.

"Didn't you tell me you sank a buncha boats when you were a kid?"

"The one I burnt down didn't count."

So the event came and went. It had been smooth and bucolic. They thanked me cordially. They tried to get me to join and I cordially declined. A couple people said they learned something but that "now it's too late."

A few months after it was all but forgotten, my wife was stopped by the wife of one of the Rotary club members in Costco. "My husband told me how impressed he and others were at how knowledgeable your husband is on such a delicate subject."

My wife just stared at her and said, "I didn't think he knew that much about it. The first time he ever did it he got sick. And the second time his hat blew off."

[If you believe **any part** of the foregoing story, you should be ashamed of yourself. And if you bought this book, you are entitled to ask for your money back. Ed.]

32

POWER BILL

I think "Karma" might be a thing. Sorta like every action has a bad reaction—'cause I've had a lotta bad reactions. And truth be told, which doesn't happen too often, I probably have deserved every one of them.

Like the time I noticed an electrical conduit coming *from* the building next door to mine, down in my garage on Commerce Street, through my brick wall, and it had been there for eighty years or more. The three-story next to mine was little more than a parking garage with a few overhead fluorescent buzzing light fixtures.

"Hmm. I betcha I could tap into that there power source and branch out all up and down that way, and that, for some free service. And no one would ever know." But I didn't because I was too lazy, probably; also, I did not *need* any more outlets than what I had installed. But I kept thinking about it and what a fool I'd be if I *didn't* do it. After a while I actually felt *guilty* for not doing it! "Man, I gotta get around to that," I would say to myself. but I was too lazy so I never did.

One morning while waiting for my coffee to brew I stood at our kitchen counter, redeyed and mouth open, scratching at everything I could get my hands on, when I noticed all of our power bills lined up ready for payment. My wife likes to show me our bills like that so that I'm encouraged to "cut back" on our expenditures; like it's my fault we mail Tacoma Power, etc., a gazillion dollars every month. She unplugs everything at bedtime—clocks, toaster—you name it. she claims the toaster "leaks" electricity all night long otherwise.

I was mid-yawn when I realized there were four power bills, all in our name, and all to our address. "We only have three meters," I muttered to myself in hoarse morning breath, still scratching. Then:

"Wait a minute!" I hollered. Cats ran in every direction.

"738 **Commerce**?!? That's not even our building! The idiot next door owns that building! I heard my wife, from the bedroom, holler, "Shut up! And *don't* plug that toaster in unless you're gonna fix me something!"

I, no, make that **we** had been paying the power bill for the building next door—the one from which I was gonna steal their juice—for *seventeen years*! I didn't feel guilty anymore for not getting around to it. That would have been like stealing from myself. I contacted Tacoma Power.

"That's interesting. We'll check on that and get back to you. Why would you pay someone else's bills for *that long?*"

"How do I know? Ask my wife. She just pays whatever bills show up in the mail; if you need something paid off just send it to us. We'll take care of it for ya, student loans, whatever."

"Where's my toast?!" from the bedroom.

"Coming, dear."

"They" did not get back to me; I got back to them. Many times, before "they" told me to collect the many thousands of dollars "they" got from me, from the owner next door, Bruce Lorig.

"He doesn't *have* my money. *You* do."

"We're sorry about that."

"The mistake wasn't *his*. This was *your* billing mistake."

"You both should be more careful next time."

"Next time! Whaddya mean *next* time?! Whose bills are we gonna get next? Oprah's? the Pentagon? Disneyland?"

"Sir. Things happen."

And that was that. So I tracked down Bruce Lorig, who, as it turns out, owns half of Seattle. So I guess "they" had let me off easy. I should've been grateful. Bruce was very understanding and thankful. He didn't even hang up on me while I whined away about it. I mean, how do you hang up on someone who's been paying your bills for the last seventeen years?—oh, wait. My kids have no problem doing that.

We did eventually settle. Well, I settled; for ten thousand dollars.

33

SCOTCH TAPE STORE

So now I've got a personal check from a millionaire, made out to me for ten grand. It's an obscure to me bank in Seattle. The name is **The Commerce Bank**. I'd never heard of it, neither had anyone else I asked. My friend, Clark, said, "You got hung with some bad paper there, buddy."

I went looking for it and found the building it supposedly was in; in an odd section of Seattle that was nowhere near any other banks or anything else for that matter. But here's the first head scratcher: it's on the *36th floor*. Who puts a bank on the 36th floor?

Who was it that said, "If it can go wrong, it *will* go wrong?" Was it that "Murphy" guy? Murphy's law? I think so. I can't stand inebriated Irishmen. If I ever get my hands on him, I'm gonna kill him—'cause he's always right. So I'm expecting the worst as I let myself into the ground floor of a tall office building.

And I look like hell. I looked like I was living **in** an outhouse when somebody tipped it over. Worn-out filthy jeans, torn-up tennis shoes, faded old baseball cap, raggedy tee shirt. I hadn't shaved for a week. I'd been "working." Not expecting to make it past security, I was surprised to see no one on the bottom floor. No one. I was equally surprised when the elevator door opened to let me in. Again, not a soul.

The elevator went straight up to floor 36, no stops. The door opened to reveal an empty corridor of silence. I flopped my ragged old sneakers and my raggedy old self down the hallway of serenity to the closed solid wood door that bore the corresponding suite number on my check.

"Good afternoon," from the guy sitting at a desk twenty feet in front of me. "Can I help you?" I'm still standing with the door open, my right hand on the knob, for a quick exit; because this was obviously *not* a bank.

"I'm here to…cash…a check?"

"Certainly. The lady behind the door will take care of you," as he pointed to my right. I thought to myself, "What lady?" I peeked around the door, which was basically in her face, almost hitting her little desk. Originally the room didn't appear much wider than the guy's desk was long, maybe ten feet, but she has a little cubbyhole all to herself with a door, closed, behind her. Very cozy.

"I'm probably going to end up with an I.O.U. or a warrant for my arrest or something," I'm thinking. Also the office equipment and furniture, desks and stuff could be purchased for about three hundred dollars at a yard sale. This here "bank" had "bullshit" written all over it. I fumbled with my soon-to-be souvenir of worthlessness. It didn't *say* "bullshit" anywhere on it, still…I sniffed at it. Something didn't smell good. It was my hand. She asked for my I.D., and as I handed them both to her, I realized that my driver's license picture looked *nothing* like **I** looked. She glanced at the name and handed it back. "What a buncha crap," I thought, "What are these people up to? This is no more a bank than I am a brain surgeon." I squinted around the room and ceiling for cameras. I checked the floor around me for seams indicating a trapdoor. "I don't know what this scam is, but they're not gonna get any money outta me." I felt my back pocket to see if I still had my wallet. "*So far, so good,*" I thought. And "*How do I get out of here?*" I reached behind me to see if that door had been locked and bolted behind me.

"There will be someone with us in a minute," she smiled sweetly.

"Oh, *here* it comes, the closer, this fast-talking dude that's about to show up is the *clincher*. He's gonna try to heavy-hand-hard-sell me a time share in Antarctica. In which case, I'm buying; our taxes around here are outta hand. They don't even have roads there, right? So it's gotta be a lot cheaper...."

"How would you like that, sir? Your money?"

This high school kid had appeared from nowhere asking what kind of money I like. I figured next he's going to say, "You can have any denomination you want as long as it's in rubles or Polish zolotniks or something."

Now I sort of "collect" two-dollar bills and they are **hard** to find. I can go to three or four banks in one day and each one will have three, six, maybe ten two-dollar bills. that's all. Still not believing this bogus little *"Scotch tape store"* was legitimate, I thought **I** would have some fun. "You got any **two-dollar bills**?" I chuckled. She stared at me blankly and the high school dweeb says with his own incredulous chuckle, "Well, *of course* we do!" as in, "You silly man." I am, at this point, speechless; but when he asked, "Would you like **all ten thousand** in two-dollar bills?" I almost passed out.

I barely squeaked out, "No."

"How much, then?"

"Two thousand?" barely audible.

"I'll be right back." And soon he returned with an armload of bricks of money. Bricks of brand-new *sequentially numbered, never spent, fresh from the mint*, two-dollar bills! And eight thousand in hundreds.

"Here's a box for you," from the desk lady. "Anything else?" I wanted to say, "Who *are* you people?" I didn't. I wanted to ask, "What *else* you got back there?" But I figured I should get outta there before they change their mind.

I left and I'm never going back.

34

WHAT ARE THE ODDS?

I suppose everybody has things happen to them that are just so random that you are left shaking your head in disbelief, asking how in hell did THAT happen? Like the time I was about to clean the gutters out for my mother-in-law.

She didn't have a spray nozzle for the garden hose, and I was working alone, so I had to turn on the faucet and throw the hose up onto the roof. Then I was going to climb the ladder and hose out the gutters. Nothing to it.

And that's what I did. Two or three coils in my right hand and up she went; water's running full blast. Nice toss. Before I could start up the ladder, I hear all this funny noise in her garage. Sounds like a thousand galloping rats on a treadmill. I go check it out. It's water pouring all down her wall and it's also drowning her gas hot water tank. The hose end had gone into the vent.

The natural gas heaters vent through the roof is three inches in diameter—with a "china cap" top covering it and it has a partially open space between the two. Small standard vent flue.

I could have stood down there in her yard for ONE THOU-SAND YEARS and for ONE MILLION DOLLARS I could NEV-ER have done that on purpose!!

This story is a little bit like that.

Here in our verdant rain riddled (please don't come to live here) Pacific Northwest—which includes Washington, Oregon, Idaho and British Columbia—we had a local and widely known car dealer. He was hard to miss.

I recently attended an open house of one of our newer "Antique Row" dealers, here on

Broadway. "Lulu's." I, of course, knew many people there but there were quite a few new faces. One of these was an older gentleman with longer hair leaning against the wall, just sorta watching. I thought maybe I should go talk to this old hippie.

We chatted for awhile about what—I have no idea—but we seemed to "hit it off," so to speak, and just what in hell does THAT even mean, hit-it-off? Who comes up with these things? You there, you've got your phone in your left hand anyway, how's about you gargle that for us, okay? Oh. Google, garble, gargle.

After awhile he sticks out his "let's be friends" hand and says, "Dick Balch."

"What a minute. Are you 'the' Dick Balch with the sledgehammer?"

"Yeah, that's me. Well, that 'was' me." Happy that I knew who he was and why he was famous.

He had become famous because of his TV commercials.

And what he did to his poor cars. He sold damaged cars. They were brand new cars, but they were damaged. And he did it. He would stand on the hood or the roof of a brand-new Chevy and tell you all about what a great car—great buy—then he'd take a great big sledgehammer, raise it over his head and with a screeching high-pitched cackling maniacal laugh, bring it down onto that brand new vehicle. "So getcher ass down here and buy it, before I do it again!!" Still cackling. And I guess they would, because he got very wealthy doing this.

He looked the same, same long hair but grayish, same grin. however much more mellow than in his commercials. We haven't had TV in our house for 25 years so I wouldn't know if he outgrew that bizarre gimmick or what. Suddenly I had a flash of inspiration. As one bizarre person to another, it occurred to me: this goofy clown might want to take a swing at another Chevy—MINE.

I always drive used Chevy cargo vans, ten or twelve years old, and already with a dent or two. And I've always referred to them as "pedophile" vans, and of course they're always white. Never been washed, but white. I was parked right outside the large picture window of "Lulu's" new shop.

"Hey, Dick! That's my pedophile van right out there. How would you like to give it a good smack? I've got a big axe hammer, blunt on the one end. How'd you like to give it a good one, like you used to do?" Boy! You should have seen this guy light up! Like he'd just won a million bucks. Apparently it'd been a long time since he'd had a chance to devaluate somebody's ride. And people DID ASK him! He'd told me some stories, like the lady that had just bought a brand new Corvette and WOULD NOT leave the lot until he came out and autographed it with a twelve pound maul. Corvettes are fiberglass, they don't dent, they break. He autographed it all right, she drove away with her shiny newly destroyed 'vette. You know the old saying about how much a new car depreciates the minute you drive it off the lot? This lady wanted to make SURE of it!

He was almost giddy when I told him I would go get my splitting maul—axe hammer and an indelible marker for him to sign my new dent. It took me more time to track down and borrow a permanent marker than to retrieve my big hammer which I concealed under my sweater when I re-entered the shindig. When I came in, he was again leaning against the wall, not in the same jovial mood as when I had left him; now he looked like he'd just eaten some two-week old sushi.

I brandished my marker, and he could already see the long hammer handle hanging out from under my turtleneck, so he knew I was ready. I grinned at him and said, "I got everything, Dick, let's roll."

He now shakes his head and says, "No. No. I can't."

"Don't worry, it IS my van. I'll show you the registration." In case he thought we were messin' with someone else's car. That would be a good one though, come to think of it, do it to a buddy's car when he's not around. I can see it now, him complaining about that big dent, and me saying, "What're ya bitchin' about? You got a nice autograph from a famous person. That piece of crap is worth more money now than it was!" Maybe this is why I don't have any friends. [It's not the only reason. Ed.]

"Nope. I just can't. "

"No, really. It's not a problem. It's okay."

"I'm sorry, Alan, I can't do it." Looking at his feet.

I looked off to his left, maybe ten feet away, where there stood a female about his age, and who appeared as though she had shared the same bad sushi. She was glaring at me, and I'm confused.

"Wel-l-l-l, okay, uh, thanks, for y'know, almost doin' it… I guess." And I departed, still confused.

And I would remain confused. For about fifteen minutes more, THEN I remembered something. I was putting my "undented" van away for the evening when I recalled hearing some stories from Dick Balch's neighbors in the Redondo Beach area between Tacoma and Seattle. Long ago stories.

Tales of his house parties, pool parties. Parties that included young teenage girls. And drugs. Stories of how some of these young girls were arriving home in a somewhat depreciated condition. And although they may have been autographed by Dick, parents were very unappreciative. So the parties were over when one party went to prison. Something that the sour sushi lady off to his left must have reminded him of when I had left.

Now, let's run the numbers. How many people in this country are stupid enough to point at their van and say, "That's MY pedophile van!"? Maybe two—three, idiots other than myself? None? Probably. Most people do snicker, but some people would NOT find that funny. Okay. Now let's see how many people in the ENTIRE

WORLD have gotten famous for sledgehammering BRAND-NEW CARS and then selling them for full price! Exactly! None! Just this ONE guy, Dick Balch, other than him, none!

All right. I think you're getting the picture. Now let's ask ourselves how to calculate the chances of these two fools meeting and one of them asking the other to go outside and beat on his car?? And the other AGREEING to it!? Until some sourpuss reminds him what the word "pedophile" means!

Yeah, that's what I figure also.

The odds on this are about as likely as me announcing, "Hey, I just finished running all the numbers on 'pi' and I finalized it. I finally found the last number for 'pi.' And it's six. It took me twelve years, but I got it. Whattya MEAN 'start over'?"

35

Coco

Everybody has weird stories. And I think most people fancy *their* story to be at the top of the list; until the next person tells theirs. And so it goes; stories around the campfire. But how many people have a story about a full-grown black panther? And I'm not talking about the civil unrest-protest movements of the Sixties, although this one does involve some uncivilized unrest. And it was the Sixties, as well as a very large cat and my new Volkswagen.

Barbara Berry was a local educational television well-known personality: "*Who's Who at the Zoo?*" on channel 9. She was the host. And we made a date. We were going to Woodland, Washington, to visit her dad's farm. She had told me she needed to deliver a cat down to her dad, and she needed a driver.

I've always loved cats; dogs, too, but they are high maintenance—and sorta gross. But first, a word: any man that announces a *dislike* of cats—and I'm not speaking about allergies— only a *dislike* of cats, does not like women either. Because I firmly believe that cats and women are nearly identical. We don't have time to discuss all the reasons *why* right now, because our cats, Buster and Sweetie, are yowling their heads off at me. "Birdnotes" on N.P.R.is coming on in two minutes; 9:00 a.m. is their breakfast time and *owww!* Buster's front top teeth stick out— sabretooth tiger style and *owww!* He knows how to dig them into my bare leg...*ow!* "Stop it!

These damn cats. Arright! Arright!"

"Stop cussing at our kitties!" from the bedroom.

Okay, they're fed. Where was I?

Barbara lived close to "Woodland Park Zoo" where she worked, and I was to pick her up there. (Woodland, Washington, and Woodland Park Zoo in Seattle are not connected in any way.) And what a sight that was to see; this beautiful young woman stride down her porch, a spectacular giant black cat beside her. I was in heaven.

I stepped outside to be introduced to this delicious creature. I stroked and fondled, hugged and kissed her until we were intimate friends. And, yes, I am talking about "Coco" the cat, not Barbara; that would come later. I hoped. Huge amber eyes and giant wide paws—the **cat**! Barbara had pretty eyes, too. I've always preferred women with small hands. We slowly introduced Coco to the back seat of my VW Bug, mostly with Barbara's cajoling and "cooing" her into it. After this small horse of a cat was safely installed, we were ready to roll. Our sleek black beauty was only mildly uncomfortable about being alone back there, without her beloved beautiful Barbara. We departed for Interstate 5.

Several traffic lights later, we found ourselves at a rather long one. I'm stopped in the right lane alongside other motorists next to me on my left when Coco got bored.

I don't know of anyone else that's had a huge jungle huntress sit with her chin on his shoulder and big cat whiskers in his right ear when she decided to *growl,* but if there *is,* I can guarantee he's never forgotten about it. Sort of, "Hey, Bob, ya 'member when that lion started growling at you?!" and him goin' "No, no, I don't!" Well, *I* never forgot it.

"I think she smells the five pounds of raw hamburger I have down here," as Barbara opens a bag on the floor. She starts to unwrap the package of dead animal and gets it halfway up to and between our

190

headrests, when one large dark lightning meat hook swiped at the big bloody blob and swooped it hard and fast onto the passenger window behind me, where she began devouring it. It's plastered flat onto the window and she's eating it off the glass. Blood is everywhere.

I looked over at the car next to me to see a face contorted much the same as the figure in Edvard Munch's "*The Scream.*" I don't know how many people there in traffic that day saw this carnage, but I know *that* guy got quite a violent display of *very large teeth* and bloodshed to talk about the next day. Not that anybody would believe him.

"She'll calm down and go to sleep in a little while," from the lion tamer on my right. And she did. But it took a while. Coco did not like being separated from Barbara. By the time we hit the freeway south, she was all done snarling, slurping and slobbering at her "kill." Our hungry little jungle vixen had washed her whiskers and licked up some of the blood off my backseat. She then spent about thirty minutes time trying to squeeze herself over our shoulders and between the seats to get to Barbara, who had rocked her to sleep while reading bedtime kitty stories for most of her early cat-hood. Halfway on the front floor and Barbara's lap she went out, snoring peacefully.

At that time, I-5 had a "missing link," an unbuilt stretch at the Olympia-Lacey area that had not been started. Something about how Washington State Department of Highways— *Olympia*—had done something offensive to the Federal Department of Highways Administration. Olympia was always clever like that. So the Feds withheld the funds—for years.

We went South to Nisqually Valley, up 99—old Nisqually Hill— to the traffic light at Tanglewilde. 'Course, I caught the light right between orangey-yellow and red. When I saw the cop car hiding in the bushes, I decided I'd better not push it. I hit the brakes, and all hell broke loose inside my quiet little car.

Unbeknownst to me, or Barbara, I guess, Coco had slid down to the floorboards to sleep. You know how kitties like to stretch *way out* with their little arms, sometimes, when they slumber away? That's what our kitty had done.

When my foot and brake pedal mashed her front paw onto the floorboard, my V.W. was filled with an ear-piercing shrieking wail that would make even the loudest ghoul in *"Dante's Inferno"* cower in fear. Followed by an enormous *"Rrooaarrr,"* much like the roar of *Leo the Lion* at the beginning of all the old M.G.M. movies, only louder 'cause she did it *in* my face, which would have easily fit into that cavern of hamburger breath. I was very grateful she had already dined. I suddenly needed to pee; in fact, I looked to see if I already had.

Barbara consoled and soothed her precious feline while Coco's long thick black tail whipped back and forth onto my dashboard and into Barbara's face. I drove a few blocks further ahead, pulled off the highway and ran into the bushes, only slightly whimpering—this was back when Lacey still had bushes, and trees. It's all strip malls now.

Coco forgave me; part of the remainder of the trip she spent with that large warm and beautiful furry head in my lap. Sound asleep. How could I ever forget that? I scritched her chin and head while she wheezed away.

36

THE FARM

Situated high on a hill overlooking Woodland, and I-5, a winding road eventually delivers you to Morgan Berry's "farm." It was a little bit of a drive, rural beauty all the way; the kind of bucolic scenery I thought I was sick and tired of when I was young, because I had no idea how much I would yearn for it in later life; yet never quite find enough time to seek it out. My friend Barbara and I, along with a majestic female black leopard, rolled along in sunshine, shadow and green sun-dappled slow road, with Coco our panther sitting up and sniffing, quite alert and watchful.

"Is she *hungry* already?" I asked, knowing I'm the only closely available grocery. My heart beat a little faster; then, my left eye caught a shape off in the thicket and grassy area on that side—where I was *not* looking. Peripheral only. "Was that…a *camel?* Ooh! There's another one!"

"Probably." Barbara was filing her nails.

"I don't think camels are supposed to live around here because…holy crap! Are those zebras?!?" off to our right.

"Uhh-yyep," without even looking up. Coco's nose is now pointing straight up toward my polka dot headliner and sunroof, while sniffing in all directions. I faintly detected a low guttural **Uhumm!**

Coming from deep within her. "Good," I thought, at least she wasn't looking at me, yet!

It would be years before they made the movie, "*Jumanji*," where all those exotic animals got loose through some movie plot "juju" and were chasing somebody's car down the street, while looking in the windows—come to think of it—this might have been the *inspiration for* that movie!

I was almost leery of looking through the tall wire fence line on either side of the small road for what I'd see next, but I let my eyes wander left again, curious what that movement was in the distance.

I'm not sure what I saw, but I think it was a Sasquatch on the back of a rhinoceros chasing around a herd of hippos or overweight water buffaloes with a stick. Or a unicorn horn. I decided maybe I should just watch the road. I didn't want to get into a wreck out here and get eaten by God-knows-what.

Eventually we arrived at the "farm's" compound. Barns full of T-rex's and giant Cassowaries probably. Barbara took me into one she said I would like. We climbed a flight of stairs to some large windows looking down onto an empty circus arena type sawdust and wood shavings rodeo performance space.

"Whoa! What *was* that and where did it go? Hey, there's something way over there…now it's *gone*. No! it's clear over there—*now* where'd it go? *Nothing* can move that fast!"

"Cheetahs can. There's two of them in here."

"*Two* of 'em? I can't even find one! Whup! There he goes!"

After some time, I did get a good look at at least one of them briefly. And Barbara was right; I did enjoy that. She knew how much I love cats.

Back outside I counted nine very large and heavily-tusked male elephants; all staked well away from one another. Each with maybe one hundred feet of extremely large chain attached to a rear foot. Munching on alfalfa, if I remember correctly. Timothy maybe. Morgan Berry was quite a guy. I would soon learn of his passion for elephants. So much so that he flat out adopted them. When male elephants reach a certain point while in captivity, they *"go rogue."* It's their way of saying, *"I've had enough!"* So they are destroyed. Something Morgan just would not tolerate. He'd have them shipped in from all over the world; and he took care of them. He gained world fame from another aspect of his deep relationship with pachyderms. Morgan was the first person in history to convince them to breed in captivity. I do remember that being big news back then, and here I was, little old me—hanging out with his daughter. I was careful to not ask him for any breeding tips.

He might have got them to breed by having them watch elephant porn.

I once asked Morgan, on a different occasion, to tell me his most interesting elephant story—as in, had one ever turned on him? Oh, he had a story alright.

He had an elephant indoors in a stall built for them, somewhat elephant-proof. 4"x12" planks stacked up horizontally inside a metal framework. He was feeding this big boy as he had done for years when, while facing each other, the big bull put one thick ivory tusk on either side of Morgan's frame and began pushing. Slowly. The tusks went sliding ever so slowly under

Morgan's armpits *through* the 4-inch-thick planks behind him; and stopped when Morgan's face met "Raging Bull's"! Then, eyeball to eyeball, he began, again, *ever so slowly* to push forward not with his tusks, but with that enormous trunk of solid elephantine muscle, cracking and crushing most of Morgan's ribs.

Satisfied, he backed up, and Morgan slid down to the straw-covered floor of the stall. And that was that. Point made. Or points made, in this case. After Morgan healed up, life carried on between them.

The day he told me that story was at the wedding of his other daughter, Janet, who I had also previously dated. While there I met Morgan's wife who was a retired "lion tamer." Because of the scars on her face and her missing fingers I *did not* ask her for any stories.

Janet Berry worked at the King County Morgue when I knew her, so I did the obviously quite natural thing, to me anyway; I asked her to take me there—*I know!* Hot date, huh? I knew after making that requisition, Janet would surely deem me irresistible. She did give me a tour; and you know, dead body here—dead body there. Janet, however, did not find me irresistible. Years later I received a phone call from Ken Berry, who was Morgan's son, whom I had not met, unless it was at Janet's wedding, but who remembers that stuff? If it had been another sister I probably would have. I was sad to hear Morgan was gone.

But I was willing to go back down to Woodland once again to the "farm" and evaluate his estate for a future liquidation at public auction, being as how that's what I do for a living; specializing in antiques. And boy! Did Morgan have some killer old Lionel train sets. Some mention of a five-karat diamond ring "being somewhere down here in the basement," was also made.

It was while Ken and I were in Morgan's home basement that his son elaborated on how his dad had met his demise. And it was not pretty. Ken proceeded to tell me they didn't know for sure because there was no body. They knew where he died, but not how. He may have had a heart attack or something; however, there was *no body.* He was gone. He had died inside one of the nine one-hundred-foot radiuses of an elephant ring.

And there was *nothing* left. Nothing of Morgan. Only fragments of clothing and his shoes. No bones, nothing visceral, no flesh. I didn't ask Ken how often Morgan had visitors, to *his* knowledge, but it seemed to me that it must have been relatively infrequent for there to be *nothing* left.

Did this one angry elephant actually and actively grind him into nothingness? Had small critters of the woods at night come in and helped? Bees, ants, bugs and worms, along with bacteria? It didn't matter, because there *was* no matter.

And that's how the world lost Morgan Berry, the elephant whisperer. *CORRECTION:*

If you like "twisto-plot" endings, I hope you like this one, because I do.

When I was told by Ken his dad had died inside one of the nine elephant enclosures, I had asked him, "How?" The following encapsulates the conversation which happened next:

"We don't know, Alan. There was nothing *there*."

"*Nothing?* Really?"

"They didn't find *anything*. They knew *where* but no trace of *why*. They looked and looked—nothing. They couldn't find anything, anywhere." His dad had just died mysteriously, and I'm *not* one to pry, so I let it go. But I've told the story many times.

Enter Judy Voelker, my ass-saving fact-checker and proofreader! June 1979—Morgan's body was found being GUARDED by "Tonga" the bull elephant!

The AUTOPSY found nothing! "There was nothing there!" Ken was speaking about the autopsy!! Only thing was, he never said that.

* * * * * *

I hope you enjoyed *that* ending over what I thought I had heard, or inferred. "Tonga," guarding his *daddy*. Makes my heart happy. Talk about "revisionist history"—sheesh!

My apologies to *all*. Especially Tonga.

37

Topsy Turvy

I don't want to bore you with my elucidations on what I think of Volkswagens—I owned one of every model they made back then—and I eventually learned to hate them all, one by one. And I know what you are thinking. *If they were such crappy cars why'd you buy so many of them?* Answer: same reason I had five kids—slow learner. And although a couple of them still snarl at me when they see me, at least they don't bite me anymore. The kids.

I rolled a VW van on my honeymoon. On a gravel road on San Juan Island in our Salish Sea, Washington State's Puget Sound. [Ed: what a keeper!]

Having only recently learned that the battery had croaked, I got it started by coasting it down the dirt driveway where we stayed, and I popped the clutch. I then drove around the island's small country roads to partially charge it up in order to catch the ferry at Friday Harbor and on to Nanaimo, B.C.

It was on one of these narrow gravel curvy roads when it happened. I came up a gentle rise on a curve when I slowed down to be safe, not that I was speeding, but VW vans are somewhat top heavy, so one takes no chances, they *are not* built for curves. And all was fine.

After reaching the crest of the very slight incline and where the curve straightened out, I gave it *some* gas.

On this *very* gradual decline I quickly encountered a *second* immediate curve—same direction—not sharp, but sharp enough. If you've had occasion to follow a VW van or bus, you probably noticed that they were all "pigeon-toed," unless heavily laden. Except for me, mine was empty.

All the foregoing variables add up. Top-heavy, pigeon-toed—unexpected quick *second* curve—tiny hill—a *little* extra gas—and a **gravel** road! They add up to…"whoopsy-daisy!" And some real loud noises. The loudest was when the bus's right side collided onto the road. The second loudest was when it bounced up and landed on its top. And it was over.

No seat belt, so it's not hard for you to do the math on that portion of the debacle. I'm on my knees on the roof and I'm picturing all the wrecked car movie scenes I've watched— upside down—car still running—dribbling gas—fire—explosion—screaming burnt cadavers. The windshield was gone. Instinctively I turned off the ignition and *dove* out through the empty windshield into the cold gray morning sky.

And the sky hurt. It hurt my face, hands and elbows. This is when I actually *realized* we were upside down, the bus and I. That cold gray sky was in reality a cold gravel road with some very abrasive clouds.

Now what? Back then these small back roads on the island had basically *no* traffic. I was on my own. I sat there for a while taking stock and playing with my rocks. What would a real man do? So far, on my honeymoon, I have proven that I can't drive, I don't know which way is up, and on my wedding night I did prove that at least I was *male* and some things can be done in record time. I decided maybe I could get it upright all by myself.

VW vans are somewhat rounded on the rooftop. I rocked it slightly, so it was obvious I could tip it over; however, was I strong enough to lift it off its side onto its wheels? I picked small pebbles from my forehead and imagined what the van would do when it landed on its side for a second time in the same day. It was bound to *bounce* a little bit, right? And if it did bounce, even a tiny bit, that would be my chance to upright this German brute. Maybe. I reached *down* to the roof to feel the curve of the small drip cowling that ran all the way around it. It felt as if it was made for all eight of my fingertips. This *could* work, I reasoned. And if not, nothing lost. It had to go onto its side one way or another anyway.

I took a minute or two to guesstimate where to grab the cowling geographically on its top; engine weight and gas tank weight, etc. I'm only gonna have a split second to be in the right spot to evenly split the load, so to speak, between the strength of two arms and two legs to achieve this. I mean, you don't see any weightlifters picking up a barbell anywhere *other* than the exact middle. And I was pretty sure nowhere on my cowling did it say—*lift here.* Although, if you own one and plan on rolling it, talk to me first, and I'll mark it for you. Still percolating with adrenaline from doing cartwheels in the country, I decided to act sooner rather than later. Plus, there was the off chance of another bad driver coming around that second curve too fast and crashing my party. I can hear his line of defense now: *"Honest, your Honor, I think that guy was already dead when I got there. I know that Volkswagen was. It was layin' on its top with no windshield. He was a bloody mess when I ran over him."* In which case he would be basically correct. I gave it a few practice lifts a minute or less apart to get as much blood as possible to all the muscles I would apply to the task before me.

Sufficiently pumped, I took three deep breaths, bent my knees once, stood up and began rocking. It didn't take much, maybe four times and I pushed it over. And it *did* bounce; I was on that cowling like a yellowjacket at a barbecue. I caught the cowling at the zenith of its bounce, while catching some of its upward inertia. I gave all I had. Once my hands and *it* made it past my knees, I knew I had it. The rest was a "cakewalk." Well, I've never once won anything at a cakewalk, not even a consolation cookie; so that was a bad analogy. It's too late now. [No, it's not. Ed.]

Victory was mine!

But wait, there's more! As I stood there cackling in celebration, telling myself *nobody's ever going to believe this*, I detected some motion, and sounds. The very slight slope of victory hill the bus and I occupied, was not done with us. A slow crunching gravelly sound was coming from the tire closest to me. It was indeed beginning to roll. Again it was no surprise that I had knocked it out of gear when I had been bouncing around inside it. Open the door and jam it into a gear—any gear would do—problem solved, right? Yeah, not so much.

The passenger door where I stood would not open. Why not? Don't know. I ran around the front to the driver's door. Same deal. It won't open either.

You know those skinny cheesy front bumpers VW's always had back then? Those narrow cheap ones that wrapped *around* the front corners of the cab? Apparently my roadside impactions had bent my bumper upward so that the *ends* of it were curled up and over the bottom of *both* doors. Curled and twisted up just like "Snidely Whiplash's" moustache. My suicidal van is gaining speed and I can't do a damn thing about it. Robbed of my momentary victory I shook my fist at it and threw rocks and profanities in its direction.

Its mind was made up. It had its sights set on the nearest ravine rich with green vegetation of all varieties. Huge blackberry vines, stinging nettles, devil's club , poison oak, poison sumac, poison hemlock, poison ivy and flesh-eating flowers. And broken beer bottles and rattlesnakes. Off the gravel road, over the shoulder and down into this lovely verdant bower she sailed, face first into its roadside retreat, leaving me standing there, bruised, bloody, shirtless and on foot.

Remembering a farmhouse about a half mile away, I pointed my scabby nose that direction, unaware of how bad I *did* look. We're all cognizant of the fact that our cars' windows are all tempered or safety glass, right? Except *not all* the glass in our vehicles is safety glass.

Not our rearview mirrors. I had shattered mine with—what else—my flesh, into a myriad of nice long daggers that had carved up my bare back as if I'd been whipped with a *cat-of-nine-tails.* I wasn't to know this until later when we were on the ferry, after a couple people asked me about my shredded back.

Walking up the long dirt driveway, accompanied by a large brown and white barking farm dog, I could see an elderly lady working in her kitchen. I explained to her my dilemma and asked if maybe she had a rope and if she'd use that John Deere tractor out there to salvage my situation.

"Nah, I'll just use the Cadillac," as she threw about a hundred pounds of chain in her brand-new car. Something was "in the oven" and she'd be right up in a few minutes. Many thanks later I left to meet her there. Her dog understood and came with me, right by my side, as if he were *my* dog. Concerned. When the two of us walked to where he could see my shipwrecked disaster on wheels, down in the dingleberries, he froze. He hit the brakes and began growling at it. I gave him some "pets" and told him it was okay—that it was **my** mess. He looked up at me with his big amber eyes that said, "*Oh, okay then, if you say so, I trust you.*" And he began happily panting away and kept on.

I almost stole that dog. Well, I wanted to.

It took this farm lady less time to pull me out from that valley of crushed vegetation than it took me to put it there. Many more thank-you's and we were done. I finished stuffing the chain into her brand-new "Caddy." That wonderful pooch wanted me to come with him; I heard him whine when they departed.

I got the impression she was widowed and that he deeply missed his "farm daddy."

When I returned from honeymooner's destruction derby back to the Lacey and Olympia area, any of my friends that saw me said something like, "*What the hell happened to your face?*

Did you spend your entire honeymoon face down? Har! Har! Har!"

To which I responded, "No. Here, take a look at my *back.*"

38

Olympic Club

Centralia, Washington State. Prohibition. Lewis County had a reputation to rival that of a later time—a *Thunder Road* type of an illegal moonshine-type reputation. I was told the hills of Lewis County had as many "stills" in the woods as Tennessee back then. I also knew people in that area were known to be prone to exaggeration. Something I've never been guilty of; I'm from Thurston County. [Umm. Hmm. Ed.]

The Olympic Club, about a block from the train station, was/is a two-story saloon and brick hotel right out of the Old West—into the horseless carriage "new" West era of long ago. And it is as spectacular now as it was then because my friends, Mike McMenamin and brother Brian, have restored it to its original—and updated—splendor. And am I glad. Because *it was close*—please read on.

In my earlier years I had been there a few times; to play some pool on **real** pool tables, old ones; to ogle antiques and have a beer. Big "Round Oak" parlor stove roaring away near the snooker tables. However, I never dreamed that, in my later life, as an antique dealer and auctioneer, I would be called on to sell *everything* inside the Olympic Club—a total liquidation. I was excited at the time, but inwardly saddened to take part in destroying such a landmark.

However, recessions wait for nobody.

One of our most recent recessions for example, 2008 and up, obliterated some of the longest-standing stalwarts of time. Royal Dauton Pottery. Waterford Crystal. Wedgewood. Others.

Paul Vogel and his brother, whose name I forget, and a sister, whom I never met, owned the Olympic Club. It was Paul who had called me. A couple days after he did, I met the two brothers there for the complete tour and inventory inspection. I brought John Swales with me. I told him it wouldn't involve work of any kind or lifting anything other than something cool and refreshing. He brought his hair spray.

It hurt my heart to scrutinize all the huge stained-glass chandeliers for the sake of dispersal, but *what a sale* this would have been. I'm having a beer at the bar right **under** one of those beauties as I write this. Soon I will utilize one of the ginormous urinals, then I'll come back and finish writing—don't worry, I *will* wash my hands. The soapy sink water has a copper pipe that runs along the wall at floor level to empty out all the hand wash water into the urinal on the right. I use that one, sort of a soap water "chaser." More about their copper plumbing soon.   The story of the Olympic Club spans many decades and has many categories, but its *main* story, if there is *one*, revolves around prohibition and how it survived the Depression, which went with or was *caused by* prohibition.

The Vogel brothers were only too happy to elaborate to John and me some of past scenarios. The bottom line regarding the prohibition years was—it didn't hurt the Olympic Club too much. In fact, it prospered. Now the "revenuers," as they were called, were *sure* there was *some* kinda liquor trafficking going on there, but they never had any luck catching it.

They'd have round-the-clock stakeouts watching every door, with no luck. Of course, the "club" was no longer a drinking establishment—not really—but they sold soft drinks and groceries. And meals. The kitchen was going full blast down in the basement.

The subtle center of attention, however, was the pickle barrel upstairs. When John and I saw it, the brothers showed us *why* it was special. Standard oak large barrel with two steel rings around it. Ingeniously modified, though. It was in the basement when we saw it. The barrel's bottom had been removed and raised *up* and reinstalled right where that bottom— knee-high—steel ring was. Three oak staves were then cut off at the same spot, then "hinged" back in place. Sort of a one-way "doggie door." The barrel was full of dill pickles way back then.

A heavy-booted logger or local farmer, thirsty of course, would mosey on over to get a pickle, tap twice on the old wood floor, whereupon some Tom Sawyer-type local kid who was sitting on a stepladder under the barrel—in the kitchen—would slide a flask up next to the small oak hinged door flap. Boot pushes that open, puts his foot on the flat pint flask, slides it out and pockets it. He then walks over to the bar and pays for his "pickle" and whatever else he picked up. Loaf of bread and a dozen eggs, maybe.

"What a cool job that woulda been. That would've beat the hell outta goin' to school," John proclaimed in a moan.

"Yeah. You would have been suckin' on one of those flasks and fallen off that ladder and broke your neck before noon."

"Ooo! You might be right. I wouldn't wanna miss lunch. Speakin' of which…"

"Shut up. I want to hear some more stories. And go fix your hair."

"Okay."

I asked Paul how the booze got smuggled in; and that was the best part. It wasn't. Stories still abound about how there was a tunnel from the old train station out back and a block away. (Ever notice how people **love** tunnel stories? No matter how many times they are dispelled.)

All of the bar's plumbing and the upstairs café's, as well as hot water and bathrooms upstairs ran over our heads as we stood next to the old oak barrel. And other old stuff. Galvanized steel pipe and lots of copper piping.

"No tunnel. It was distilled right here." And he pointed at all the copper tubing right over us, running every which way.

"Didn't anybody smell it?"

"No. Back then *everybody* cooked and heated with either wood or coal. So, no, you couldn't smell the mash. Local hog farmers got all the used-up grains. We'd see the federal tax agents sitting in their cars in the cold rain and snow out there hours on end waiting for deliveries that never came, just food. Lotsa 'food.'"

I thought about the coal-fired power plant just a few miles away that's in full operation at this moment, and the large coal deposit at *Tono*, a few miles further. And all the wood stoves back then. It all made sense. John wanted to know what kind of soup was on today's menu.

"Corn chowder or beef barley; local favorites."

I finished making notes of what to highlight for advertising the auction and which newsrooms in Oregon and Washington to contact for what would be a **huge** West Coast news story, as well as an upcoming date to hold the sale.

As exciting as it was to have the honor of performing the task of selling every piece-bypiece of this incredible landmark, it was with a heavy heart I drew up that contract. Paul and his brother both signed it. And I signed. Then Paul told us they had to take it to their sister for signature and she lived out of town. Hands were shaken and I paid for lunch.

Knowing full well I would be hated by every historian for a thousand miles, we began leaving. I was already having abhorrent feelings toward myself when I pointed to a paper sign at the entrance.

"I'll bet we get $500 for that sign." It read "**Street Ladies:** *Daily rent must be paid in advance.*" John and I climbed into my truck which smelled, as usual, like hair spray.

A week later Paul called to tell me their sister wouldn't sign.

Never would I be so happy to not get hired.

39

TIN MEN

The one and only time in my life I have ever craved a cigarette, I was ten.

And the truth is I didn't want a cigarette, I just wished I smoked. And it was the "Tin Men's" fault. If you saw the movie, *"Tin Men,"* you're familiar with Danny Devito and Richard Dreyfuss being the two main characters; competing and feuding aluminum siding salesmen. I don't think they smoked in the movie, but *these other two guys did.*

One winter evening we were visited by two siding salesmen that had noticed our current siding was—tarpaper. So we were an obvious candidate for a couple of fast-talking chainsmoking borderline con men to come in and be told what a lovely home we had and how much it needed to be protected and preserved from the elements: weather, temperature, disease, termites and bands of marauding tarpaper thieves.

My hardworking dad made a buck an hour, so to sign us up for new green and yellow metal siding was a slim to none bet. However, door-to-door salesmen have their ways; oh, yes, they do. Or did. Now it's the home shopping channels and TV ads that snag all the weak-minded nitwits that own fifteen popcorn poppers, six treadmills, four exercise bicycles and thirty-five new pillows along with every kind of hypochondriatical medication that's **just recently** been discovered that are fed on by the professional sales force that infests our airwaves, attention span, and what's left of our intellect and reason.

So we buy it all. Because we have credit cards. Back then it was the *easy* time payment method. Or *plan* as it was called then. The plan was to keep you making monthly *easy* payments until you were older than Methuselah. But don't worry about the interest on the balance due, it won't be *too* much. Just sign here.

Apparently the one fast-talking, fast-smoking and fast-thinking tin man registered my annoyance at my folks getting emotionally bulldozed into this deal. I never asked for *anything* because I knew we didn't have the money. Enough for Little League would have been nice, but…

"C'mere, son. I'll show you somethin'," as he nodded me away from the upcoming finalities for our gorgeous twentieth-century cure for the common cold and our future vaccination from social shame. And I've always done what I have been told; I mean, whenever a strange greasy-lookin' dude who smells like a wet ashtray beckons you, don't we all? And this guy didn't even have any candy. But he wanted to show me something—betcha never heard *that one* before.

We go over to one of our single-pane 1950's windows and he takes a deep whistling drag from his ash dribbling skanky fuse of less future and prepared to exhale it against the top portion of the glass.

"Now watch this." He wheezes out after holding his breath for a second or two. He leaned in near the pane and blew slowly.

I watched in ten-year-old amazement as the bluish white cloud billowed across the top part of the window—when suddenly all of it went straight *down* the glass, immediately to regather at the bottom sill.

"It was warm air when it left my lungs, but cold air drops; that's how much your windows cool off yer house." Grinning at me, yellow teeth and all. Then he started coughing. "So this heat-saving siding is gonna go **over** our windows?" And I glanced over at my folks at the kitchen table with the other tin man, preparing to sign away any hope of me ever playing in "Little League."

"NooooO! Why would we do that? I wuz just showin' ya somethin'." He shook his head and began to turn away.

"Shouldn't you guys be selling those new double-paned windows?"

He turned back and stared right through me, somewhat deep in thought.

* * * * * *

Do you remember back when people could smoke *anywhere* they wanted? How did we all put up with that insanity for as long as we did? I guess that's somewhat of a rhetorical question. It's just the way it was.

How many mornings I can recall trying to choke down my breakfast sitting at the counter of the **Rib Eye** restaurant in Olympia or **VIP's** in Nisqually next to a chain smoker on my right *and* my left. An ashtray with lit cigarette on both sides of my plate as both guys ate off theirs, not even picking up the little smokestacks in front of them. About the time their food was done their smokes would burn themselves out—so, they'd fire up another one—to go with their fourth cup of coffee.

Boy, those were good times. Always loved the smell of my clothes and hair when I got home.

I should have asked those tin man sales guys if maybe they could put some siding on our little outhouse for free. The wind blew right through that puppy.

40

THE SPAR

The first time I visited "The Spar" on Fourth Avenue in downtown Olympia, I was a little kid. My mom and I went in to split my very first café-bought hamburger and my first ever Coke. After telling her I had "to go," she pointed past the pool tables and the smokey throng of men milling around there.

"And don't talk to *anybody*, you understand?"

And I didn't. but I kinda took my time, in case one of these nice men had a spare candy bar or maybe a Tootsie Roll. I didn't pat any of them down, but on my return trip I concluded the only things these guys owned was matches, cigarettes, lighters and cigars; along with a vocabulary I would not possess until **I** had become a decent pool player, much later. The only thing I learned there that day was to not belch after guzzling your coke; not with your mouth closed, that is. Damn near blew my eyeballs out. Before a decade and a half was over, I was to learn a lot more while there.

By the time I was hired to be the night-time janitor at The Spar, those pool tables were gone, as was the glass-domed **Western Union** ticker tape machine. Most of those guys there had died of lung cancer or heart disease by the time I showed up.

My job was to lock out the last drunk and semi-drunk bartender at two a.m. every night and let Kenny, the cook, in at six. Other than that I did what janitors everywhere do. I ate all their food.

When I wasn't doing that, I *did* mop, sweep, polish, vacuum, scrub toilets and buff the floor as well as play the nickel *pay-out* "Bally" pinball machines. And it was that Bally "horse race" machine which got me into this little peccadillo, and the reason I don't work there anymore.

In my spare time at The Spar, and I made sure I had plenty of it, I'd stick my nickels into one machine or another. Then when I lost, I'd give it a good whack and yell some filthy names at it. In doing so, one time I apparently made it feel sorry for me because it gave me a *brandnew* game. As if I had just put another nickel in the machine!

It worked every time. If I hit that front panel at *just the right spot* I got a free game; so I upped my game. Those machines were made to take multiple nickels. Multiple coins—multiple whacks for increased odds. *Now* we're talkin'! Except now my hand is sore and swollen. So I started kicking it the next night. That worked also.

When I came back to work, though, my right hand was so bruised and purple from pounding I could hardly steer that big buffing machine around. I fought with it until my hand weakened and slipped off. Then the machine chased me around that shiny floor until I fell over a buncha chairs and a garbage can. Satisfied, it came unplugged.

After I cleaned up *that* mess I plugged it back in, completely forgetting it was still in gear and **on**. So it got to chase me around some more. This time it ran me down and I hit my head on a wooden barstool. Then it celebrated by dancing in circles while whirling the power cord around itself until unplugging it. Again.

After turning the power switch off [Actually he had *duct-taped* the lever to *stay* on when he let go of it, so he had it coming. Because he's an idiot. Ed.] I went and got a wet cold bar towel for the goose egg on the back of my head.

The next few nights I got better at kicking my odds up, but now my leg was getting sore. I tried with my leg on the other side—which would be…the *left* one. I'm pretty sure. I think. Anyway it's on the side I don't write with. [Just got done telling you he's an idiot. Recycle this book *now*. Ed.] And that's the side that's not very coordinated so most of the time I *tilted* it. Game over. I went back to my…right side and began kicking my favorite Bally *"Beach Ball"* machine. And that's when I pulled a groin muscle and fell over backwards again, smacking my goose-egg onto my nice glimmering shiny floor.

As I sat on that time-worn, but polished, brown linoleum floor rubbing my head *and* my leg, calling down retribution of all kinds onto this machine, something occurred to me. Don't monkeys and crows and others use *tools* to get things done? If I could rise to their level maybe I could master this bastard.

But, *they* didn't get a job at a café. I did. And there were no rocks or hammers anywhere to be found. All I had was brooms, a big mop and…well, that's about it. So I hit it with the dirty wet mop which made a huge, stinky mess and "shorted" it out. The thing made a buzzing noise and went dark. A little while after I cleaned that up, the lights came back on. Clearly, it was taunting me.

Sufficiently goaded into further escalating this war, I went into the kitchen to see what armaments I could come up with. The knives were all locked away, or I might have stabbed it. [Or himself. Ed.] Wait a minute! Here's some big uncooked raw potatoes! They're pretty hard, right? I thumped a big one up against my forehead, bruising my eyebrow—Yoww! These things are *hard*! Hard enough to beat the livin' hell outta that contraption out front, I figured. I grabbed another towel and put my war mace into the center of it, spun it around into a twist and slowly pushed open the swinging saloon-café door, ready to hammer that blinking electric contrivance into submission. I think I heard the "High Noon" music theme playing on the radio in my sore head. I wished I was wearing some nice jangling spurs.

For the next week or two they lost a lotta potatoes at The Spar, and I played a lotta pinball. None that "clicked" up any actual winnings that could be *cashed in* to the cashier, "Stan the Man," as he was called, the following day. But **I** was getting much better. My potato only worked on the *one* "Beach Ball" machine, so I stuck with that; I mean, I was playing for *free* on that one, for cryin' out loud. I managed to ignore all the starchy dents on the chrome front panel where the "sweet spot" was, which had been severely assaulted by a bushel of spuds, my fist, a mop, and my foot. Then, one day it was not there.

"Hey, Stan, where's the 'Beach Ball' machine?"

"It's gone."

"…Yeah. I can see that. Where'd it go?"

"The dump, I guess. They said it was done. They're bringin' in a new one—somethin' about horses. And whatta you care, anyway?"

Now knowing, but never admitting I was hopelessly addicted to these evil monsters, I began to tremble. Am I gonna have to *actually pay* to play these damn things? Withdrawal was not an option. I am **no** quitter. I began bringing nickels, whatever I could spare. Or not. Then, one night my odds were going great. However, to beat the new "Horse Race" device of vice, I needed to "bump" the odds way up into my favor. I needed *more nickels*! And I had none. I *knew* I could beat this new machine!

Back then places like this had these tubular coin holders on a stand which the cashier would pull a small lever on the bottom of the tube and, *kaching!* five nickels drop into his palm. We had one of these and it was always full when I came to work. Well, it was empty when I left, this time.

You know *what was* rather plump when six a.m. rolled around? My winning little clicker ticker ratchet type clacking number counter that had counted up and registered my "honest" winnings! Two hundred ten dollars!

I made around two hundred dollars a month working two jobs. So now I'm going to be wealthy. I waited around for Stan to come in at seven a.m.

When he did, I immediately and proudly showed him my tally of winnings on the clicker, waiting for him to congratulate me on my pinball prowess and hand over my 210 bucks. Stan always looked like a Mafia sycophant anyway, so I wasn't at all surprised when he took on the demeanor of a Mafia hitman.

He squinted at me and said, "Not so fast, Junior, lemmee talk to the boss. Ask me tomorrow," as he walked over to my horses and hit the toggle switch that began to click away all my hard-earned nickels. Clearly, collecting my earnings wasn't going to be as simple as when I'd seen other people do it.

But I had high hopes. I mean, fair's fair, right? So there I was, hand out again, facing a now *smirking* Stan. We never did like the looks of one another in the first place, but I couldn't *stand* that smirk.

"Yer not getting' a nickel, kid. For *ONE* reason, you're not twenty-one yet. *And* we were closed, you did it after hours. *And* you used all of *our* nickels to do it."

"That's *three* reasons. Yeah, I forgot to tell you about the nickels I borrowed."

"Yah, you borrowed 'em arright. Here's yer paycheck, now get out. Yer done here, Junior."

"Can I collect my money when I turn twenty-one?"

"Get outta here before I have Kenny take a cleaver to ya!"

* * * * * *

If you go into The Spar, and please do because, much like Centralia's Olympic Club, it is also a refurbished but now original *McMenamin's*. You will see a large painting that *includes Stan*. And believe it or not, Stan is wearing *exactly* the same smirk and exactly the same **damn tie** he was wearing the day he fired me!

41

REGRETS

Two quick stories about how money corrupts
-and-
Ancient baseball stories never told

When Wes Bunnell opened that old family book to show me the intricately beautiful Canadian five-dollar bill which was inside, I was astounded at the colors and patterns. *Real money—and from another country!* I hadn't owned, in total, five bucks in my twelve years of scrounging for a living on this earth.

Wes lived with his parents, Bill and Irene, up at the South end of Kinwood Road, in Lacey, in one of the several small cabins behind the "Log Cabin Tavern" on the old Pacific Highway 99. Although two years older than me, we hung out because, well, there was no one else around. Wes was a pretty muscular kid and he had once accidently saved my life when I had choked to death on a strawberry—by grabbing my arms and dragging my lifeless corpse out of our garden towards my house so my parents could call the coroner. And that's what caused the strawberry to dislodge and slide down into my dormant digestive apparatus. [Why can't he just say *stomach?* Ed.] He'd brought me back to life when he pulled my skinny arms up over my head and yanked. He saved my life. Later I would pay him in appreciation.

It would be a couple years or so before they, Wes and his folks, realized their gorgeous Canadian five spot had evaporated. So that's how I repaid them. Impressive, huh? And just when you thought your moralistic expectations of me could not get any lower…well, you just need to lower your expectations. Please keep reading; I'm not done with you yet.

* * * * * *

Another five-dollar bill. This one was given to me. *Honest!* Although I do understand if you don't believe me. But, dear reader, have I ever lied to you before? [Yes. Ed.] My uncle Clifford came to our house in Lacey on one of his, maybe three times in my life, visits. He brought my cousin Jimmy Aarde with him. Jimmy was one year older than I, and in high school would prove to be somewhat of a prodigy in music, sports and academia—everything I would prove not to be. After high school Jimmy went to Vietnam. My cousin Jimmy was there less than a week and I didn't have a cousin anymore.

When my Uncle Clifford privately handed me **this** five-dollar bill, it came with a caveat. "Take this and buy some nice candy for your mom and yourself." Back then *five bucks* could buy a lotta good candy.

As fortune would have it, **Stone's Candy Cane Company** was a candy cane *factory* right at the north end of Kinwood Road where we lived! I could've bought about a million nickel candy bars with five bucks, but that's not what my mom would've wanted. I knew what to do.   At the time my mom was a cook at *Lee's Restaurant and Steak House* kitty-corner from the candy cane factory, and she had mentioned how "good it smells" when she gets off work to walk home. And that was true; whenever a north wind would kick up and blow that sugary peppermint aroma our way, I would yearn. I think my teeth would start hurting in eager anticipation. But this was a real five-dollar bill! And I was **told** to go buy candy! So I went shopping. I was about to deplete that there factory of half their inventory.

They had little candy canes. They had middle-size candy canes. They had big candy canes and some bigger than that. Then, over here in this corner on a short sturdy table in a huge cardboard box, wrapped in crinkly cellophane adorned with a big red ribbon and bow, stood a candy cane that *King Kong* must've ordered but never picked up because he'd made a nuisance of himself in New York City and got *put down*. And guess what? It was five bucks.

"You sure, kid? That's bigger than you are."

"Not for long."

They gathered up a crew that mumbled in disbelief—someone finally purchased this monolithic shepherd's crook pillar of peppermint swirled sugar from which two hundred dentists could retire in comfort, and then they fired up the forklift.

"Once we git it out the door it's all yers, kid. And good luck."

I drug it across Martin Way on the asphalt okay, but Kinwood Road was gravel so the going got tougher, and kinda noisy. I knew I could make it home, but I began to worry about being attacked—at the speed I was moving—by sugar ants. I tied myself to the cardboard crate by the big red ribbon around my waist, the oversize bow at my left hip. I noisily ground away. Every once in a while, a car would slow down, look, and speed off in a dusty cloud. I could imagine the conversations in those cars.   "What the hells' that kid draggin'?"

"I dunno, looked like a coffin to me."

"A cardboard coffin?"

 "You know, Bob, not every family can afford a real nice comfy expensive casket. He looks like an orphan to me."

"Yeah, probably. Hey, isn't that that weird kid that's always pickin' up beer bottles outta the ditches around here? Here, throw him one."

By the time I made it past our house and into the bushes where I had a small "fort" within the vegetation, unseen, my shirt was all wet. Not from exertion. From slobber. I pried open my cardboard crate they'd taped shut, ripped a hole in that annoying cellophane which was in my way, and inhaled all the peppermint paradise my lungs could hold.

Lifting the end of the mint log to my face didn't do much good. My mouth wouldn't fit around it. I gnawed on the round end's edge. It tasted wonderful but unsatisfactory because I wasn't able to break anything off to chew. Once again, I'm covered in sugary saliva—my face, chin, neck and chest. Pink drool ran down my forearms and my red and white barber pole. I unstuck myself and went looking for a big boulder to bang away at it, knowing it would be brittle.

And so it was. By the time I had worked my way up the huge shaft to the big curved cane's handle, Spring had arrived and I could be seen with a large swirled "U" across my chest as I lay there banging away on it with a two-pound boulder **exactly** like a sea otter does with a clam.

And then there were these conversations: "Is that all you're gonna eat? Roast pork and homemade sauerkraut's your favorite."

"Full. Gotta go…lay down. Tooth hurt."

"Your teeth always hurt. You been brushin' your teeth at all?"

"Yeah." [Oh, he brushes his teeth alright. Usually with another piece of candy. Or a cookie. Ed.]

But the best part, and true to form? I managed to somewhat "forget" to share that industrial strength sweet treat with my mom. [No one is surprised. Ed.]

* * * * * *

I realize I titled these short *"reveals"* of my social ineptitudes as "Regrets"; however, the preceding pair are more sorrow—sorry for my selfishness. Regrets, yes, but mostly I'm just sorry for having all the nobility, ethics and empathy of a self-serving psychopathic scor-pion. The following is a story I *truly* regret, because I didn't do any-thing. And that's just it.

* * * * * *

I was still in the roofing business while owning a pack of kids and a half-built outofpocket house to shelter them within. I was busy.

A nice old house just off Capitol Way two blocks away from the state capitol grounds in downtown Olympia. I was finishing off the ridge cap on the 1920's eight/twelve pitch Victorian. After cleaning up the yard I grabbed my receipt book and contract with *Al Fleetwood*, the homeowner, and knocked softly on the front door.

The front room was immaculate, proportionate and well kept, to the point I complimented the lady of the house, although I hadn't met her; but it was obvious. She was everywhere.

"No, no. my wife's been gone for years, but thank you," the elderly gentleman said. "Wow. Sorry to hear that, Al, but you've kept it the way she liked it and it looks spotless. She would be proud."

He was sitting in a big mohair overstuffed art deco armchair while I sat on the matching sofa, cranberry in color. Neither showed any sign of wear but that old wool mohair is resilient; it lasts forever. I could not take my eyes off the array of *Frankart* art deco nude female figures which adorned the antique carved oak mantle. They were all turquoise and in motion. Static, but in motion. My favorite was the athletic naked long of limb beauty dropping a round ball onto her right foot and kicking it mid-motion, arms straight out from her shoulders as if she were taking flight. That bronze was exquisite, from head to her dainty toes. "She sure had a good eye," was all I could say.

"Mr. Fleetwood," I began, "Are you related to my fifth-grade teacher, Mrs. Fleetwood, Lacey grade school?" already knowing the answer.

"My sister. Taught school her whole life." *Yeah. And she did her best to ruin mine*, I thought to myself.

My fifth-grade teacher and I did **not** get along and it's all chronicled in my first book, "*All the Ways I Found to Hurt Myself, Vol. I.*" She did, however, teach me to greatly appreciate good poetry, and she did it by tricking me! I did not relate to Mr. Fleetwood my recalcitrant attitude toward his sister. He was obviously lonely and began to tell me some of his stories.

The Fleetwood homestead where he grew up included a small lake—the same exact lake that was *my* lake—or I should say **our** lake when my friend, Ed Doench and I had grown up "on" it, so to speak, because we spent so much time sneaking in there to fish. By that time, however, the property had passed into the hands of Jeremiah Long. So we called it Long's Lake, not to be confused with *Long Lake*, less than a mile away. Again, please refer to the beforementioned book for many of those stories.

I listened to several of Al Fleetwood's tales of *his* long ago (and here I am, writing mine), all of which I could relate to, but when he began telling me *baseball* stories, professional baseball stories, I mentally shifted gears. Up until then it was as if we shared the same childhood through the location, although separated by sixty years or more.

He'd given me my check for the finished new roof two hours ago; however, when he gave me a dose of his baseball past, I was enthralled. Anecdotes of **behind-the-scenes** pro ball was not something that would ever cross my path again, so I stuck around. I was starved for this opportunity, *and* I was equally starving for *dinner*. Okay, maybe one more, these were *great* untold and unrecorded stories.

After a couple more incredible tales of some of the personalities that Al got to contend with while traveling in the later years, especially on the "exhibition" circuit with a colorful roommate, I pulled the plug. I told him I would return for more stories when I could. And I meant it. I even went out and purchased a pocket Dictaphone type recorder; this old lonesome guy had a whole bookful of unheard information stored and saved for future eyes and ears.

But I was busy. Too busy. I never made it back. And I think I saw that little recorder which I never once used in a box of old junk a few days ago. All of Al's stories went away with him.

* * * * * *

Every time I think about it, and I have, hundreds or thousands of times, I picture Al Fleetwood walking over to the window of his front door to see if I was coming up the walk, and then turning away to sit in his big mohair chair to stare at the art deco nudes on his mantle. That, for me, is true remorseful guilt and, oh—his roommate's name? Babe Ruth.

42

NYET

We like to think we're so damn special. We Americans. Anyone who travels a lot knows better, though. A person can learn more about *themselves* through traveling to other countries than remaining in their forever stagnated bubble of American self-importance. A person can be easily humbled from the graciousness exhibited by some of the very poorest people of other lands.

Just like a catered-to child, we Americans grow up believing we all get a gold star because we're special. "American Exceptionalism," we call it. Quite a few other countries call it something else.

How many *of us* grew up knowing that in *1630* there were 50,000 Europeans living in Mexico City, riding around in gilded coaches on cobblestone streets, and wearing diamond stickpins in their ascots? *We* had just finished up hanging, burning and drowning all of our witches in the muddy streets of Salem. Just one of **many** tidbits left out of our *exceptional* history books.

We, however, are by no means exclusive copyright holders to the dangerous disease of arrogant nationalism, nationalism being the largest religion on the planet. Probably tied with the other largest religion—hypocrisy. I know people who belong to both.

Two months before the Berlin Wall came down, I went for two weeks. It was a reconnaissance trip, "Antique sleuthing." East Germany had been locked out of any chance to sell off the boatloads of generational hand-me-downs which other countries had been shipping off to American antiques buyers for the last half century.

Everyone knew it was coming down. No one more so than the East Germans. They wanted Western money, they were poised, ready to sell.

Each day there, I would leave my pension near the Berlin Zoo and board the train to "Checkpoint Charley." There I got a fifty-cent haircut one morning and she was **thrilled** I gave her a dollar tip. I would sometimes take the train outside East Berlin to areas you were told not to go. Once you were away from the area near the gate at Checkpoint Charley, you wouldn't believe the indescribable lack of color. The gray dismal bleakness, no advertising, no nothing. "Black and white" would indicate color, but there was **none**. An old black-and-white television show, and it was everywhere. Not a dearth of color, a death of it.

No matter where I went, I was noticed. Why? I had no idea. I hadn't talked. I looked just like them. They wore jeans and tee shirts like I did. No jewelry, maybe one little ring. My half used-up tennis shoes maybe? Although they had some old enamel overspray on them, they might have been a brand they couldn't get, otherwise I don't know.

The area around the Charley gate was "glitsy" by their grayed out standard, looking somewhat "westernized," their updated *Grand Hotel* being the area's anchor. There was also, close by, a very large one-room café; think oversize "Denny's" on steroids. Ten thousand square feet I'd say. I only went there once. Once was enough.

Packed for morning coffee. Three, maybe four hundred people, all men, I believe, lotta smoke. And **loud**. No music, just loud.

Big round tables and curved bentwood café chairs which would on a shiny floor, if you tipped forward *slightly* immediately shoot out behind you, whereupon you hit your chin on the table or your face into the gooey, hot pizza the server had just brought you. And then you fell on your ass. Not that it ever happened to me. [Three times. Ed.]

As you know, in America one would *never* try to insinuate themselves into someone else's space, or *table* by *asking* if there were room for one or two in a busy restaurant. However, in England, and Europe, I had learned not only was it okay, it was encouraged. And it was *always* a brilliantly uplifting experience. New people. New perspectives. No matter who they were. People, just people. Try it and if you find them boring, chances are *you* were the boring one.

After walking around and in between tables amid the thundering roar and smoke I spotted a loose chair, and it wasn't too far away from a table with a blank spot. The chair was in my right hand when I stepped up to the empty place at the table and gestured towards it with my left hand, palm up, and open. After making eye contact with a guy across from me, I raised my eyebrows, asking for permission. Silently.

Before he could respond to my request, a firm answer came on my immediate left, two feet from my left hand, sat a man looking up at me.

"Nyet!!"

Not actually surprised at this answer, given where I was, what happened next not only took me by surprise, I still find it eerie and chilling today, all these years later.

The gentleman that had turned me down was in uniform, which was not unusual—it *was* Checkpoint Charley, after all—and I did notice some brass and braid on him once I looked. But by the time he had finished *saying* that **one word**, the room was **silent! Not . a . sound.** He had no more than pronounced the "t" in "nyet" than the whole place was "pin-drop" quiet. I was the only person in the entire auditorium on his feet. Aware that hundreds of eyeballs were on only me, I put the chair back where I'd found it, and left. When I closed the door behind me, I could hear the murmur behind me begin to pick up momentum. "I'm really not that much of a coffee drinker anyway," I told myself, as I left the loudening noise behind me.

I also did not have any more luck making inroads into the purchase of antiques in East Berlin than I'd had getting a cup of coffee. Oh, they all wanted to sell stuff alright, but anywhere I would see something, I'd find out they were all armed with *Miller's Antiques Price Guide*, or something similar; and that's how much they *wanted* for *it*. Whatever *it* was. Full retail.

I've no idea what actually triggered everybody there that day to hit the mute button, but since that time I have experimented a couple times to see how it *could* happen.

If you are in a room similar to what I described, large, crowded and without *music*, try this:

Shush the people at *your* table and right away turn to the table closest to yours and keep *shushing*. You wouldn't believe how quickly contagious everybody becomes. They all shush each other until the whole room is quiet.

Then they're all sitting there looking around for an announcement or *something* which never comes. Everybody in the room sits there with a blank look glancing around, blinking in confusion. Then they go, "What the hell was that all about? What happened? Did something happen? Did I miss something? Why'd it get so quiet? Is somethin' supposed to happen? What caused that? Who *started* that?" and it is at this point when you want to bend down to tie your shoes; several times, maybe.

So many people who would like to travel cannot. Yet *so many* people who could and can afford to, especially those my age, *will* not! They're afraid of the new; strange new places, lands, peoples, ways of life—color. They will sit and vegetate in personal stupification of their own private grayness, motionless on the sticky tarmac of their safe and preferred solitary confinement gazing at their wide screen TV, not knowing it's all in gray.

43

A RIGHT FINE TIME

I somehow recently acquired another brother-in-law. He and his family (along with several concubines) hail from Salt Lake City and from what I understand, they are the only ones there that have been inoculated against this recent, and very popular plague we have also inherited, so we, my wife Cheryl and I, invited them to our little lake house in Chelan-Manson, Washington. We were in the middle of the worst heat wave ever to grip our parts; by the time their week-long vacation with us would be over, we'd *all* be gripping our parts.

Bill left his family at home where they'd be safe and comfortable and drove out here with Jenny, his girlfriend, and no one else. Except for his ants—lots of, ants. (If someone is reading this to you—that's ants without a "u"). Now, come to think of it—the way they do things in Utah, Jenny might also be a distant aunt as well as his girlfriend—wouldn't be my only inbred family member—been going on for centuries, all the way back to Salem.

Cheryl informed them where she hides the key (something she's never told me), as they'd be arriving before us. My wife and I were only too happy to leave 106° Tacoma to get to our air-conditioned lake house.

North Central Washington in summer is much warmer than our Tacoma climate, so when we got there, it was by my calculations, about 190° and climbing. We ran from our A/C car into the house. We were greeted by a half-naked sweat-soaked and whiskey-soaked famous Salt Lake radio personality, Bill Alred. Bill is the host of "Radio Waves from Hades," or some such irreverant (and go heavy on that last syllable there) name like that. Huge following by the way— he lost count of how many listeners once it got all the way up to twelve. He sat sweltering at the kitchen table with his arm around an only slightly tampered with gallon bottle of "Maker's Mark" bourbon. Within two more days it would be drained, as would we. Jenny was hiding downstairs. Turns out she would be the only intelligent one in the group; Cheryl and I later told Bill he should marry her, too, even if she is his aunt. Also much more handsome than that other fishwife that was waiting for him back in Salty Flats, and Jenny was obviously not encumbered with kids, stretch marks or nervous fits, either.

Me: "Why the hell isn't the air conditioning on?"

The sweat hog: "It is—I fixed it."

"You fixed it all right—I think I hear the popcorn in our pantry popping!" "That noise has been going on since we got here. I think you guys have ants or somethin'. We gottem at home, too."

"What'd ya do to our thermostat?" I saw shards of beige plastic on the carpet and wires dangling lifelessly from the wall.

"I took care of it—it was way worse when we got here." His glassy eyes informed me that he was just plain numb; he had convinced himself through self-medication and drunken meditation that the temperature had lowered through his "fixing" things.

"I think you're just dying from alcohol poisoning."

The sweat hog's response? "Cool."

Within a couple more days we would learn that a capacitor in our A/C had croaked and the refrigerant had evaporated and it was full of ants and almost every A/C unit in Washington State had gone heavenward and so had every A/C technician because there were none to be found *anywhere*! They'd all caught the midnight "trane" skyward.

By nightfall Cheryl and I had consumed all the cold beer, seltzers, wine, Kool-Aid, and antifreeze we could find and the next morning she began a desperate search for a couple hotel rooms. She found some. Hotel rooms that were around a hundred fifty bucks were *now* because it was Fourth or July week, and because of the plague, and short staffing and because everybody's A/C crapping out, right around a *grand*!

Between my many trips down to the "Red Apple" for crackers and beer we all sat quietly in our own dark corners of the house waiting for death to arrive. I wanted to ask Bill, my blearyeyed hellfire and brimstone radio guy a few things. I wanted to know what he'd done to our A/C. I wanted to know why our house had ants all over the place. I wanted to know what he knew about the afterlife. I wanted to know if this is how hot hell is. I wanted to know why Jenny never comes upstairs. I wanted to know why nose hairs grow so fast. I wanted to know why blackberries are red when they're green. I wanted to know if Elvis is still alive. I wanted to know if bipolar bears are more dangerous than polar bears.

But I didn't. I did not ask him anything. I don't grill people. I don't like being interrogated myself; so I don't submit others to it. "Ask me no questions, I'll tell no lies." Besides, it's too hard to remember what my last lie was, so just don't. Don't interrogate me; if you don't believe me, the next time you see me, just ask.

It was in the middle of me not asking my smoldering mumbling shadow dweller in the far dark corner that I heard a light curious clink…clink…clink from one of his many married ring fingers faintly and thoughtfully tapping on my $100 gallon of "Maker's Mark" growler followed by a blurry "…think them ants came in with our luggage." Mournfully, nearly apologetically, a confession of sorts.

"Yeah, Bill. Quite the coincidence, huh?" and "Hey, Bill, yah think you might be able to gather 'em all up and scoop 'em back into your suitcase? When you leave, I mean?" No answer. The house began filling with dust. And noise, big growling rumbling like army tanks and helicopters coming in through the windows and walls. It was an invasion! It was the Commies! A blitzkrieg! Armageddon!

It was the empty lot across the street, on Totem Pole Road. Excavators and track hoes everywhere. Dynamite. Lovely trees pushed over and chewed up, spit out and into idling semitrucks off to Presto Log land. Our daily Lake Chelan winds swirling grit and sandy dirt in all directions—mostly ours.

The large one-acre empty lot across and uphill from us was about to become *really* empty! Within two days there would be nothing alive or dead on what yesterday was a lovely small, forested hillside. Well, it's no longer a forest—or a hillside. It's two flat plats. The dust storms continue today.

The good thing about all the demolition and dust storms was I could no longer hear hellfire Bill gurgling somewhere in the darkness. I went to bed expecting locusts and at least one or two other of Pharaoh's favorite plagues to be visited upon us, and just what did I do to deserve all this in the first place?

At no point, unlike that stubborn idiot in Egypt, did I hear blurry Bill say, "Let my people go!" This whole tribe, army ants and all, could pack up and split—the Red Sea—and anything else they wanted to. They can go talk to burning bushes and all the golden colorful cows they like. Go hiking in the wilderness for forty years! (Bring mosquito repellant) and take all the firstborns you want—including mine. In fact, take all my kids hiking! Make it a hundred and forty years. And do *not* come back with any grandkids.

But I do wonder, though, what *does* manna taste like? So now it's morning and there they are—the locusts. Creeping up to and down my steep driveway.

Over three or four days of our blistering quarantine infested with ants and guests, my wife—my fine, fine wife—thinking of all others—never herself—has ordered online every single air condi-

234

tioner, of every size and every single inflatable pool—of every size that Amazon had for sale in the free world! Not only beautiful, intelligent and caring, but frugal! On the A/C's alone she spent thirty-six hundred dollars because *one* was on sale for $239 off! *That* money bought us another plastic pool!

Now they're gathering; the locusts; in fact, they're slowly swarming up Totem Pole Road to our house.

These locusts are a dark and kind of gray color and each and all bear a distinctive "Prime" marking on each side, as well as an obviously phallic symbol, blue in color, arrow shaped and with an upward curve. (I'm tellin' ya, that Jeff Bezos guy and, by the way, my wife is the one who pointed out to me that phallic thing.) Each inflatable pool and each air conditioner apparently required its own delivery van and driver. They're all up there now, lined up in swirling brown dirt, doors open, coughing and sneezing while bickering about who gets to descend the driveway to deliver what.

None of these A/C's ever got hooked up, but we used several of the kiddie pools; and that's about when Salt Flats Bill sobered up and said, 'Let's fire up yer barbecue!" I sat there contemplating what could possibly go wrong, envisioning that scenario, when a *child* appeared from downstairs.

Her name was Flora and already walking! Sweet, quiet and did not drink alcohol yet, so I was impressed. I was even more impressed by the fact that these people, Bill and Jenny, had been able to copulate and procreate in all this heat! It explained also why Jenny hadn't made it up the stairs.

That's when barbecue Bill informed us that, "Nah, she mighta been in the luggage, too." I looked at adorable little Flora's face and appendages. She was covered with ant bites.

Somewhere along the line we—through working our way among the Chelan-Manson extensive underworld—procured a qualified A/C repairman guy—fresh outta prison. I didn't ask if he'd been released, paroled or escaped. I didn't care. I didn't want to know, like

I said—I don't grill people. In any case, the house got a lot cooler and after a while Jenny came upstairs proud as a peacock of her three to maybe twelve-year-old brand-new daughter, Flora the sweet. The same Flora that had been, since birth, I think, savored on by their very own Utah, imported to our house, *pissants. The* Flora that had been born and raised in our very own basement. So now we're gonna barbecue.

We do have a barbecue, but I never use it myself; it's only pressed into service when we have people visit. I leave the barbecuing to the real men. Real men like wild Bill.

Our favorite, and shadiest part of the house is on the deck just off the kitchen under the wisteria-laced wooden pergola and it has a very cooling, soothing, verdant Old World peacefulness to it with all the vines, leaves, limbs and purple blossoms dripping over and around us. Paradise.

Things were better now, and we were nearing the conclusion of our family visit. Bill and Jenny produced several beautiful steaks and a large and lovely pink slab of salmon. We set about putting together everything needed for a serious potlatch. Barely a breeze ruffled the wisteria leaves; the dust storms had subsided, replaced with hummingbirds and honeybees. Bill and Jenny hummed separate soft tunes while my honey clattered around utensils, plates and wine glasses. Flora and I sat, watched, and drank beer, which is the only thing I'm good for— something my wife points out at least fourteen times a day. Flora gave me her beer, said she'd had enough, such a little sweetheart. A hummingbird sniffed at her ear.

Late on a summer afternoon and nearing evening in this part of the country is the best. I watched blissfully as Cheryl brought out the *very* vintage treasured bottle of "Dom Perignon" champagne and inserted it carefully into the ice our antique wine bucket held. She had saved this champagne for a special occasion just like this.

Now, remember, I already discussed that I don't know much about barbecues and that this one gets rarely used. And only then

236

by the real men that come to visit. Several times a year Cheryl drives over to the lake house alone and I'm unaware of how many real men come to visit then, although there are a couple pairs of shoes under my bed that don't fit my feet. Much bigger than mine.

What I *now* know, and did not, at the time, is: there's a pan or bucket or something down inside there somewhere in the bowels of Hades that collects, for future merriment, all the extra grease and fat from every BBQ party you *ever* had. And it doesn't go away. It never leaves, doesn't evaporate or dry up; it just gathers and waits, gets thicker, bigger and more scrumptious each time you drizzle more tallow, lard or chicken fat on top of last year's savories. *Real* men are supposed to *know* about this yummy stash of candle wax and periodically do something about it! Like maybe take that bucket of *suet* out and feed it to the local birds or a mountain lion or a homeless person or something.

None of Cheryl's real men had done this; no one had ever emptied this nasty-assed thing. Bill knew what to do, though. Bill got it empty. Bill knows all about hellfire. Fireman Bill. Did I tell you that this is also the Fourth of July? Oh, yeah, and that we are surrounded by wildfires? I mean, what's to be concerned about? It's just a little barbecue. I think that's what they said on the Titanic: "It's just an over-size ice cube."

By the time the time capsule from hell, this drum full of napalm festering away under the grill itself, erupted into our very own Fourth of July "Mount Vesuvius," our steaks were just getting warm.

The flame thrower in front of now eyebrowless Bill shot up into and past the wisteria bower and pergola that I treasured so. Flora snatched both my cans of beer—one from each hand, shook them up, and started spraying the wisteria. I grabbed the back of Bill's shirt behind his neck and yanked him backward; I figured if that open flame got a whiff of his breath, he'd blow up and take me with him.

Several stunned and extremely annoyed honeybees dropped down onto Flora, found some spaces *between* her blotches of ant bites and began stinging her. As I opened another can of beer I watched a smoldering blind hummingbird trying to put out one of Bill's watery eyes. Jenny said she was "gonna go downstairs for a while." When Flora wasn't moaning I could hear my wisteria leaves and curling tendrils sizzle, whistle and crackle as they cooled and began drooping and dropping. I sat down again anticipating dinner, listening for sirens. Cheryl, my siren, had run into the house as soon as Bill's fireworks started, fearing her copious amounts of luscious red curly hair had caught fire, which it usually does whenever this type of thing happens.

The ensuing several minutes ensured us that surely the worst of it was over, the hissing of the plants slowly subsided. The sizzling suet slackened, and soon enough, a nice salubrious calm settled. Flora stopped sniveling and handed me an opened beer, one eye swollen shut. Soon the spice-sprinkled and parsley-slathered slab of salmon was slapped on the…the…thing. Oh, wait! I know! The smoldering grill. There. Satisfied?

Long-legged Jenny reappeared, glass of wine in hand right about when the steaks might have been about half done, radiant. That's about when fire chief Bill announced, "Something's wrong." I know he wasn't looking at Jenny. Or Cheryl, who also reappeared looking equally beautiful, not one singed curl out of place.

"This thing's getting cold."

Me: "What'd ya do to *it?*"

"Nothing," while banging on the grill with some kinda flapjack turner thing. "You musta 'fixed' something on it, right? I mean that's usually how it goes with you, right?

Hey, Bill, do you work on a lotta things around the house? You know, little repairs?"

Jenny: "Not anymore."

"This thing's outta propane!" He hollers at me, glaring with his one good eye, like it's my fault. Now, I don't know about you, but I have never liked taking the blame for anything. *Especially* if it was my fault. The honorable thing to do is always blame someone else. I'm a professional blame shifter; possibly this is why none of my friends ever want to sit next to me. Wait—I just remembered I only have imaginary friends; and most of them are female. So don't judge me because I know for a fact that I already told you that I know *nothing* about greasy, stinky, firebomb grill hellbelcher things all you hillbillies have on your porches and pickup trucks, remember? Cheryl's *real men* friends should have exercised due diligence and maintained the damn thing. Me? I don't exercise anything. And tell them to come and get their shoes.

Today being July the Fourth there are no places open to refuel the grease monster and everything on it *seemed* to be sorta cooked, and we're pretty hungry by now so somebody said, "Let's just eat it before it gets colder." Seemed like a good idea and so we dove in.

I cut Flora's meat for her and fed it to the poor little darling because by now both eyes were swollen shut; I felt like I was feeding a newly hatched baby bird, with all her polka dots and big closed eyes.

Such a beautiful night it was. Good family, good food, very memorable…memories, while dining on our unburnt *front* deck facing the lake and soon to arrive sunset on the very eve of the celebration of our very own two hundred and fifty year ago *Amerexit*. The salmon made for great sashimi. From what I heard from others their steaks were almost "just right." My steak— and I do like it medium rare, in case you are thinking of having me over—still had a heartbeat.

A couple bottles of nice peppery pinot noirs and a pinot gris for the salmon finished, Cheryl is now ready (and able) to shave the cork out from the "Dom Perignon" with her bedside machete; which she does seamlessly. (And if you, dear reader, have *any* questions at this point— you'll have to ask her. And then, please tell me; I'd like to also know.)

The champagne? What a moment. Glasses raised by all—sun setting behind stormy mountain as well as Flora's lumpy swollen head and her tiny arm with her sippy cup of "Dom Perignon" raised into the warm evening breeze of freedom from our quarter of a millennia enslavement to kidney-and-mash, Yorkshire pudding and warm beer!

Flora was the first one to spit it out—the wise little sommelier that she was. Yep. Cheryl's much saved and sought-after treasure trove was "corked." I tried to convince myself and the others that it was okay—that our palates were haywire from eating raw food; but when one-eyed Bill spit it on my leg, even I had to concede. I took the remainder of France's finest to the side of our lake retreat and poured it slowly into the gravel; similar to how one does a loved one's ashes, trying not to weep.

Have you ever seen ants dance? I had no idea how much they loved spoiled champagne. They may have been French ants—frisky little insects.

I've always thought manna bread from heaven tasted just like my heavenly bodied wife's banana bread, right outta the oven.

Bill, Jenny and our cute swollen little humanoid Flora? They all froze to death in the mountains on their way back to Utah.

44

FORK IN THE ROAD

Years ago, having a penchant for classic old MGA convertibles, I had
acquired yet another one while on a road trip in California—from a
young Navy kid that brought it into America via military shipping;
so it hadn't been cleared by customs, etc., as of yet. I would have to
go through government (federal) hoops to drive it. So I drove it up
to Seattle from Olympia to get on with it, wearing a nice new pair of
slacks and my finest Hawaiian shirt.

I was pleasantly surprised how smoothly the British to America—Washington State title transfer went; quite rare, in my case. So
I was able to enjoy an afternoon in a couple of my favorite restau-
rant-pubs. I left for home a little after dusk with a large moon rising,
top down and the promise of a warm summer eve's pilgrimage south
towards home. I left for a pleasant one-hour drive.

Halfway into that one hour, just south of Tacoma, passing Lake-
wood, the pleasantries ceased.

Now, most of us have, at some time or other, run out of gas; and
it's never pleasant. Nobody ever goes, "Yay! We're outta gas! Isn't
that cool? Yay!" Nope, it's not pleasant. But it gets worse.

So now I'm out of petrol and in need of a gas can. Not wanting to attract the attention of the Washington State Patrol, I left my little convertible and climbed the eight-foot-high chain link fence. I picked a corner spot so that I could stabilize myself—one foot on the top rail of each of the right-angle connecting sections. I did this so that I could carefully scrutinize the terrain onto which I was about to launch; the moonlight helped. I've jumped off or over, when younger, a lot of fences in my day; I knew I would be okay.

I did not want to jump onto large or jagged rocks, sticker bushes, holes, odd pieces of cars, splintered boards or anything else other than soft grassy earth. Although a nice freshly lost mattress would've been welcome.

Picking a dry, ankle deep, dead grass safe spot while balancing on my corner launchpad, and secure in my own abilities to land safely, I was ready to act.

Yogi Berra, years ago said, "When you come to a fork in the road—take it!" and that's what I did. When I sailed off into the moon graced summer air I was confidently anticipating a smooth landing onto the hillside with little vegetation and no obstacles.

Then it happened.

Incredible pain! Shocked to feel my head and face grazing the gravel and earth of the small upward hillside slope along with the painful mid-air suspension of my torso and legs, I could not believe the white-hot searing misery and hellfire that was roaring at 500 miles an hour through my right thigh.

Normally I don't cuss and swear profusely—just mildly. Years ago I heard swearing was a sign of a weak mind—so you'd think I would do more of it. That warm supple midsummer peaceful evening was lit—bright electric blue—with every curse word I had ever heard into the stratosphere and beyond. And they're still there, so don't buy any space travel tickets; if you do, bring earplugs.

I had taken all of the precautions I possibly could have, given the circumstances; however, even with my little above average night vision (I used to be able to tie my fishing lures onto my monofilament line in the dark—correctly)—I had been utterly unable to discern the fact that I had been looking *STRAIGHT DOWN* onto a five-foot-high branchless and dead but still rooted mini tree trunk of SCOTCH BROOM!

The painful realization that I had impaled myself onto an invisible something was obvious by now, but the other obvious part of my new equation was that, as I hung there, upside down, I *had* to unimpale myself.

Fearing that I was already bleeding out—I knew from the immense roaring pain the injury was through my inner right thigh—and that I *had* to do a handstand to extricate my flesh, included what I was sure had pierced through my femoral artery. I expected the worst. Placing my hands, palms down, onto the warm summer soil and pebbles I took a deep breath and shoved my torso and legs moonward and felt the gnarly bark of the scotch broom sliding out of my upper leg; more cursing.

Sitting there, looking at my legs and what was left of my new slacks, I watched for pulsating blood loss—a sure sign of a punctured artery. There wasn't any, so I'd be okay in that area. In fact, as it would turn out there was *very* little blood loss, even though that *blunt* stick went clear through the meat of my inner thigh. It had gone under the femoral artery and came out through my upper groin.

Knowing now that I was at least not going to bleed to death gave me the energy, fortitude and blind rage to grab that demon stick and thrash it back and forth until it snapped off just below ground level, giving me some satisfaction as well as assistance up the small but steep twenty-foot slope to the road. The 76 gas station was only a few hundred yards away— my goal: a full gas can.

I was no longer in much pain—comparatively—unless I took a stride with my right leg, which, of course, I had to do in order to motate. I stabbed at the small mountain with my staff from Hades and leaned into the hillside while I dragged myself, one-and-a-half steps at a time, for another stab and another painful step-and-a-half, cussin' and swearing my head off the whole time. There was, of course, no one to hear and I was totally drowned out by I-5 traffic anyway. The whole process of overcoming my second obstacle in order to obtain a gas can took forever. I'd say somewhere around thirty to forty seconds or so before I gained level ground. Like I said: forever.

I also realize that I told you I was in horrible pain and then I mentioned that I wasn't in *too much* pain unless I moved my injured leg; and that's true. But it was a completely different pain, not the searing white-hot horror of maybe placing your face on a stove burner, similar to what the initial impalement was like. At the risk of grossing you out, dear reader, I'll try to explain: evidently when you get a blunt puncture through your entire upper inner thigh, a lot of meat and fatty tissue blossoms out of the wound upon extraction; because that's what I was looking at in the moonlight and some streetlight. When I ripped wider the new hole in my new slacks to inspect the new hole in my leg, I was looking at what resembled a sea anemone. Shreds and tentacles of my inner thigh. Next to no blood at all. And speaking of sea creatures, I had on my slacks and all around the wound, a goodly number of what I had to assume was fatty pink tissue, all of them resembling smaller salad shrimp. I didn't eat shrimp salad for years after this ordeal. But back to explaining the pain issue—*all* of the tissues blooming out from the puncture still had nerve endings, still attached—but exposed! When I took a step with my right foot, all of the exposed meat brushed either my torn slacks or the slacks of the other leg, a *very different* type of pain! One that I knew I would not be able to endure for a couple of half-mile walks; to the service station and back. Plus , I envisioned what I would look like to a state patrolman driving by. An illegal pedestrian on the freeway carrying a gas can and a bloody stick, wearing tattered (but otherwise nicely pressed) flapping pants smeared in what appeared to be a fresh seafood deli counter's leftover inventory, gnashing his teeth and screaming nonstop obscenities and dragging his right leg behind him. All with beer on his breath.

I've never been much of one to ask others for help—as in a flat out humanitarian favor— but after making it to the first sign of civilization, a rundown older small motel occupied mostly by month-to-month American GI's from nearby Fort Lewis—I knocked on the first (and only) door. he saw the condition I was in and after convincing the nice young soldier I only needed a brief ride, he said he'd help me out.

And he did. Everything went smoothly after that. Gas can. Gas. Dropped me off at my car; I got it started, he drove off after I thanked him profusely. I made it home and tended to my wounds with the help of my ten-year-old son—didn't awaken my wife. Took four months to heal up.

It, the stick, had gone *under* my femoral artery and exited— slightly higher up my leg (nine inches, to be exact—I just measured it). Bark from the scotch broom floated out of the wounds for over a month; no infections. How it missed my artery is still a mystery to me. My walking staff that I intended to polish, varnish, and keep for the rest of my life, I forgot in the poor soldier's car. I kinda think he was not as emotionally connected to it as I was; so I can only assume his wife didn't want it around either; I guess it went back into the bushes.

A tiny footnote: it was a *slightly forked* stick; and the smaller fork you really don't wanna hear about.

45

The Lost City

On one of my myriad antique trips to Montana and Eastern Washington a very surreal occurrence befell myself and John Swales. This is our return trip.

My van and trailer were both pretty packed, but we still had room for a few more things should I find any, and I still had some cash left. Summertime. Cruising through Spokane and heading West I decided to take a slight detour and bear off onto a small side road to see what I could chase up in the rurals.

My road atlas showed a thin meandering line running northwest; it was a nice warm morning, and we had the time, so I jumped off I-90 and onto the back of the eyelash thin little squiggle which went…somewhere. This, of course, annoyed John. Well, he was always annoyed anyhow.

"What the hell's this all about?"

"Let's see what's out there in the dingleberries."

"Nothin.' That's what's out there. Rattlesnakes and mean farmers with shotguns draped over their laps sitting in old rockers on rickety old porches just waiting for some city slicker idiots like us to show up and try and cheat 'em outta their stuff—remember what happened back in **Roy**?"

"First of all, we have room for a few more rocking chairs—we can just **tie** those onto the trailer. Second of all, nothing happened in Roy; we just got scared nosing around somebody's barn, and "they" sicked a mean-ass Doberman on us, except it was **your own damn dog** that was chasing us down the road when we almost *died* of heart attacks we were so scared! *Third* of all—don't farmers have daughters?—I've always heard stories that they do."

"Yeah…that's right. Me, too." And I recognized the faraway dreamy look in John's eyes. He was now deep in thought. Lost in the land of lust. John was a ruggedly handsome young—Robert Redford looking—horndog from hell. I knew he'd be stuck there like that for a while.

Many is the time on these road trips in other states when we'd pull up to some roadhouse shitkicker saloon/dance hall place and while he's outside fluffing and spraying his Redford hairdo, I'd already gone inside and up to the first two or three beautiful women I could see and quickly said to them, "My buddy's coming in any minute now, and he's **real** good looking—you won't miss him when he gets here—but I just wanna letcha know—he's gay." Then I'd go play pool.

Couple hours later I'd get to listen to him whining on about what a crappy place we'd picked to stop and that the only people that would talk to him was that one old *weird*-looking guy over there in that real dark corner who's got his pants unzipped and he's talking to himself. One time, and I don't remember where we were, somewhere in South Dakota I think, while I'm waiting for my opponent to miss an easy corner pocket bank shot, John grabbed me by my shirt and threw me against the wall.

"I cannot get **one** woman in this *entire damn place* to dance with me! *Did you* have anything to do with it!?!

"What the hell are you drinkin' anyhow? How would I know?—It's my shot. Maybe it's your hair?"

"What wrongmyhair—I mean, what's wrong with my hair?"

"How should I know—maybe it needs—I dunno, a little more body or somethin'—whatever that is; anyway, you should go fix it. Dude, get outta my way. I gotta chance to run the table for a beer here and I can't help you with yer woman problems. Ya shoulda got married, like me, then you wouldn't have any," as I sank the six ball—perfect leave on the two.

"Oooohh, no ya don't." And off he goes, grumbling about how "this never happens anywhere else," to fix his hair and try again.

* * * * * *

"There's nothin' out here but brown grass."

"John, I think they raise a lotta wheat here."

"Are you kidding me—now we're on a *gravel* road. We just ran outta asphalt. Where we goin'?"

"According to the map it eventually curves back around and we'll end up in good old

Ritzville."

"Oh no, not *Ritzville*. Bad things always happen in Ritzville."

"*Tell* me about it." He was right; many bad things had befallen me when passing through that place. But *good* things, too.

"Hey, look! There's some kinda town or something up ahead."

"You're right. Maybe they'll have a little junk store to check out. I'll pull in."

"Good. Igottapee!"

If one pictures the main street of all the towns we've seen in a million "westerns," only twenty or thirty years *newer*, that's what we were looking at—desert dismal, dusty and desolate. Not much life— we would soon change that. Without. Even. Trying.

If memory serves, the first wooden structure on our right was in the old west false front style *with*, I think, rooms up on the second floor. Although I don't believe it included the usual trite balcony for the ladies to lean over and the ubiquitous "bad guy" to crash through after getting picked off by the "good guy" across the street. On the bottom floor where I parked my van and heavily-laden trailer was a—guess what? That's right. A saloon. Other buildings consisted of cinder blocks as well as weathered brown clapboard and shiplap. Maybe a brick or two. Even though it was only eleven o'clock or so, it was hot enough for a cold one. I walked to the well-worn front bar; John hit the can. Two people working, two customers having coffee. Black. No one was talking.

This place hadn't always been a saloon. There was everything there to indicate "country store." Unused double wheel "Enterprise" coffee grinder, a "National" brass cash register with a nice dusty film on it, a chopping block, a glass and oak encased cheese wheel with original cleaver and so on. All of it was unemployed. A couple women came in wearing bathrobes and slippers; big curlers plastered all over their heads. More coffees. All black.

I was not referring to the coffee. I hadn't paid attention to what anybody did or did not put in their morning joe. The customers, the staff and management, every person present except us, was African-American. In comes two more bathrobes and curlers along with a grimfaced handsome young man I'd guess to be maybe eighteen. Still no conversing, none I could hear anyway. They were conversing loud and clear to us, however, through demeanor and burning stares—they did *not* want us there. Stink-eye was everywhere.

The older lady working near the end of the bar at a small kitchen area I judged to be the owner and in charge. So I went to her with my half glass of beer.

"Ma'am, would you be interested in selling the cash register on the floor? I like that type of stuff."

"S'not for sale."

John was already jittery and was standing nowhere near me with his long-ago emptied beer glass in hand, drumming his fingers on it, when I drained mine and asked for two more. I heard him moan.

While she pulled two more cool ones, I politely inquired about the future of the large coffee grinder knowing I did **not** have room for it and I needn't worry because I received the answer I expected.

250

"*That's* not for sale."

"Okay. Well, thank you anyway, ma'am." And I drifted to the back of the room with a glass of brew in each hand to where John was nervously looking around and around for a second exit. They were still comin' and none of 'em were happy. I handed him his beer and he wasn't happy either.

"Whatja go and do that for? They all just wanna kill us—we need to get out of here." "Yeah, I know. It's kinda cool, isn't it? To know what it's like to be treated like these folks have been for generations. Hand me your empty glass."

I did my best to act all naïve-like and clueless to how we were being treated **only** because of the color of the skin we wore. I could quietly perceive, though, from the looks on all the faces there that day, they seemed to be only one or two ratchet notches removed from those four thousand or so *recorded* lynchings not so many years ago, mostly down in our polite southern states where so many people in this, our so well-educated and well-informed America either don't believe or won't believe it ever happened.

My imagination was playing Billy Holliday's "Strange Fruit" as I slowly meandered over to place John's empty on the bar. Still no perceptible dialogue. At least if we're gonna get hung it will be by a nice quiet crowd, I thought to myself, not like all those loud screaming white mobs I'd seen in all my old westerns. Orderly.

"Do you think you could maybe part with those old empty "Beech-nut gum" dispenser display racks?" I took a sip from my mostly full glass awaiting an answer.

With an exasperated sigh she put down whatever it was she was doing, pointed at my beer, and said, "The only thing that's for *sale* in this town is that **beer** you have in your HAND, HONEY!" and I heard a veritable chorus of "uh-huhs" and "um-hmms" as I watched most of the hair curlers nodding up and down in concurrence. John passed me on his way out the door on his way to the van. I joined him a couple minutes later. When I did, he of course had locked all the doors.

* * * * * *

What we experienced that day in that dusty forgotten little town and what I rather enjoyed because I'm used to being ignored, was righteous indignation, in my opinion. I mean, you take a people, beat them down, overrule them, enslave them, murder them and otherwise humiliate them for **centuries,** they might notice. People can get annoyed when you whip them, murder them and sterilize them; they're likely to remember and hold it against somebody who looks just like *you.* Or me. And can you *actually* blame them?

I hadn't noticed or don't remember if that small community had a name. It certainly was not "Brigadoon." When I've related the story to others, every once in a while someone would tell me of a similarly sequestered town or city in other states, like Oregon, and so on. By now we've all heard the story of Tulsa, Oklahoma, and the quite prosperous city that had emerged over years of hard work, industriousness and civic pride, by all the offspring of generations of enslaved forebears.

And of the white jealous supremacists who came and burned it all down. And murdered them.

In any case, I think it would be an excellent project, and timely, as well as historically important, for someone to take on the project of researching and recording the locations of similar towns hidden in out-of-the-way locations elsewhere. And the stories. A great historical coffee table book. But you'll have to hurry. Most of those stories will have been forgotten, ground away by the coarse gritty sands of time. Those that still survive are locked away in the fading memories of an aging generation. So act soon. Catalogue quickly those crinkly old photos whirling around in the sepia silence before the whole idea is exterminated, vaporized by the clock.

46

APPLEKNOCKERS

John Swales and I were "junkin'" east of the Cascades with my van only—no trailer—one hot summer foray into the hinterlands around the Spokane area when we found a barely there town called "Ralston." I remember asking a local if the town next door was called "Purina."

"No." And *that* without even so much as a smile.

I have noticed the further afield I travel, the less my humor is appreciated, although at home people don't think I'm too funny either. Take my wife. [If he says "please" throw this book out the window. ED.] She only laughs at me when I'm begging her to get nekked. Then there was that Pierce County health inspector. Her I did not ask to get naked with me, but the outcome most likely woulda been similar.

We had opened a small coffee shop on our bottom floor where we built a two-story gothic style Victorian library with ten thousand old books (ten bucks each!) "American Gothic Coffee." So one day this nice lady shows up to do the health inspection. She snapped on her rubber gloves and no, I *did not* drop my pants and bend over! [He thought about it. ED.] Everything checked out. We passed—colors flying—but because Nannette, our barista, now sold *cookies* there was an issue. These people *love* issues.

"You need a full blown 'restaurant' permit now."

"Because of a few *cookies?*"

"You've got a total restaurant going on here; you're not fooling anybody. Just look at all these dining tables and chairs." Well, she was right about that last part.

"I'm an antique dealer—this is a three-story antique shop—that stuff is **inventory**. It's all for sale!"

"Sorry, that makes it a *RESTAURANT!*"

"Okay. I'll move all this stuff *upstairs*. Then I'll gather up *all* my antique bed frames. I'll bring 'em all down here and put them together. Will that make this place a *WHOREHOUSE?*" She left, not laughing. Well, *I* thought it was funny.

Anyway, enough about that. I'm trying to tell a story here, so stop interrupting; I get off track. [What track would that be? ED.]

This one-horse town did have a second-hand shop. So I was able to "top off" my load although I soon found myself embroiled in a death struggle with a commode. [We already don't like the sound of where this is going. ED.] Antique commodes of years ago were basically a small cabinet with a door at the bottom for the then everyday oversize appearing "coffee cup" receptacle which preceded indoor plumbing. "Thunder mugs," the British antique dealers call them. "Chamber pots" here. Normally the commode cabinet has a "wishbone" on the top back of it with the usual towel bar horizontally connecting the two "ears" of the wishbone. Back in the old days, again, before indoor plumbing, a pitcher and washbowl sat on top of the washstand-commode. "Good" ones would be Victorian black walnut with a marble top. Or oak.

Cheap "hotel" commodes were constructed of soft wood—Douglas fir, and that's what I had scored for myself that hot afternoon. They weren't worth much to begin with and by the time I got done with it and it with me, neither one of us was worth much.

"Alan, we don't have any more room."

"We'll get it in one way or another." I'm on my knees, sweltering in the back of the loaded van. John is checking himself out in the window reflection.

"When was the last time you washed this thing? I can't even see through the glass."

"Here, pull out these coupla boxes so I can scoot this dresser over two inches... *There!*

My knees are killing me but I think it'll fit now. Trade places with me. I gotta straighten my legs."

"How hot is it in there?"

"Cooler than where you're headed—get up there. I need to take the "wishbone" offa the top and we've got no tools." I started looking for my tire iron. And this is when the fun began.

"John, reach behind you and feel for the tire iron. It's in that space by the wheel well."

"We gotta flat tire?"

"No, I need to pry the wishbone off of this commode."

"There's a bee in here! A big one!"

"Slide me that tire iron when you feel it."

"Holy *crap!* Looka this spider! He's comin' right *at* me! Hey! They have Black Widows over here! How do I know that's not a Black Widow? There's that damn hornet again!" "Black Widows have a red stripe on their belly. Turn him over. If he has one, feed him to that big bad bee...*OWWW!*" He had flung the tire iron out at a hard enough velocity that I never saw it coming.

"I think you broke my kneecap! Ya coulda said something! You might've warned me, damn!" Blood dribbled down my right shin.

"There's yer tire thing. Jeez, it's hot in here. Will you hurry up? Where'd that bee go?" I began wiggling the wishbone "harp" back and forth to get the tire iron a place to pry. "I think I saw him on your back."

"*WHAT!!*" Bam! I heard John's head hit the inside of the van's metal roof. "Oww! Dammit! He's not on my back! Why'd you say that?"

"I wuz just tryin' to take your mind off the heat. How's your pet spider doing?" Working the harp back and forth while prying. "I'm almost there."

"He's not moving, I think he passed out in this blast furnace."

"Roll him over and check his tummy." I yanked on the wishbone's right "ear." It split off right where the "almost loose" screw was and hit me above my left eye. "Ow! Shit!"

"How's about *you* come in here and roll him over. I'll come out there and finish destroying yer pet hotel commode for ya? And how do I know I'm not allergic to all these critters in here? I could swell up and die."

"Only one way to find out. Tickle his tummy. And if you die, they'll have something yummy to feed on." While accidentally kicking the towel bar dowel, which had fallen onto the ground when I had disconnected the ear of the harp, under the van. I lifted the small cabinet up, to position it for placement into the space created for "packing," when the top came off in my hands. The 2'x3' cabinet case itself landed on my left arch as well as my right toes. Me no happy!

"Why do you stand out there and cuss alla time? I'm dyin' in here, we gonna do this, or what? I hear that giant bee again; he sounds pissed."

"Well, grab 'im and tickle *his* tummy too; I hear they like that. But maybe that's alligators or skunks or something. Here, grab the bottom." As I turned it on an angle to fit into place.

That's when I took a magnificent stride to smack my left shin firmly into my trailer hitch. [For the 384th time in his life. ED.]

"Geeyoww! God, I *hate* trailer hitches!"

'I've watched you do that so many times, I'm surprised you can even feel it anymore.

Hey, where'd that tarantula go? He woke up and went somewhere."

"He's on yer neck—left side." As I wobbled the cabinet sideways for positioning, spilling a small drawer out and onto my already tender right foot. "Son of a b...!" I looked across the way to see some old coot sitting on his porch smoking a pipe and slowly shaking his head in disbelief.

"There's no spider on my neck—that's a hickey."

"You got a hickey from a spider? He musta really liked that tummy rub."

"Now how am I supposed to get outta here?"

"I don't know—crawl over something—all's I know is—if I was stuck in a hot oven with a buncha poisonous creatures *I'd* find a way out." As I got down on my stomach to reach under my van to retrieve the towel bar, I could hear John scrabbling around and cursing above me.

About the same time I got the fingers of my right hand wrapped around the towel bar, John backed himself out of the van to step on my left hand. "Get offa my *fingers*, you idiot!" And I raised my head up to whack it on the underside of my favorite trailer hitch. "*Shit!*" I crawled myself upright to dust off.

"Alan, you look like hell. Botha yer legs are bleeding. Why didn't ja just pull the van forward a few feet?"

"Shut up! You've arready done enough damage."

"What'd I do? You had me locked away in the ovens of Auschwitz with things with fangs and stingers and God knows what else. You probably threw a rattlesnake in there when I wasn't looking; I know you like to do that kinda stuff to me."

"I looked all over; I couldn't' find one. But I know I'm thirsty." The arduous task of loading a forty-dollar commode [that's now worth twenty. ED.] over, we walked the one block it took to the tiny town store. Straight to the cooler.

I snagged a six-pack of "Rainier" while John's head disappeared into the glass door fridge to shop for something more exotic and expensive. I stood at the counter to pay for our refreshments once he was all done "selecting." Finally I heard him holler, "Appleknockers?

Appleknockers! Whoa, look at that. Appleknockers! What a name! I gotta try this."

Now, I can't say for sure, but I believe what caught his eye that day, other than an odd name, was the graphics. If I remember correctly [which seldom happens. ED.] there was a buxom half-naked beauty on the can. I mean that's the best way to market *anything* to half the planet's population, right? Beer, cars, movies, vacations, "Rogaine," gum, toothpaste, liver transplants—well, maybe not. I'll bet there was some guy back in "caveman" times who sat around drawing *pictures* of boobs on flat rocks and then went around selling them.

John put his can on the counter. I was ready to pay, money in hand. He opened his can and looked away. I dropped a penny in his "Appleknocker" and paid.

Back in the van and out of town a mile or two he's still goin' on and on about "Appleknockers." I was kinda worn out, sore and in no mood to emote anything over his "discovery." When I was about to open my second "Rainier," John chuckled and said, "What a weird name. They prob'ly got a little piece of metal hangin' by a wire in each can" as he swished his half full Appleknocker back and forth, whereupon *it did indeed* go—click, click, click.

"*Whaaatt?!*"

He was looking at me—speechless—eyes bulging, then: "*What the hell?!* They *do* have something in there!! What a gimmick! Click—click—click. Listen to that! I wonder how much they spend on that little trick. Maybe they just put a rock or something in there. But people would choke on that." Click—click and he takes a swig. Now it's clack—clack—clack. I could tell the can was nearly empty. Soon all will be revealed. Then maybe he'll shut up, I thought silently. It was not to be.

For the next fifteen miles he was head down with his right eye glued onto the can's top trying to see inside. Every once in a while I'd tap the brakes so he could hit my dashboard with the top of his head.

"Hey! Ow! Whaddya doin'?"

"These prairie jackrabbits are all over the place."

"I'm tryin' to see what's in here."

"Why don't you just dump it out?"

"I'm afraid of what I might find; probably a big ol' rat fang or something. You've heard the same stories I have about dead mice inside Olympia beer bottle." (Indeed I had. Not only that, but I know where they came from and who sold them back to the brewery. Please refer to my first book: "*All the Ways I Found to Hurt Myself*" *Vol. I* chapter "Trudging and dredging."

He dribble-shook the penny into his open palm.

"It's a *penny*. They put a *PENNY IN* the can! How many people have they choked to death on this gimmick! They're outta their minds! Appleknocker. I'm never drinkin' that crap again. I coulda died. Appleknocker."

"I dunno. I don't remember. I was too busy tryin' to figure out why it rattled."

"Do you hear something buzzing?"

"Oh, no. Is that damn bee still in here? Now I gotta worry about *that* alla way home." "John, that purple thing on your neck is starting to fester."

47

Cat and Mouse

So a trucker goes into a diner and sits down next to a kid that's staring at a bowl of oyster stew; he's shaking his head and he keeps repeating, "I can't do it, I just can't do it."

"Do what?" says the trucker.

"I just can't eat these."

"I'll show you how if you want."

"Okay." And the kid slides the bowl towards the trucker who takes a spoon and eats a nice big one.

Wide-eyed, the kid is amazed as he continues to stare at the big brave trucker. Finally the kid says, "Wow! Mister, you *did* it! I ate that same oyster three times and it came back up every time!"

The following true story is a lot like that oyster. No animals were harmed in this "event." Well, not really.

I think I was twenty-two and Lonnie Woollett was twenty-six and living life in a wheelchair as a newly minted paraplegic when I would go visit him at his parents' home on Long Lake to play some chess.

Raining outside, big crackling fireplace inside, big orange marmalade tomcat upside down and passed out on his back in front of the fire on the flagstone hearth. Nobody else home. We wrapped up our first game and were a few moves into our second when we agreed we needed a snack. Lonnie sent me to check the upper kitchen cupboards for something. I was in the breakfast cereal department when I discovered a really cool distraction that was soon to take our minds off our cravings for snacks.

"Hey, Lonnie, there's a dead mouse in here—in a mousetrap."

"I don't want a dead mouse, but I hear they're pretty good with some cream and sugar; you can have him. Look for some cookies."

"You got any string around here?" I had already formed a plan.

"I'm not hungry for any string, either; that the best you can come up with—dead mice and string? There's good stuff up there somewhere. Mom puts it up there where I can't reach it."

I undid the poor little cereal poacher from his death grip, then found maybe fifteen feet of sturdy string in their junk drawer. I gently, but firmly, tied a nice respectful belt around his lifeless little hungry tummy and walked back into the living room, grinning.

"*That's* all we've got in our cupboards—dead mice? I mean, Dad works nine days a week and that's all we've got to eat around here?"

I quietly walked over towards the fireplace and the catatonic cat who was now twitching. I've seen tons of dogs twitching and jerking, running in place, almost, while sleeping, but normally cats don't do that too much, but I know they *do* do it. A couple years back, our little sweet calico, "Sweetie," had one helluva dream one night while sharing my wife's pillow; around three a.m. Apparently she'd confronted a cobra in her slumber and needed to leap *straight up* to get away because when she launched to avoid her sleep nightmare monster she nearly broke our bed. Our bedroom is *pitch black* but that woke my wife and me up! Although we see nothing, Cheryl hollers, "What the hell was *that?*" her head still on the pillow. That's when our little sleep leaper came *straight back down* in the total darkness to land on Cheryl's face.

"Yeeeeeee!!!" into the otherwise quiet dark bedroom. This is when Sweetie decided to leave, *quickly*. She had landed on my wife's mouth and didn't care for all the noise coming out from her face.

(It's one thing that cat and I have in common.) [This guy *must* have a death wish. Ed.] One of her rear claws had found traction on Cheryl's sweet upper lip when my wife screamed and so the cat launched a second time.

"Will you turn on your damn light!" All this had taken place in *maybe* two seconds. "I am! I am!" and I did. Blood everywhere; all because of a bad kitty night terror. 'Course the rest of the day I was treated as if the whole thing was *my* fault by both of them; but I'm used to that.

I silently tossed the poor little dead guy past the cat and softly onto the hearth, too close to the fire logs. Both the cat and mouse were about to embark on the most active adventure of their lives. Although one of them was clinically no longer alive; but that mouse was about to get very active for being dead. I gently lowered the string onto and over the peacefully slumbering feline's fluffy belly.

Lonnie, behind me, had turned his wheelchair away from the coffee table and chessboard to see what I was up to. The mouse fur closest to the fire began smoking slightly.

"So you're gonna *roast* our dead mouse lunch treat? Oh. I see, this is gonna be good."   As I slowly pulled the smoldering tethered mouse toward the cat, he realized something was crawling over his midsection. It was only the string, but it caused him to wake up and roll onto his left side, facing the fire and approaching zombie mouse. When he flipped up onto all fours, I yanked the string and mouse airborne and over the cat. Now I realize this wide-eyed "mouser" had nabbed his fair share of vermin, but I'm pretty sure he had never seen one *fly* before. I had yanked it backwards, and it landed in Lonnie's lap.

"Eeew!" from Lonnie, who grabbed it and threw it over his shoulder. Within two bounds this cat had made it up onto Lonnie's lap and seeing an airborne mouse sail over Lonnie's head, ran up his chest and spring boarded off his right shoulder to snatch a dead flying mouse that wasn't there. I had yanked the string back toward me, and my feet. The cat saw this, whirled around and ran straight at me.

Although I *was* laughing my ass off, I kinda panicked when I saw the look on this cat's face. I screamed and jerked the string straight up—towards the ceiling, which was a mistake. He used all of his claws on my legs, stomach, chest and right arm to get at this flying pest; 'course the mouse by this time wasn't up there anymore, he was on the carpet off to my right. The cat jumps off my right arm onto the motionless critter.

Now, cats are sorta finicky about their table manners—compared to dogs. Dogs literally "*wolf*" down their food. Not this cat. Not today. I knew he wasn't even *hungry*, not the way he was passed out on his back. He was just plain *pissed!* Lonnie was nearly falling out of his wheelchair laughing when this cat stuffed the little corpse into his mouth, bit twice, and swallowed it, *whole.* I was laughing so hard I almost fell over into the fire.

Eventually the dust settled, eyes were dried, and we returned to normal breathing. We looked at the cat who just sat there, blinking, the string hung out the left side of his mouth. The other end was still in my right hand. Lonnie and I looked at each other. "Well, we can't let him go through life with a rope dangling out the side of his face," I told Lonnie, who moaned, while grinning.

I backed away from the cat the length of the string and gently tugged it taut. Two cat eyes got real big. Lonnie began laughing. That poor kitty had that, "*I don't believe it, I think I'm gonna be sick!*" look on his face. I told him that "If I ate a raw dead mouse, I know I'd be sick." I pulled really slowly. Lonnie was laughing and pounding like hell on his paralyzed numb thighs. The cat leans forward and…"plop." A dead mouse reappears. For a second he stares at it in amazement. He starts to go for it, I jerk the string away, and to another part of the room goes a newly resurrected rodent. With lightning instincts he's after it. He runs over everything that's in his path—coffee table, chessboard, Lonnie, end tables. Trinkets and chess pieces go flying.

I'm running around the room to keep out of his way because each time I yank it *back* toward me this cat from hell heads right at *me* again, so I would scream and run away from where it landed, falling over end tables or Lonnie's footrest; onto chess pieces and candy dishes. Remember, Lonnie is paralyzed from the chest down so he has no diaphragm. He's wheezelaughing and doubling over, so as I run past him I push his head and upper body back so he can catch his breath. Hellcat ran up my back and jumped onto the long window drapes because that's the last place he saw "Mighty Mouse" who, of course, was no longer there. He's over there, warming up his tiny cold corpse by the fire, same spot where the cat had been quite peacefully sleeping. I'm not fast enough; the demonized cat grabs it, takes *one* chomp and gulps it down a second time.

Eventually I regained composure and told Lonnie to "*Stop laughing.* I am not giving you 'mouth-to-mouth'!"

And here we were *AGAIN.* A panting cat with some form of feline P.T.S.D. and a string hanging down. If you want to reread the previous several paragraphs, and I don't blame you if you don't, you will have a replay of what happened next; more merriment, more destruction, more mousecapades, another dangling string. Only *this next time* would be the *last* time; the string came up but the mouse stayed down. And everyone was grateful, especially that poor mouse.

Everyone was worn out; the cat watched me throw the string into the fire. I didn't want to be there when Eileen, Lonnie's mom, came home, so I was preparing for departure as I surveyed the carnage. When I headed for the door Lonnie says, "What's that stuck on your butt?"

I reached back to find a big sticky wad of hard "Christmas candy" people used to call it, clinging to my jeans. I threw that into the fire, too. The cat was still sneering at me as I closed the patio door and ran to my car. *Before* I closed the door, though, Lonnie says, "Look at this place; what'm I gonna tell my mom?"

"Tell her the cat got ahold of a tainted mouse that disagreed with him and he went berserk. He just went *nuts*." All of which was true, and that mouse had *not* agreed to any of this.

* * * * * *

I can only imagine the nightmares that cat had, remembering a smoking zombie mouse that crawled out of a roaring fire to "get" him. Lonnie said the cat became a vegetarian and just sat there growling at the fireplace, and if a burning log shifted, he would jump back and hiss at it.

48

Clark and the Kitchen-Aid

My friends for the most part are not normal. I read a book, "88% of Americans are Abnormal" so I'm not surprised. My wife is definitely not normal which to you comes as no surprise; she *did* marry *me*, after all.

My buddy, Clark, was in our apartment one day and when I opened the pantry door he spotted our shiny red unused Kitchen-Aid mixer. "I've always wanted one of those."   Now, my wife had been on a verbal campaign to "get rid of stuff. We have too much stuff." Clark is a chef and Chief Steward aboard mostly secret government ships and goes all over the world. Chief Steward runs the whole ship and is the third to last person to abandon the ship before the First Mate and Captain.

"Well, *here*; we never use it. Take it," as I pulled it out and set it down on the counter in front of him. Cheryl will be proud that I had given it to the closest person I'll every have to call a "brother." I couldn't wait to tell her.

I just now heaved an exasperated sigh as I write this, because you probably already know what happens next.

"Well I love Clark, too, but he can't have my mixer. Get it back!"

"I can't ask for it back. He's always wanted one and we *NEVER* use it."

"Get it back."

"You said to get rid of stuff, so I did."

"Get me my mixer back or I'll get ridda something," as she reaches for the cleaver.

So a couple days later, Clark and I are having a beer, sitting in the afternoon sunshine outside "Meconi's Pub."

"I'm in trouble. Cheryl wants her mixer back."

"Why? You told me she never uses it."

"I can't help it that she's nuts. Why don'tcha call her up right now and ask her yourself?"   "Ohhh, no ya don't, I know better than that, that's between you and her. Leave me out of it; the transaction we had was just between the two of *us*."

"You chickenshit. Wait a minute. What 'transaction'? What did I get in return?"

"My eternal gratitude."

'You're gonna get me killed."

"I'll buy her another one, any color but red."

"Why not red? You're *tryin'* to get me killed."

"She'll think it's the same one—I don't want her thinkin' that. *Hee hee hee.*"

My wife actually liked that idea when I told her, so she told me "lime green." Next day or so I relayed that information to my ratbastard of a friend who said, "Okay, I'll get her one."

"When? She's in a hurry. I have to sleep with one eye open."

"All over a mixer she never uses? Your wife is crazy."

"Nobody knows that better than me, but hurry up, she's gonna put my nuts in the blender."

And so he did. And there it sits, in the pantry in the same spot the red one occupied.

That was seven years ago and it has not even been plugged in! Not once.

Clark moved away six years ago to mend his ex-wife while she "healed up" from a *horrific* car wreck. When he was packing to move to Prescott, Arizona, naturally I got roped in to help him. We were in his storage space when he pointed upwards to a steel shelf and starts giggling. "*Hee hee hee.*" There sat the red Kitchen-Aid. "*Hee hee hee.*"

"Have you ever used it?"

"No! not once, *hee hee.*"

"You've had it a year and never used it?"

"Nope. How many times has Cheryl used her pretty green one?"

"Never." And that's when Clark *really* started laughing.

* * * * * *

Now, Clark moved back to Tacoma a little over a year ago; when he did, one of the first things I did was ask him if his Kitchen Aid had been pressed into service while he was cooking for Jasmine, his ex, those five years.

"No, but it's back here now, with me. In storage. How 'bout her? She used hers yet?" "Nope." And he *lost* it!

I shook my head in disbelief, utter amazement actually, that these two even met. How does a person go find people like these two dunderheads? And how *would* they meet? I guess they'd have to have an agent, somebody to be a "go-between"; so I guess I know who that is. They may be idiots, but they're my idiots. Stubborn and consistent. Fourteen years and counting of unemployed appliances.

We've got a whole lot of stuff to get rid of, so come on over to our house if you need anything. You can't have any of it, but you can come look at all the "stuff we've gotta get rid of." Well, maybe you *can* have some of it, but you'll have to bring it back the next day, 'cause that's how we roll.

49

CURSE OF THE MUMMY

In my somewhat earlier years as an antiques dealer, I maintained a mental short list of what I wanted to be able to say I either *have* or *have had* in my inventory. First of all, outsiders need to understand that *all* antique dealers are first and foremost *collectors* themselves. We love what we do.

I wanted someday to say I once had, or still *do*, a quality cigar store Indian. Maybe not the high quality of a *Samuel Robb*, but good caliber. And I have had a couple.

I'd always coveted those "monumental Apulian bell or column wine kraters" 300-400 B.C. with red figures and voluted handles. I'm looking at my magnificent example at this moment. Reasonably sure I would never afford one, I only drooled over them if "Sotheby's" or "Christie's" had one in an upcoming auction of "antiquities." The *reason* I have one is unfortunate, and I think *you* will agree.

The Twin Towers had *just* been destroyed, and America, indeed much of the world, ceased to function—no air travel, etc. I had been, since that moment, pontificating to friends and other dealers about how *many* auction houses still had sales planned and advertised for the very near future. Somewhere between rarely and never do we auctioneers cancel a sale.

One exception would be an alternate "snow date," in Upper East Coast cases, for example. "If you guys have any recent sale brochures or catalogs with anything 'good' that's comin' up, you might want to do a phone or absentee bid."

The reason I was saying this was because *nobody was buying or selling anything!!* Pampers, gas, groceries and beer—that's about it, for weeks.

Then I remembered a catalogue which I'd received two weeks before, from one of the two major houses in New Orleans. Either "Neal" or "New Orleans Auctions." So I looked it over again. "Maybe I should shut up and listen to my own advice and leave other people alone," I told myself. I then arranged for a live phone bid; and that's how I procured my Apulian prize. At a good price.

But I would cheerfully *give it* to the first person who could go back and make 9/11 unhappen.

An interesting side note: after I had owned my "Krater" for a few months, I learned that William Randolph Hearst had *planned* to build six, *I believe*, more "San Simeons" on the East Coast and Deep South, but he had money problems, too, during the Depression; so he liquidated all the rare "knick-knacks" he would have filled them with.

It you've been through "San Simeon" you may remember a large, impressive room. (Well, I know it's *all* impressive.) It may have been a "drawing room" or "study." In any case, it has a valance running around all the walls high up, near the ceiling. And *on* the valance sits one hundred fifty-five early Grecian and Apulian urns, pots, jugs and kraters.

Another item I've always yearned to own, and still do because I never got one, is a ship's figurehead. Preferably a bare-breasted beauty.

Now, about this here mummy case, or "sarcophagus." We have a good one. I'm still amazed at how I was able to acquire it, because I *never* expected to be privileged enough to own one.

Cheryl and I were in Paris for leisure; we had wrapped up loading two forty-footers bound for Tacoma. Our friend and local (Brussels) truck driver, Francois, had loaned us a chauffeur for the drive. The three of us were spending the weekend perusing an annual antique *enormous* "paper" show. Antique manuscripts, wallpaper, advertising, posters, you name it, with other stuff mixed in by the boatload. We spent three days there and didn't see everything; we weren't buying anything; besides we only had three thousand dollars left, anyway. My wife said we needed that for wine. Our chauffeur was Chantal, Francois' wife. The four of us had gone to many auctions and shared many meals. Francois was unable to accompany us this time. On Saturday we visited the booth of a gentleman who specialized in medieval antiquities, mostly early bronze and iron, an impressive inventory. Long black velvet drapes hung down his back wall offsetting an ivory-colored Egyptian sarcophagus lid, like the ones I often visit in the British Museum. I stared at it for a while, shook my head and moved on.

That night in bed I asked myself why I hadn't even *asked* the guy how much he was wanting for it. "Go back and ask him tomorrow." From Cheryl.

So I did; knowing full well he knew what it was worth. First, though, I asked for some provenance, how *he* got it. Chantal did some of the French translating.

A large country ancient chateau, once owned by one of Napoleon's generals with a collection of medieval objects to liquidate, contacted this guy. A deal was struck which *included* this much, much older mummy case.

It's no secret soldiers bring home war souvenirs, and the higher the rank, the bigger the souvenir (think free shipping). So all the way from Alexandria this general hauls this six-foot tall artifact; only to have his wife say, "You're not bringin' that nasty thing into MY house!" Down into the basement it went, never to see the light of day again (but then, it was never *meant* to in the first place, was it?) until this guy hauled it out. And it was at this point in the story when Chantal whispered into my ear, "You know, Alan—Napoleon—

that's really *not* so old." Well, Napoleonic is plenty old to me and most Americans—and *any* dynasty of Egyptian antiquities is *too old* for most to comprehend.

When I was told the price, I was bowled over. "Can I give you three thousand dollars for down payment?"

"But of course. Send me the rest." He was happy to be rid of it because it lay outside the brackets or parameters of what he preferred to specialize in; he just couldn't be bothered. Two days later we were back in America from our buying trip, and we wired the money to Francois to finalize this transaction and bring my sarcophagus to Brussels. Shortly after the money was sent, two weeks maybe, is when everything goes sideways. I answered the phone.

"Alan! I am in jail!" Then, "We are *all* in jail!"

"Who's *we*? And why?"

"Rita's in jail!"

"Who's Rita?" Silence, then…"Umm…my girlfriend." So now I knew why he was too busy to go with us to Paris.

"Rita's little dog is in a different jail, and my truck is in jail! All my money is in jail!" He always carried a lot of cash—ten grand maybe.

"Your mummy is in jail."

"Why? What the hell did *it* do? What'd *you* do?"

"Nothing! I pay the guy for the mummy. He give me V.A.T. papers and we go back to Brussels."

Value added tax, V.A.T. (Tax value added. T.V.A., in England, was around 20 percent added to any transaction, which these governments collected.)

They had been stopped at the France-Belgium border because at this *PARTICULAR MOMENT* in France, there was a ring of antique thieves operating with trucks *exactly* like Francois', backing up to rich collectors' homes and cleaning them out. When the cops demanded he open the overhead door of his big truck, they were amazed to see *one item* only, a sarcophagus lid with a blanket over it, in the shape of a body. Verrry slowly they peeled back the blanket. Maybe they were grateful; or maybe disappointed; then they said, "All the way to Paris? For one thing? 'Papers' please." They didn't, for a second, believe the document. The dealer from whom I had bought it declared I had only paid four thousand, in an attempt to save himself thousands in V.A.T. dues, yet it was Francois who was in jail.

Within a couple of days, though, a prisoner exchange was made; they went and drug this guy out of bed, kicking and screaming at four a.m., and "my" people were all set free.

If that guy had told the truth he probably would have saved himself a wad more money than lying on his paperwork got him.

And that's how Chantal found out Francois had a mistress.

50

Hilda Peach—Revisited

In an earlier book I wrote about how many of the more elite "cool" kids treated Hilda Peach. Her crime, somehow, was being poor, plain *and* pretty, as well as quiet. So they treated her even worse than they treated me. But I probably deserved it; Hilda did not. This was back in sixth, seventh and eighth grades; I don't believe Hilda was with our class once we scaled the ladder to graduate the eighth grade into North Thurston High School. And if she wasn't, I don't blame her one bit.

These guys thought it was fun to wipe an open palm onto your shoulder or chest, as if to smear something onto you, while saying, "Hilda's fleas" with a snicker. As in "pass it on." With poor Hilda in the room. They soon learned I did not participate; the smear campaign died on the floor once they wiped me. I just glared.

Once I knew I had graduated my senior year, I said "Bubye," and was about to head for home.

"Aren't you going to walk?

"No, I think I'll run!" It was only two miles.

"No. I'm talking about the graduation walk; to receive our diplomas. Saturday night. Ya gotta have your diploma in order to get a job!" which *is* what they'd told us our whole lives, and since receiving mine (in the mail) not once has anyone *ever* asked to see it.

"Not a chance in hell! I just want outta here; that door better be unlocked. Get outta my way."

"Okay, well, see you at the reunion."

"What reunion?"

"Our five-year reunion—it'll be in five years. Our *class* reunion!" These people actually wanted to get together and *relive* this shit? This whole miserable twelve-year stint of unspeakable torture, failure, embarrassment and shame they wanted to *rehash*? Maybe gang up on people like Hilda Peach or worse yet, me? Yeah. I can't wait for that. My twelve years of servitude within these hallowed halls were *EXACTLY* like being nibbled to death by ducks. "Then we're gonna have another one in ten years. Every ten years, until…well…I don't know when."

"So you thought these last twelve years were so great you all wanna get together for a redo? All the way to eternity?"

"Well, yeah. Just to catch up on each other. Why not?"

"I mean, I learned to not pick at scabs a long time ago—they take longer to heal. But I'll tell you what, I'm not going to *any* of them, *but* if I live long enough (which I knew I wouldn't) I'll be at our 50th!"

And the years went by. Then I could see that stupid declaration looming in the cold gray distant dawn of my dim existence. "I'm going to my 50th. You needa come with me so I don't kill somebody."

"Good, honey. You are actually going to *see* all your school friends. Bring some of your books. They'll be impressed you finally learned how to write."

"No, I still print." [True—Ed.]

I brought a case of each of the "All the Ways" books, one volume each into the room early enough that the "proceedings" hadn't started yet. Whatever "they" were. If we were going to march around the room with our diplomas in hand, I was outta luck. I used mine forty years ago to ignite my fireplace.

Louie Pahlitch, our emcee fellow graduate, said he had a few minutes of spare "mike" time if anybody wanted to say something before our dinner showed up.

"Boy, Louie, you are going to regret saying that," as I rose with my book in hand, to grab the mike before some other classfool got to it to talk tearfully about what wonderful people we all are—cheerleader fashion.

"Taffy Pull" is a chapter I wrote about a ten or twelve-year-old boy trying his hardest to examine his furthest south extremities which do not include his legs and feet; with a flashlight between his heels, pointed up. I have read it many times at signings and larger book events. When that was over with and while some people were actually *trying* to eat, we sat at a larger table near the door *just* in case, signing away free books.

* * * * * *

The reason I had written, long ago, the story of how Hilda Peach had been mistreated was not so much my guilt over it, although, yes, I feel guilty *today* for not doing…something. But because Loren Tiapale had said to me: "Alan, I can't believe how our class treated her." A guilt that he'd carried, and still does, decades later.

My arm candy wife, Cheryl, not always so sure of the veracity of my stories, sat next to me while I signed copies. She was witness to three more classmates from Lacey *grade school* from out of nowhere who said to me some version of: ""I can't *believe* how our class treated Hilda Peach."

To which I replied after signing, along with a smile, "You are gonna *love* this book— you're in it."

"I *am?*" elatedly.

51

Naked and In Tears

Yesterday my thoughtful wife smeared some kinda crap all over my face before I left for softball. It was gale force winds blowing up at the ballfield. In fact, yesterday was the launch of the "Iditarod on the Water" race from nearby Port Townsend to Ketchikan. Seven powerless boats capsized. This yearly event is billed as "the best worst idea ever." I'm surprised I wasn't in it.

Whatever she'd put on my face mingled nicely with my windy tears from this tornado we were playing in, to cause my eyes to burn like hell for about two hours. But it was nothing like what she'd done to me in Maui. And I don't *think* she does stuff like this to me on purpose, but, you know…she does leave "post-it" reminder notes around for herself and I saw one that said, "Get even," once.

My friend and fellow softball player, Dave Farenbach, said, "Alan, you're a nudist; if you're going to Maui, go to Little Beach."

So we did. Well, I did. *We* went there once. Cheryl soon left, with clothes still on. The second time I went alone with some beer and a sandwich, in our rental car from our hotel in Kihei.

"Cover your eyes," she'd said. Not because of the upcoming scenery at the nude beach; because she was about to hose me down with a can or two of "baby strength" *SPF*. Just before I left she did it again. "Cover your eyes."

So I climb the cliff to get to "Little Beach," leaving all the dreary "normal" people with all their stupid swimsuits on behind me, to join others of *my* ilk. And it's hot—and getting hotter, the sun, I mean.

It's so cool seeing small families at a place like this. Little kids being raised to not be ashamed. Fifteen, sixteen-year-old boys and girls frolicking on body boards washing up to the shore, laughing; just to run out and do it again. They'd probably been coming here since early childhood. Brooke Shields and what's-his-name were all over the place. About the time I told myself I probably would have committed a lot less crimes if I had had the chance to grow up like these kids, all the hot battery acid sweat I'd been saving up in my hair and forehead came cascading down into my eye sockets. I am now officially blind *and* in burning pain. I went over to where my lunch cooler was; there were paper towels there. Tears streamed down on my sandwich as I sat there hoping it would stop, wiping my eyes, moaning, cursing, and chewing. No relief in sight, the misery kept coming.

Mumbling and bumbling, I gave up and headed toward the small rolling waves, hoping to not trip over or fall onto some big naked hairy dude that might think my whining ass is there for consolation. The acid pain would not let up. A wad of paper towels in each hand, I am now kneethigh into the ebb and flow. But I kept on trying to make it go away—wet towel, dry towel, muttering and crying like a baby the whole time.

What a downer I musta been that day to the beachgoers within view of my sorry display, or my display of sorrow.

"Should we help him? I think he's blind."

"What the hell's he doin' at a nude beach if he's blind? Let him drown; I think he's here to commit suicide anyway."

"He looks so sad."

"Well, he just cracked another beer."

"He's blubbering like a two-year-old."

"Most two-year-olds don't cuss and swear like he does."

"Ours did, thanks to your filthy-assed mouth."

"That's bullshit and you know it, Mona. Just gimmee a beer. That suicidal dipshit's makin' my ass thirsty."

"Lookit him out there, like he's lost his whole family in a plane wreck or somethin' an' his pecker's *still* bigger'n yours."

"Goddamit, Mona! I'm getting' ready to drown *him* and *you both* if you don't shut the hell up!"

"Stop it. Here come the kids. And I think he's leaving. Stop bein' a prick."

* * * * * *

Now I can't testify to a conversation I never heard—or saw— but that's how it would have gone if it were the other way around.

* * * * * *

After driving, with alternating eyes, back to Kihei to the closest pub and ordering a beer and a glass of ice, I waited for my young bride to find me. I had come back early from my donating salty tears into salty water. Two hours later, she did.

"Did you sunburn your *eyeballs*? They're beet red! You actually strained your eyeballs looking at naked women to the point where you *cooked* them? You are *such* a pervert!"

I dipped my napkin into my ice water and up to swab my eyes for the thousandth time in the last four hours, and answered her. "No, honey. It's from that stuff you slathered-sprayed me with this morning."

"That's bull. It's 'baby strength,' you big baby!"

52

TIJUANA TOOTHACHE

When people start whining to me about their past dental horror stories, I gently suggest they should just shut up. "Don't get me started," I warn them. Inevitably, they keep going, so I warn them again. "You keep goin' you're gonna be sorry." And they keep yammering away in the mistaken belief I'm even listening.

"Oh, are you done? Good. Now it's my turn." It's not as if I hadn't warned them. And don't worry, I'm not going to regale you here with mine (unless you start it). And mine are *ug-u-ly*.

Just this one, and my most recent; but in truth, the dentistry itself couldn't have been better or smoother. The procedure was great. Lengthy, but that's because it involved six root canals and six porcelain crowns. My teeth were fine, but "chiseled" down in the bottom front due to my bite. Too close to the dentine to grind down for crowns; hence the root canals. The problem was, I nearly ended up in prison because of my teeth.

They take an hour off for lunch down here in Tijuana, the dental staff. So they threw me out into the street and locked the door, after shooting me up with three quarts of Novocain and drilling out six roots. They told *me* to go have a nice lunch at one of the nearby cantinas, then come back for four more hours of fun. Food was the last thing on my mind but I desperately needed to rehydrate.

"Forvafa," I slurped out to the lovely bar "mesera."

"Como?" looking cautiously at my mouth.

I tried once again to say "Cervesa" but it came out again as "Forfafa" while blowing a big bloody bubble that popped all over my face. She looked disgusted and held up a small square aluminum packet which contained one "Viagra." Now she's all cute and coy with one raised eyebrow as she shakes the packet near her cheek; as in, "Come and get it."

Moaning, I walked to the cooler and grabbed two "Pacificos," opened one and poured it all over my lower face, ears, neck and chest. I think some went down my throat. This was clearly the wrong way to drink. I looked around the bar top for a straw. Seeing none, I resorted to sign language.

Doing my level best to demonstrate how you use a straw while making the necessary sounds and while, in my case, slobbering all over my right hand which holds my imaginary straw, I stop to look at her to see if she "gets" it.

She unbuttons the top button of her shirt and pulls out of a drawer a large flat silver packet which displayed *twenty-four* "Viagras." Evidently one of us is horny and I'm pretty sure it's not me. *Now* it dawns on me; she thinks I'm asking for oral sex.

I'm trying to explain to her in gurgling English I just had oral *surgery*—and I am now pointing at my mouth, which *convinces* her *that's* what I want, up goes that eyebrow again.

Catching a glimpse in the bar's mirror I realize my tongue is hanging out the side of my mouth and apparently I've been chewing on it. That made me wonder, Is this what *all* sex-starved gringos look like when they visit? I poured more beer out onto my shirt and swallowed some air.

I paid and left for a sunny spot on a bench to watch traffic and try to suck on my other beer. An old man was setting up a street cart shoe repair sidewalk small business endeavor. An apparently out-of-work middle-aged guy leans on a light post, passively watches. They both hear me choking and belching from all the air I'm drinking. When I finish, I get up to walk over to a small "shotgun" style bodega for another beer and hopefully, a straw. A 32-ounce beer and one Spanish lesson later, I had a nice fat "Popote" to drink from. I reclaimed my bench. He's still here, watching the shoe guy.

Halfway through my liquid lunch, the leaning man walks over to advise me not to drink in public. On *this* one I took issue. I told him in plain English how my wife had told me that, twenty years ago, in blistering Porta Vallarta; so I had asked a cop; he extended his arms and with a big grin hollered, "It's *Mexico*!!"

Unfortunately, this is what my plain English sounded like to him: "Whumf hugptat corfa mif dongsploot feeff thrakkettt porfoo meefa forknok theet shooofaa garsssshha feeepo," with a lotta slurping in between my "words."

He frowned and pulled back one side of his jacket to reveal his police identification on a lanyard. No longer thirsty, I dropped my jug of half drunk liquid gold in the nearby trash can, because he wants me to take a walk with him. I actually *wanted* to run.

He threw his head sideways towards a guy across the street and said, "That's my sergeant over there watching us, so walk down this way with me."

During this "walk" he did all the talking. A brief encapsulation on this walk includes the following: "We can make this all go away…" and out from my front pocket comes a 20-dollar bill.

"Well, that's not gonna *do* it. I have my sergeant to consider. You gotta do better."

"Sallgoft." (translation: "That's all I've got.")

"No it's not. *C'mon*! Or you'll be here a long time." With my short arms and deep pockets

I fished out another $28 in cash.

"That's it, huh? S'all you got? How you pay tooth guy?"

I gestured in the direction of my "tooth people" and said," mafegodempaaalmeefmooony." (Translation: "They got all my money," which wasn't true. I had not yet paid them.) I had over twelve grand in my *back* pocket. He set me free with a warning.

As I walk briskly back to buy another beer (I kept my "Popote") I saw his "sergeant" trip on the broken sidewalk, drop his "Modelo" can and fall into a planter. Where he stayed. I gave my "tooth guy" his ten thousand after they were done with me, and Fernando, their driver, picked me up to deliver me back to San Diego to my hotel and wife.

The Novocain now dissipated, I told Fernando the story, and we both concluded it was a simple scam and that, "Alan, you *had* to do it that way! You could not take the *chance!*" "I know." He dropped me off at the "Westin" lobby and I brought my new teeth up to the eleventh floor of the north tower overlooking the harbor and what was then "Anthony's Seafood," to show my wife.

"Wow! Those are nice!" I heard the "rumboat's" cannons go off when she asked me if I bought anything while there.

"Yeah, I bought a lotta Viagra."

53

MALROBE WARDFUNCTION

Lacey grade school had rich kids, middle kids, poor kids, and me. My sense of style or fashion could be boiled down to "You're just lucky I'm wearing *anything.*"

But I guess I was conscious of what they were pushing on TV, which included

"Brilliantine," a sticky paste to make your hair stand straight up in the front. Something else I had no money to buy but needed, to "fit in."

We always had a coffee can full of bacon grease under the sink but I thought if I used that on my hair, it would just make me hungry *all* day. Being resourceful, though, I found myself a workaround. I was gonna make my hair stick straight up in the front just like the rich kids, without smelling like breakfast.

I noticed a square white cube on top of our bathroom sink and when I sniffed at it I detected something clinical and sinister. So I asked my mom about it.

"What square thing? Oh, *that?* We call that stuff…*soap.*"

After some rudimentary experimentation, I found out a couple drops of water on this alien "soap" thing could produce a slightly sticky, yet slick, film between my thumb and forefinger. The bar's surface had the same texture.

Without getting too much of this strange new substance on many more fingers than needed, I brushed the bar upward from my hairline, and it worked! My hair stayed up. It quickly dried and stayed like that. They can keep their "Brilliantine." I would keep my buck and a quarter; if I'd had it.

Every day for a couple weeks, my counterfeit hairdo "fit in." My quarter mile walk to my bus stop and ten minute wait in the pouring rain would soon "unfit" me, again.

We are gathering for class and I hear some sniggering when a girl points and, grinning, says, "What's that all over your head?" Now everybody's looking, and laughing.

"I don't know. What?" I felt the top of my head and looked at my palm full of nice white soapy suds.

In the boys' room while dealing with the evil muck, some smartass goes, "Hey, aren't you supposed to rinse *in* the *shower* after you shampoo?"

"Rinse" and "shampoo"—two more words I had to look up.

* * * * * *

'long about May, on exceptionally nice hot spring days, "my lake" would call to me; there were fish to be caught. So every once in awhile, in order to get outta class, my zipper would "break."

"Miss Sweeney, I can't go back to class like this." Quietly.

"Alan, how in the world do you keep…never mind. Just go. See you tomorrow. Come back with some homework for a change."

'I could bring her a *fish* maybe, but I can't do any homework with a broken zipper; too distracting,' is what I was thinking as I threaded a big fat nightcrawler onto my 'catfish' hook. "How in hell do you keep messin' up this damn zipper? I'm gonna put you inna dress!" from my mom. "Look, Mom. Two catfish."

54

OLD BONES

Most people, I guess, don't have an extra skeleton other than the metaphorical ones "in the closet." And some of *those* "closets" are large and packed. On the other hand, there are people who've had quite a few extra skeletal remains, a club to which I belong.

The antique business turns up some interesting stuff. I *think* it was the "Odd Fellows' Fraternal Organization which would occasionally deaccession some of their initiation ritual paraphernalia that included human remains in the form of complete skeletons. Some of those would find their way to me. Trust me when I say, I never went looking for them. But for some reason they are quite sought after.

I did have some fun with my last one. In fact, I grew to be rather attached. [Do *not* go there—Ed.] I sat him up in the passenger seat of my van where he stayed for most of the summer about four years ago, window down, with one boney foot on the dash and elbow out the window, big "smile" on his "face."

Softball tournaments, as well as a million trips to Home Depot. Up and down I-5 as well as Costco and elsewhere. Lotsa open mouths and downturned mouths of disgust and utter disdain. No cops ever came near me.

I thought about utilizing him for the H.O.V. lanes just to see if I could get away with it but elected not to because of where that could lead....

"Sir, you are aware the H.O.V. lane is for vehicles with two or more passengers?" "Sure. That's why my friend, Milt here, is with me—goin' to Home Depot to get him some new wire for his neck. His head bobbles around too much. People think he's choking." "Yeah, I saw that—I thought he was laughing. Sir, he's not a passenger. He's dead." "*Don't* talk like that in front of him! Look, his head just fell forward in total sadness. The sign says 'persons' so he counts as a passenger."

"He's dead."

"Sign says *nothing* about dead or alive."

"You cannot transport dead bodies, either."

"Not a body, only a skeleton—and you just hurt his feelings—look now—he won't even look at you."

"Yeah, you know, you may be right. The fine for an H.O.V. violation is $124.00. This one here is for $136.00—he's not wearing his seatbelt. Have a nice day."

"Oh, yeah—*thanks a lot.*"

"I was talking to Milt."

Quite a while back I was commissioned to do an estate auction in the Carlyon area of Olympia-Tumwater vicinity. The name of the gentleman who hired me was John Dart—grandson of the famous "Professor" John Dart, of African Anthropology notoriety.

It used to be that antique-estate auctiongoers liked to know the circumstances of the dispersal. More folks would show up if something horrible happened. Cancer, bankruptcy, plane crash, murder, whatever; just something cataclysmic and final. So they could come and fight over the carcass. And that's what I told the owner and his wife, jokingly; all they were wanting to do was downsize and move. So we settled on "by the order of—" which was the standard—but not dismal and negative enough, so John said, "Well, Alan, our daughter just moved away to college. How about you just say, 'Due to the departure of our daughter.'?" While setting up the auction—in their home—I found two things of interest down in the basement in their trash pile: an American early "Bannister back" armchair *and* a very old human skull. Upstairs displayed on the walls there was an impressive collection of ancient African tribal artifacts, testament to Professor Dart's work in those parts of the world, so I had no doubts about where this skull I dug out from the garbage pile had originated.

Many of the items in this collective display were, to me, "chief worthy." By that I mean they looked important and elaborate enough to have been a tribal chief or elder's prized possession. Having seen collections like this before, usually amassed over years of being in close contact and on good terms with whichever indigenous culture was involved, I gave it respect. I don't know what kind of terms you have to be on to get them to donate or trade their own cranium to your collection, but there it was. We got six-hundred bucks for it. My friend and sometimes co-conspirator, Jack Gunter, paid seven hundred for the chair.

The last, but by no means the least, of the parade of dead humans I have sold on the open market, I sold it for $5,500; but it was a special one. (Isn't it odd that you are not allowed to traffic in *legally* obtained wild game, but you can buy and sell human skeletons? As long as they're not *too* fresh, I guess.)

Also from Africa, from the area commonly known for people mummifying their deceased, I not long ago acquired a spectacularly preserved version of the afterlife (?) although I'm not so sure the original owner or his mourners would have approved of his travels and treatment after he'd croaked. I bought this skull from a dealer in Brussels, took him to my shop in Tacoma, then sold him to a collector in New York. So I'm pretty sure he logged more miles dead than alive—he most likely never even got out from the Nile Valley while upright. This skull possessed a nearly full head of tightly packed hair, much skin *with* gold leaf overlay, including over one eye socket packed with cotton—the natron the Egyptians used to embalm their "client" would quickly dissolve the eyeballs—hence the cotton packing.

* * * * * *

Ever hear of mummia? It was "medicine" available in pharmacies for hundreds of years. Back when they used to dig up Egyptian coffins—for firewood—they decided to grind up their dead ancestors and sell 'em off to hypochondriacs who were stupid enough to eat them.

The North African steam railroad was fueled by chopped up Egyptian coffins. And Mummia was outlawed a long time ago 'cause they sorta ran low and went for somewhat "newer" mummies—like last week for instance.

Hey! Let's take a break for a snack. How about some nice shredded beef jerky and crackers?

55

Cowpies And Indians

'Course I grew up worshipping westerns, like many males my age. And playing "cowboys and Indians" would be a natural pastime except for two things. I had outgrown what little cowboy gear I once had, which adorns the front covers of my first two books, and there weren't any other kids around for me to "shoot" at with a cap gun I didn't have.

By midsummer any given year I'd already been sunburned enough times to no longer qualify as a paleface cowboy anyway, so I decided to switch sides. I would set about seeking revenge upon the evil white menace that now plagues our lands, our prairies, our forests, rivers, buffalo and casinos! [Casinos are a *little* later—Ed.] I basically only wore a "loincloth" all summer anyway. I was to be a heathen terror, tan and lean—slightly Swedish.

* * * * *

Incidentally, my wife signed me up for "Ancestry.com" not long ago, but she got it wrong the first time and signed me up for "Incestory.com," so I found out I'm related to almost everybody in Alabama—but seriously, I am 41% Swedish and, get this: I'm from the *most* northern section of Sweden; the area called "*Angermanland*"! So do *not* piss me off.

* * * * *

So I'm all set to wage war with the "whites." Not having any weapons, I went to work crafting a bow and arrow. After several failed attempts at a "bow," I came up with a sorta decent one, with fish line for string. Arrows?—that was a different story. Our entire forest of five acres would *not* yield up *one* straight stick, so I made a couple curved arrows and I compensated by *not* aiming *at* my target. If my arrow curved left, I'd aim *right*. Now I can't say that that actually worked, but it was impressive. It *really* impressed one of our chickens, as well as my dad.

"What the hell you think you're doin'?"

"That wasn't on purpose; my arrow's no good. My arrow's crooked."

"Well listen, 'Crooked Arrow,' don't do that around the house. Yer gonna kill the dog or somebody. Go out into 'Newkirk's' field. That hen's probably not gonna lay for a week."   I stuffed one of our gunny sacks full of tall dead grass and threw it past the fence to drag it over the dry and wet cow patties for "target practice." My dad watched from our front window as I, in complete futility, tried to hit it. Never did. They would sail away left or right. Once in a while one would go straight. Straight up in the air—or straight into the ground. When the returning war party came home in defeat, my dad said, "I guess we don't have to worry about our gunny sack. Son, I'll make you an arrow tomorrow."

And he did. He picked out a nice straight piece of cedar board, split off a slender stick from it and whittle-carved an arrow's length, suitable for sanding round. My arrows looked like bent green logs compared to his work of art. Complete with our own chicken feathers for "fletching."

Next morning I took off to shoot and butcher me a burlap buffalo.

Now, I have no idea where that arrow went, but I think it had fun getting there because I watched it dance as it disappeared, far *and* wide. It didn't weigh anything, so it *travelled*!

Those chicken feathers on one end with *no tip* on the front caused my errant arrow to act so erratic it probably sailed all the way on the jet stream to kill one of my relatives in Birmingham.

Not long after, the folks bought me a "junior archery" set from Sears!

Cowpies were now cowboys and other greedy interlopers, and they were multiplying. No cowpie in that pasture was safe from "Crooked Arrow." Well, the wet ones were spared, and it was just me against all of them. I guess I was the last of my kind, so I was busy. My four new arrows of righteousness lasted me about one week before slipping into invisibility. My second to last vestige of vengeance I actually accidentally shot in half when it was sticking up out of a dead "mountain man" or cowboy before *it* slid horizontally into the weeds. All my arrows were gone now.

After telling my dad I could really use some more, he said, "No."

How *dare* he? Standing right here, on *our* sacred *stolen* grounds, deny me the right to bear arms and the right to defend our *stolen* lands from intruders? I did *not* ask him for a "Gatling gun." Just *some* arrows, for defense—or food. It was not to be. What's next? Now, completely without defense, or a means for food sourcing, I—"we" *wondered,* yes, what's next? Rotten meat? Reservations and new diseases, on *our* land, never heard of before? Will we sit in our wickiups and teepees and watch them slash our food source for *profit* while we starve? The answer to that and many similar atrocious questions is, *yes.*

The Great White Father had spoken. "No." As usual, we had to settle on the white man's terms. Knowing what the word "powerless" meant, having been used to it since birth, I never asked again. I hung up my powerless, useless bow on the last nail of my coat rack which was my closet.

Somma them damn cowpies sure suffered, though. "Teach 'em not to mess with a surefire pissed off Scandinavian-Native American militant twelve-year-old defender of "our" soil.

56

CHESSMASTER

I've been in the "sports" pages twice; once was a picture of me tryin' like hell to get to third with a second baseman on my heels with the ball. His name is Jan Wolcott and he was further away than the camera made it appear.

But the look on my face is pure desperation. In fact, my son said, "Dad, is that guy a cop? 'Cause you sure *look* like yer running from the cops." And he should know.

The first time I wound up in the paper, though, was in the "Daily Olympian's" sports section. I was nineteen. [He was on the front page twice before this, though, because the cops were searching for the perpetrators of two different crimes.—Ed.]

My addiction to "Flipper" pinball machines sucked me into the Lacey Lanes bowling alley to donate all my hard-earned quarters to the "Bally" and "Gottlieb" people. Once a month the Olympia Chess Club met in the foyer; it was on one of those meets I was asked to play. My money nearly gone, I said yes.

Surprisingly, I won, and a couple days later someone told me they'd read how I had beat the president of the Olympia Chess Club.

"I did? Wow, I mean, I didn't know who he was or anything; just some guy sittin' there by himself. I hope I didn't get him into trouble or anything." Up until then I didn't *think* I had any special aptitude for chess; my buddy Bob Richards used to beat me more often than I beat him, so…

One month later found me lusting for more blood on the old checkered battlefield of kings, queens, and jumping sideways horses.

Only it was a different format this time. They had a "guest" player, it was an "event." No one was playing except for six guys. And this "guest" guy who was maybe four years older than myself. Six tables were set up in a row with a local chess addict seated at each—eager to play this kid. Everyone else got to watch. This kid from out of town was pacing around, waiting to get started.

Somebody says, "Begin," and he walks into the far corner and stands there facing the inside corner of two walls.

"What's he doing, meditating?"

"No."

"Is he pouting?"

"No."

"Did he get sent into the corner 'cause he did something bad?"

"No, he's *playing*. Sshhh!"

So I watched this guy and the six seated players holler chess moves back and forth like it was a tennis match, for about an hour. After the third guy gets his ass kicked or concedes, I withdrew. I had seen enough of this bloodbath. I headed for a pinball machine. And I never looked back.

If this kid can come to town and beat the hell out of our *finest*, I am *outta* here, I figured. But I have played chess a few times since, just to prove to myself that I'm actually no good at it—and I've never been disappointed. Except when teaching the game to my kids. I looked pretty good then.

But I was in the sports page once, though, for something I accomplished.

* * * * * *

Like you, I just now made the mistake of reading the story I just wrote, and for the first time in my life, I realized I didn't *win* that game! That old guy totally *threw* the game! He lost on purpose! It was a tactic to attract new members. And these people are tacticians, right? Dammit!

It's the same thing my wife did to me when we first met.

"Alan, you are sooo *funny!*" Now she only glares at me *or* interrupts so many times I have *no* idea what I was even talking about. Then she sends me back to the store to return everything

I bought yesterday because it was all the wrong stuff.

Ya, I beat the president of the chess club, alright. I'm no fool. [Only for a half century. Ed.]

57

Nisqually Wreck

It might not seem like it a lot of the time, but I believe that most all of the time, people the world over would like to think that at any given moment they want to do the right thing. That they are a "good" person.

But then Putin, Hitler and Lucifer probably thought that also. And the three of them are possibly all the same person.

Of course, all of the wrong people are the ones who grab the headlines. Good people— no, make that *great* people—like you—don't often make it into the papers *because* you are "good." I have been in the papers way too many times. Like the time I balanced a brand new Chevy sedan up on top of the guardrail on the Nisqually River bridge. Almost In the *middle* of the bridge, river below.

Once again, color picture, front page, "Daily Olympian," my fault, slam dunk. Except it wasn't my fault. [Nothing ever is his fault, is it?—Ed.]

I was leasing a 24-foot U-Haul from Randy, the manager of the local U-Haul franchise in Olympia, for a "flat" $600 a month. Once a month I drove cross-country to gather antiques, while also going all over Washington and Oregon auctioning off thermal windows and doors. I wore *out* some of these trucks.

I was returning home to Lacey from "Milgard Windows" in Tacoma with a full load of thermal patio door "units" the afternoon of this escapade. Traffic was light, almost nil, on I-5 as I began the maybe three or four percent downgrade hill towards the river. U-Haul trucks had "governors" on them, not to exceed 60 m.p.h. This one, you can get 62 or 63 if you have a load; I have easily four or five tons of glass behind me.

Three lanes, I'm in the middle with one car in front when I begin to pick up a tiny bit more speed, enough to hit my blinker left, and pass him.

In a tall truck you have to be able to see the vehicle behind you which you just passed *in* your starboard side mirror because one never knows, he may have stomped on the gas and be sitting right there, *under* your mirror, in your blind spot. To make sure, I often sorta bounce up and down in my seat, looking for some sneaky fool in a sedan or, worse yet, a convertible with the top *down*. Sometimes, when I'm performing this "bouncy" thing, people with me look at me as if I'm trying to look up their nose or I'm having a serious autism episode. Today, though, I am alone; "company" will arrive soon.

Signaling right, I passed the car by 100-150 feet and began drifting back into the middle lane. A *major* explosion with corresponding jarring impact on my right front fender as a white sedan swings around backwards and attaches itself sideways onto my front bumper. Downshifting as best I could, my right foot and leg is locked straight out on the brake pedal. "Don't roll! Don't roll!" was all I could holler as I "chattered" his four wheels sideways down the highway.

I finally got stopped enough to watch him leave my bumper, spin around again and climb up onto the guard rail, where he stayed, balancing.

Assuming the soon to arrive firetrucks, aid cars, cops, cranes, tow trucks, lawyers, news crews, and food trucks would need me to move, I pulled ahead onto the shoulder just after the bridge, left side. Walking back to the carnage and half expecting "Barnum and Bailey" after hearing about a new balancing act, to be on their way, I wasn't too far off when I saw the hundreds of cars, buses and trucks beginning to "queue up" all the way back to Fort Lewis. And leading the charge was an entire convoy of army trucks and jeeps.

A jeep roared up in the gravel to stop on the right shoulder. This loud "general" type guy jumps out and starts barking orders to people who weren't even there. I stood and watched him wave his arms around for a while, then joined the melee on the "bridge of sighs." By now people had his passenger door open and they could talk to him; he was lying down on the front seat. Said his ribs hurt. I just wanted to get close enough to tip him and what's left of his car into the river; let the salmon nurse him back to health.

This was the same river at the same spot when the "Fisheries Department," with shotguns, were chasing Jane Fonda and Marlon Brando around in boats. They had threatened to chain themselves to the bridge or a salmon net or something. The government didn't want the Indians catching their own fish.

During my brief interview with the state patrolman, I tried to tell him how this happened and that I had done everything right. He wasn't much listening.

"You didn't signal. We have witnesses."

"The *hell* I didn't! Look! It's still on."

All of which was true. Didn't matter, he rips off my "ticket" page from his book, hands it to me and says, "We get lotsa these 'improper' lane changes in a truck. You can go."

"But…"

My negligent driving court date arrived and although I didn't expect to vindicate, my time came to testify. I explained everythning *which you have already read,* along with: "I don't care what 'witnesses' said, I was *absolutely* signaling right when I changed lanes. And the ONLY way this could have happened *is* that guy *HAD* to have been traveling at a *very* high speed when he passed the car behind me. And he *HAD* to have come outta the far right lane, because he was *NOT* in my mirror! That's all I have to say."

The judge sat there a few, then said, while unfolding a piece of paper, "Thank you, Mister Gorsuch. I'd *like* to read a letter received by this court."

I thought, "uh-oh." I was *fully* clothed and sober when this happened. Can I have an attorney? Can I make a phone call? May I please have a glass of beer?

Judge: "To whom it may concern: We were behind the U-Haul truck when we saw a white car traveling at a *very high rate of speed* go around us on our right and collide into the truck which had its turn signal *on*. My name is Mary…."

"Case dismissed!" Bam!

When the judge had said, "I'd *like* to read this letter," I *still* have the impression he was as happy as was I someone *did* step forward to do the *right thing* and actually took the time to write an old-fashioned letter.

By this time, however, the U-Haul folks had already given the 84-year-old "Dale Earnhart" a brand-new car and ten grand because he said, "I can't get erections anymore." So I guess that was *my* fault.

Thank you, Mary.

58

The Rodeo Comes To Town

When it comes to ugly rumors, whether it's that social (or unsocial) media plague which all of mankind now seems to willingly suffer from, I don't wait around. I just don't have the patience for it to hear what the next nasty thing it was that I supposedly did. I simply start my own rumors. And they're good ones, the ones that people *love* to pass on.

Like the time Renee was "preggers" with Dave Meconi's baby. I told the whole town it was my baby, with Renee's blessing. Something most women would *not* do. But Renee's kinda "special," if you know what I mean; she'd *have* to be, to get tangled up with Dave Meconi. But when little "Wayne" was born with eyelashes a foot long—just like Dave's, that was the end of *that* rumor. Half the time mine look like they were burnt off. [Because they were. Ed.]

* * * * * *

Cheryl and our friend, Gretchen, are in the front seat of my wife's convertible, whereas I am relegated to the [trunk? Ed.] backseat. We're gonna have a nice dinner at "Pacific Grill" down on our main drag; Friday night.

Cheryl's having trouble parking, curbside.

Now, don't you *dare* tell her I said this, but she has ground some of our Tacoma curbs with her hubcaps or wheelrims, down to half their original thickness over the years. And somehow, If I'm riding with her, it is, of course, *my* fault. Sometimes, I pretend I'm sleeping so I might not get yelled at. And it doesn't work; she yells 'cause I'm not "helping" her.

So this night, I thought I would help her.

"Okay, honey, crank it, and you be good."

"Shut up! I know what I'm doing."

"Careful. You're…"

"Leave me alone!" Sparks fly into the evening breeze and the metallic gristmill grinding added to the sounds of the city.

"If…. ." and that was the last word I spoke that evening, or the next day; to my wife anyway. Because she *and* Gretchen turned on me, hollered obscenities at me and threw me out of the car. My own car.

I held the restaurant door for my two pretty lovely ladies of the evening and fought the automatic door "closer" to shut it quickly and ran. I went to the "Marriott" hotel next door, up to the bar and did some healing up.

Young men in cowboy hats were all over the place; then I remembered the fancy billboard electronic ads at the "Tacoma Dome" for a *HUGE* rodeo event, this weekend. Isn't it nice that "drinking" and "thinking" rhyme? [It is not—Ed.] The longer I sat there, before walking home and going to bed, the better my idea looked—I was gonna join the rodeo! I made just enough phone calls the next day, Saturday, to *other* people, not my wife, that I had signed up for the cash prize, $10,000 mechanical bull ride on Sunday, for her to find out second hand—the rumor mill. And it spread like wildfire! [More like a grass fire in a mud puddle—Ed.] She found out on Sunday morning.

"No, it's already done, honey, hope you guys will all be there, Gretchen and everyone.

Where's my antique ten-gallon hat?"

"Upstairs in that thing you call a closet. I think two of our cats are stuck in there somewhere." I grabbed my hat and lit out for the badlands.

Now just to clarify, I did *not* go anywhere near the Tacoma Dome to sign up for anything. Before you go off thinking I was gonna break my neck getting on *anything*, I wasn't and I didn't. [Barstool—Ed.]

I had told everybody "my" event was at 3 p.m.—gate #17. So every sadistic, bloodthirsty, schadenfreudenistic [Where did he get that one? Mary Poppins?— expealladocious—Ed.] rat bastard "friend" of mine went there and paid $30 to watch me kill myself in front of thousands of other bloodsport thrill seekers. I was across town at "Magoo's," a pub where nobody knows me, wearing my giant hat and watching a baseball game. They wandered around in confused futility, asking where Gate 17 was, only to be repeatedly told, "There is no gate 17, I don't think. Well, maybe it's over there—yeah, go try over there."

Then, "It's almost 3 o'clock—where's the bull ride?"

"It's right in front of you—it's goin' on now—whoops, there he goes. Wow! That musta hurt."

"No. the *mechanical* bull ride."

"What mechanical bull ride?"

"The one at 3 o'clock."

""There isn't one.—Wow, seven seconds—not a bad ride, cowboy. Let's see, who's up next? Oh, yeah. Ozzie Wallace. He's a good rider but he drew a tough bull."

"The mechanical bull ride should start right now—a friend of ours is in it. Her husband." "Friend a yers, huh?"

"Yeah—he does crazy stuff like this."

"Ya know whatcher *lookin'* at out there? This here is called a "RO-DEE-O!! Ain't *no* mechanized bulls here! I think yer buddy— her husband—rode *you* in here on *some* kinda bull." Then he spit some smelly brown juice into a Pepsi can.

"Can't you folks go siddown somewhere?"

So they did.

59

Hhhaaats!

Used to get some good stuff going to the "U.S. Customs" auctions. Sometimes not so good—like the time I bought three sealed and banded 55 gallon drums of "eel skin leather," cured and stored in some kinda liquid hell.

I wasn't allowed to unseal them until after the auction. I wish they'd just stipulated that under *no* circumstances are you *ever* allowed to open these drums of death, from now to eternity!

I'd also bought ten thousand "Resistol" wool hat "blanks" in bundles of 250 in burlap bags, so it took a while to load those into my 20' box truck, and now it was time to inspect my exotic leather eel skins; curious to see what I had scored. The crowd had thinned out once people paid and left with their insignificant little purchases. A crowd gathered around me— which included "KING 5 TV" news. Clearly, I had made the wisest transaction of the day, I mean if the news crew is here—it must be *somethin'* good, y'know?

I popped the band and used my hammer to bend all the clips upward to unseal the big lid. When I unsealed it from the rubber, a buncha wet slop got all over my hands and shoes. I saw dead fish things floating in there when the smell hit me. Then it hit everybody. I was the first to motate. While they began to scatter, amid lots of noisy sickened groans—I had already run to the ladies' room—the closest one, to scrub on my slimy, putrid hands. Over and over. I kicked off my shoes and left them, covered in some kinda horrendous, skanky nuclear fish waste. When I ran through and past the drums of death I saw no one, no one alive anyway. I got into my truck and got the hell outta there.

Next morning I received a call from a nice, well-spoken customs agent man who gently explained to me how I should come get my prize putrification.

"Getcher ass back here—pick up this shit—six people out on sick leave—two people quit—hate crime—fumigate—terrorist charges—twenty to life—or we're comin' to haul yer ass into a cell *with* that open tank of poison and seal *you* off *with* it!"

'I'll be there soon as I find some shoes."

"Yah! Come and get *those*, too!"

A gas-masked forklift driver deputy slid three pallets of certain chemical warfare into my truck and I departed to donate it to the "Hanford Nuclear Waste Facility," the "Manhattan Project" had come full circle. [That is not what he did but we're bound by a non-disclosure this time. Ed.]

Now, about these hat blanks. I really thought I'd never get rid of them, but I did. They were big floppy hillbilly looking things, thick wool, ready for the mold for process, through steam and chemicals, to form into a three hundred dollar "Stetson" type shape. I'd paid nine cents apiece for them and was selling them for five bucks, as a novelty. But they *were* excellent rain hats too, impervious to water.

Brimfield, Mass. Was my biggest vehicle for sales. If it looked like a summer storm was pending I would put one on, flip the brim up in the front, grab an armload and stroll the miles of aisles of the never-ending "booths" of other antique dealers, hollering an obnoxious *"Hhhaats! Getcher official wide-brim-field hats here!"* And "best rain hat money can buy—five bucks." They sold like hatcakes! I had a callous on my thumb from counting five-dollar bills. Of course, I "wholesaled" quite a few bales out to other dealers around the country; if you stopped by "Wall Drug" in South Dakota—a huge tourist trap— you might have seen some; they bought a lot. I did have fun selling those hats, and sometimes trading as well.

On one of my many cross-country road odysseys, John "Hair Spray" Swales and one other truly unique individual named Jack Gunter were with me in a 24' U-Haul truck. We were heading east, still in South Dakota, after leaving Wall Drug, when I made a good trade. First, though, I need to enlighten you about Jack Gunter.

The only thing in the back of the truck were bales of hats. Jack wanted a nap, so we stuffed him in back there and pulled down the rollup door and latched it. It was hotter than a skillet in there.

Maybe two hours later I stopped for gas. Expecting Jack to be dead, I unlatched and uprolled the door, to be greeted by a smiling naked Jack wearing a filthy sweat-salted crusty old leather cowboy hat, lying down "reading" a "Penthouse" magazine, eating an ice cream bar while drinking a bottle of beer *and smoking a joint!"* Yesser, I only travel with the best of 'em. So now he's back up front with us again and we're gearing up for another refuel. We're in the middle of overcook, nowhere. I always tried to sell—or trade at the gas stations, some hats; so the guys were instructed to be wearing them when we pulled in. And we were as I pulled up to the pump.

And that's when the three of us wearing our big floppy hillbilly hats noticed the three old hillbillies sitting next to us on the bench next to the store's door. All six of us pointed at each other, laughing.

All three of *them* were wearing baseball caps with a *pheasant* on them which read:

"South Dakota is BIG COCK COUNTRY!"

When we pulled out, each shoe, so to speak, was on a different foot. We waved at the hillbilly hats on the park bench while sporting our "BIG COCK" HATS. And we drove away laughing. John was pissed off that his hair got all messed up, and he threw his hat onto the dashboard of the big Ford. He shook his head like a wet spaniel and tried to fluff it back into place.

I had traded for a few more hats *inside* the store as well—sold those in Brimfield, too. More than one good looking woman who read my hat gave me a *big* smile which disappeared as soon as I told her I was from Washington State.

I've *never* been accused of false advertising.

60

WASTING AWAY

Life is a flesh-eating disease.

AND, by the way, I have studied all the data, and apparently all food is poisonous, because anybody who eats it—dies. Irrefutably true. Not even fake news.

Years back while junkin' in Buffalo, New York, I'm in some old geezer's junk store trying to get a price out of him on a "Limberts" oak armchair, and this was his answer:

"Everything leaves a mark."

Clueless as to what that meant, this was my reply: "Yeah, the chair's marked 'Limberts,' how much? To a fellow dealer? Best price?"

"Everything, *everything* leaves a mark" staring out at nothing. I didn't ask him again. He was gone. He's still there, but gone. "*Everything* leaves a bruise," is the next thing he says, staring out, seeing nothing, clearly off on another planet. Planet dementia, I figured. I had *no* idea what this guy was saying.

Well, I *know* what he was talking about *now*.

That convo came back to me only recently because I am now currently and for the last couple of years, *covered* in bruises. I look like a walking human plum tree. And I don't even have to try. I don't know where most of them even came from. I think my wife bludgeons me in my sleep or I get attacked by a pack of toothless wild dogs.

Now, this big scab on my right shin I'm well aware, I was *wide* awake when that softball thread twisted off a nice patch of my skin in the outfield last week. [Not "wide awake" enough to catch the ball—Ed.] We were playing at "Steel Lake" which is a very inferior outfield— unpredictable. Our outfielders are also inferior—but predictable. In fact, if somebody catches a flyball, everybody is surprised. Couple weeks ago Bud dropped four, Bobby got knocked down by two, Dave lost one and our other outfielder just got lost and went home. Eventually Bud *did* catch one, a tough one, going *away* from him, and *he* was the last one to figure out that he'd actually caught it. In fact, he was arguing with us! "No! You caught it! Look in yer glove, you idiot!"

And you should see us run; I've seen taxidermy run faster than us. Half of our team has to hit it to the fence just to make it to first base. But what can you expect from a team named "Casket Ready"? Our hats say R.I.P. on them. Big hit with the ladies. Other teams are *not* happy when they lose to us, and many do. Our team credo is, "We don't care how riddled you are with cancer, *just catch the damn BALL!*"

There is *nothing* soft about "softballs" either. They just leave a bigger bruise. More than a couple players have collided with one and did not live to talk about it.

Maybe three years ago, my daughter Jenny looked at my forearms and said, "*Dad!* You have *OLD MAN* arms now!"

"Wonder why?"

Our second baseman, Warren, has a lovely wife, Paula, who asked about all the spots on my lower legs as well as upper. She's a nurse.

I pointed at the big one above my knee. "Well, a raisin fell outta my mouth and hit me here, then it bounced down my shin and did all these. I dropped a marshmallow on this leg right here and a moth ran into me here."

"What about the back of your legs?"

"Cheryl whipped me with a peacock feather and she's a lot younger'n me, so that *is* elder abuse, right?

"Miscarriage of justice, I'd say. I woulda whooped ya with the whole damn peacock.

You needa start taking collagen."

"Okay, thank you. I'll put that on the list. Even though I don't want anything to do with higher education."

She stood there and blinked a couple of times, thinking, then, "Don't worry, Alan, it won't make you any smarter. That's not possible."

"Good." And that was *nice* of her to say that.

* * * * * *

I think we think *if* we've been in good health our whole lives, we always *will* be. But we know that's wrong because there are so many things to *go* wrong. So we'd rather not think about it and then one day something does, or worse. My buddy Dave Roberts just tells me to "drink through it." He's smart like that.

Most of the bruises on the back of my hand and forearms are from fighting with those "flaps" on the ends of cardboard beer cases, especially when reaching way back.

It's four o'clock, time to go stir some'a that "college" powder into a beer.

61

MAN-EATING HORSES

My dad used to break horses in Montana and although he never told me how to do it, I thought he might be kinda proud when I came home to tell him I did, too; I tamed a wild horse.

In fact, I knocked this full-grown thoroughbred horse on her ass—and she had it coming.

My first "real" job came up when I was fifteen, as a stableboy for a guy named Lee Bentsley who owned "Lee's Restaurant and Steak House" at the north end of Kinwood Road. I was paid a whopping $20 a month to, seven days a week, twice a day, clean out the stalls, restraw them and feed as many as four purebred quarter horses. Most of the time there were only two, Franfire and Sister Fran. Sister Fran was a year old when I had to knock her block off; and I felt terrible about it, yet proud enough to tell my dad; who, of course, just like you, didn't believe me.

She was frisky, playful even, and that became problematic because horses play with their *TEETH*. She didn't used to be like this, it sort of evolved; she *was* calm and gentle, but now she's developed this nasty habit of snapping at me. And she's also realized that it scares the livin' bejesus outta me! So she does it even more. Eventually she would stand under the "transparent" apple tree by the fence on Kinwood and wait for me to climb over to go the hundred yards to the stable; she thinks this is fun. I don't.

Jimmy, the neighbor kid, had accompanied me a few times, so he knew how to do my chores, just in case. One weekend that's what happened; I got to go to the ocean to camp out with my cousins. When I came home he, Jimmy, showed me the *nasty* bruise on his shoulder; *big* teeth marks. And he retired as my backup. He said something about, "Getting your face bit off for 33 cents twice a day just isn't quite worth it."

"Thirty-three cents? Is that all I'm making?"

"Yes. Do the math."

"I hate math, you know that. That's why I'm shoveling shit for man-eating horses for a living."

"Well, you should stick with it. By the time you're forty you'll be making probably a dollar thirty-five a day."

"Ooo! How much is that a month? Is it over a thousand dollars?"

"…um, no. I gotta go. My mom told me to stop hanging around with you—she said you're going to get me killed. Or jailed. I have a lot of homework to do, so…"

"Hey! You do *homework?* I have some math…"

"No."

So there I am one afternoon after school, eyeball to eyeball with a grinning hellhorse, ready to eat me alive. I climb down off the fence and back away from her, towards the barn. She's shaking her beautiful head and mane as I do so, and she's clacking those monstrous teeth every once in a while.

That's when I hear Lee Bentsley on his porch, laughing. He thinks this is *funny?*

"Alan, *DON'T* let her do that to you! You gotta break her a that, or she'll do it to everybody." Still laughing. I'm still backing up. My cannibal hellhorse is still hungry. Not for oats.

"Who's everybody?" I never saw anybody except me around these monsters. "Longacres. My jockeys and trainers. I can't have her biting them. Ya gotta break that habit." I mean, what does he want me to do, *spank* her? I'm almost to the stable when he finally hollers, "Hit her! Hit her in the nose! She'll stop. Jesus!" and he goes in to watch "Leave it to Beaver" or "Queen for a Day" or something.

Then he quickly returns. He just remembered something. That's when I hollered, "Hit her with *what?*"

"That's what I came out to tell ya. Anything! Anything you can getcher hands on. Feed can, whatever. But *do not* hit with a bridle! *Ever!*"

Finally! A lesson. Of course, next day, there I was , climbing the fence, after throwing my schoolbooks in the tall grass, the homework Jimmy won't do, to face my nemesis. She wasn't there, not at the apple tree, but she spotted me and was she *happy* to see me, her after school favorite snack. She came running. So did I. I'm running straight at her and the barn. I had brought nothing—nothing to hit her with. I suddenly wished for that "U.S. Government" book I'd thrown in the bushes; there was something in there about "checks and balances" she might appreciate. She ran past me and now behind. Now, even *I* have the powers of deduction enough to know a human is not going to outrun a racehorse, no matter how bad you have to pee.

She's right on me and I hear her huffing. Now I feel her whiskers and I have no choice; I hit the brakes. So does she, eyes wide, total surprise and sliding, her back brakes locked up and plowing sod. Up she slides with a "what the hell" look on her sweet face, as if betrayed; like I'm cheating. I swing the biggest, hardest haymaker of my young, or old, life I will *ever* deliver, right onto that soft squishy nose. And I stand there as my sweet "Sister Fran" soon to be "Longacres" first-place winner sits—and thinks.

She got up, put her big cheekbone over my shoulder up against my left ear and quietly, softly snorted, "I'm sorry." Then left for the stable, as in, "Let's eat!" I followed.

She was once again the same adorable little puppy personality that she had been. I nearly cried that I'd hurt her. I, to this day, still feel my right fist hit, and squash, that *most* tender of horse parts, and wish I hadn't done it.

Later, Lee said it had to be done and I was the one to do it, that yearlings get to be like that, right about that age.

Now, don'tcha think he mighta told me that beforehand? For 33 cents, I coulda lost my ear. Or my jugular.

How come so many lessons in life *have* to come so late? *ALL* the *real* ones come later, waaay after school. I think those books of mine are part of the roadside ecosystem next to the fence, under the apple tree, doing the soil some good—more good than they did me. On the rare occasion I get to "pet" a horse, *after* making friends, I try to always brush lightly that bristly tender snout, my favorite part. Like the soft creamy rich inner thigh of a woman.

* * * * * *

My woman is not bristly. [Whew! That was close—Ed.]

62

HORSE PISS

If you think second-hand cigarette smoke gets into your clothing, hang out in a stable full of horse hydrants. Horse piss can permeate spacecraft. The vapors, I mean.

Every morning at 7:00 I would open up the stables and put a bridle on each horse to lead them to whichever small pasture was that day's. After school I only had to bang on the two-pound coffee can for them to come in for dinner. Their dinner bell, so to speak. After cleaning out their stalls, I always smelled like an equine port-a-potty in August. Another big hit with my classmates.

But everything I ever did was social suicide anyhow, I figured, so who cares. Plus I had already ostracized myself when I, in art class, threw a broom into a barrel and it glanced off, changed direction, and broke Claudia Kimble's perfect nose. She was Carol Kimble's twin sister; well, until then. They weren't twins when I was done—with one of them. Nobody has trouble telling them apart now. That was the part of my life I started living under bridges.

Understandably, in the middle of all this, my fits of ineptitude, stupidity, scholastic and socially pernicious ammonia smelling insolent attempts at "fitting in," nobody would have anything to do with me; until this one day Mr. Calhoun's horse got loose.

Mr. Calhoun was the North Thurston School District Superintendent and lived across from our high school. It was winter.

His house, like our school, faced Sleater-Kinney Road with a short insignificant gravel road in between. If it had a name, I don't know what it was; I don't think it deserved a name. Anyway, in the middle of Miss Finley's English class someone hollers, "Look! There's a horse on the road!"

Sure enough, there's Mr. Calhoun's big gray, meandering the ditch on Sleater-Kinney where people often sped by at 50 or more. Couple girls became loudly worried and looked to Miss Finley for a solution. She watched a couple cars roar around and past the horse. She was wringing her hands. She was quiet. She was pregnant. She was crying.

"Miss Finley, I'll go get him," I volunteered.

"How?"

"I know how to do it."

"With what?" He had no bridle on.

"I'm a stable boy for some racehorses. *I'LL* go get him." I heard some doubtful male moans, along with a murmured, "So that's why he smells like that." With someone else's "Yeah, I though he just pissed his pants alla time." Laughter.

When I approached him slowly, while telling him soothingly what a nice big boy he was, I unbuttoned the sleeves of my long-sleeve flannel shirt and, gently caressing his cheek, drooped one arm of my shirt over his neck.

With both of my shirtsleeve ends in my left hand I led him across the road onto the school's lawn into the direction of home, flexing, to the best of my abilities whatever bare chest muscles and biceps I could muster as we went past my classroom windows.

Upon my triumphant return Miss Finley quietly said, "Thank you, Alan." The guys said nothing.

Quite a few girls smiled, nodded in approval and looked at me as if seeing me for the first time.

I'm not sure, but I don't think I smelled quite as bad after that; in fact, it was much later, a month maybe, when some kid who had made the mistake of standing too near me goes, "Whoa! What the hell is that smell? Is that *you*?"

And a girl whom I didn't know and not in any of my classes answers him, ""Shut up! He works with racehorses! What do *you* do?"

* * * * * *

In my entire life, I've never been on a horse.

63

THE RAFT

My biggest fear when I was a kid, was growing up. Grownups had to work, and I wanted no part of *that*. My dad got up and went to work every damn day and I knew I could never do it. I was a miserable failure already just bein' a kid, for cryin' out loud, so you can't expect me to do meaningful adult stuff. I was lazy and I was aware of it. Although no one ever said that to me. A couple—well, *all*—of my teachers might've dropped a hint or two. "When will you start using that 'inane' brain of yours and get something *done* in this class?" And, "at the rate you're going,

Alan, you could be stuck here in Lacey grade school until your grandkids graduate from college." So I would do *just enough* "hard labor" homework to pass. And they were just as relieved as was I.

Seventh or eighth grade rolled around and with it came the obligatory "Tom Sawyer" or "Huck Finn" short story. Now *this* I could identify with, I was *in*.

Lois Lake was a pathetic small lake probably two thousand feet from our house which occupied a fair amount of my free time and, as I already mentioned, I made sure I had a lot of it.

The fish probably were not biting this day so I thought maybe I should do some "Life on the Mississippi " adventuring. While on my favorite fallen into the water uprooted old fir log, fishing for boney yellow perch and catching none, I noticed the other half-submerged shorter and smaller deadhead logs. "Maybe I should make a nice 'river raft,'" I conjured. It mighta been ten in the morning.

Vine maple was all over the place, up into trees and branches, mingling with nice supple ivy vines. I had all the rope I would need to raft myself down the Missouri or the Gangese. Did you know that Lewis and Clark—in their early thirties rowed and *TOWED* their boats 2,700 miles *up* the Missouri River?!—I had all the "rope" I needed to lash my barge of wilderness odyssey together, so I set about preparing to conquer some new lands—the Northwest Passage maybe.

After stripping down about a hundred and ten miles of stubborn vines and going around pulling fat water-sodden broken tree sections and pooling them together for assembly, I began winding.

By the time I was done "weaving" this monster together it was maybe one o'clock; and I was covered in "garfs" from getting poked by broken sticks, bark and branches. But I was ready to launch.

A fourteen-inch rainbow swam between my naked thighs as I swung one leg up onto the deck of my fine vessel; then my foot slid off and down between two waterlogs, squishing my ankle—a maneuver I would repeat several more times before stabilizing.

I had already selected a nice thin pole about fifteen feet long, sorta straight, that fit my torn-up hands from struggling with stubborn vines; I would pole myself across this ocean of unknown danger. Planting the end of my pole onto the firm gravel lake's edge I shoved off. I…said…I…shoved *off*. This damn water sogged pile of rotten wood—would *not* move. Finally! I got it loose and I moved my pole down the bank for a second shove, and eventually a third— now there's no turning back; as if I could *turn* this thing. My pole was getting shorter. I hadn't known until now the mud below was about twelve feet thick. My pole's end *along* with my arm, disappeared into the water each new push. Then I played hell pulling it free from the sucking muck below. *This* required both hands and much effort. And

I wasn't hardly going anywhere. Clearly this was a stupid idea—there's that stupid trout again. I spit at him.

But I don't cave in easily, I kept at it until I reached the far shore. Exhausted and sore, I waded the last ten feet or so to claim the new "land" for myself. Now I had to scamper back around the shore to get my clothes and fishing gear. It was almost dark, around 9:30.

I surveyed the miles I had traveled in my intrepid labors—about eighty feet. In twelve hours.

I crawled home, still dreading the day would eventually arrive when I'd grow up and had to actually *work* for a living.

That was the *only* trout I ever saw in that useless pond.

64

THE BACKBAR

On Highway 99—Old Pacific Highway—Secoma, Washington, there once was an auction "barn" that entertained a succession of auctioneers over time; C.C. Jones, Sourdough Don, Mike Junger, Joe Welch, Randy Lazwell, and last and least, Jim Ness. Jim Ness was pure reprobate that Tennessee had somehow generously delivered to the Pacific Northwest. I wish they had kept him, but I had not dealt with him until this one time—and it only took once.

He advertised an "antique auction," so I checked it out. A lotta junk with a few good things, but he did have a nice 12' stick-and-ball backbar; unusual, and original varnish, American, 1880s. I did not have much in the way of competition when bidding on it, so it was mine for $1,250. When I paid I told them I couldn't pick it up for a month or so, and they said no problem; it's fine where it is, and thank you.

* * * * * *

I have an empty truck and am ready to pick up the two-piece backbar, so I back up to Ness's loading "dock" to haul it home. Upon entering his front door I glance right to where it should be.

"Maybe they had to move it," l thought, so I patrolled his whole—maybe three thousand square foot facility—it's not here. I scare up somebody that has no idea what I'm talking about. It is a summer day and although warm, I'm getting exceptionally hot where I'm standing. That's when Ness walked in with half a sandwich in his hand—he stopped chewing when he saw me.

He gets all angelic looking and, "Heey, Alan, how you doin'?"

"Where's my backbar?"

"You picked *it uuup!*" incredulously.

"How come I don't remember doing that? And guess what—if I picked it up, I would have it; and I don't. But maybe I should go back home and look around for it? How does a person misplace a twelve by eight-foot bar?" He's chewing again; but he stops when I yell, "You know god-damn well I didn't pick it up! Where *is* it?"

"Well, not *you!* Those two hippies with a flatbed you sent here."

"Those hippies have my auction receipt?"

"Don't know. They just said you sent 'em."

"So you just let people haul off other people's stuff with no paperwork? That's a crocka shit and you *know* it! You really think I'm gonna roll over on this? Do you even *have* an auctioneer's bond and license? 'Cause you *won't* when I'm done and you might end up missing other things, too—although you don't have too many of those left to lose," pointing at his mouth. He tossed his half-eaten sandwich out the door into the crushed gravel parking lot, and left, towards the back of his "barn."

Furious, I departed also, peeling out in my one-ton van, spitting as much gravel into his little shitshow as I could. He knew I would be back.

It didn't take long for every antique dealer in three counties to have heard what Ness had perpetrated on me. I mean, an auctioneer, especially in antiques, is only as good as—guess what?—his reputation.

My friend, Randy Lazwell, who at one time had leased out the same place Ness now infested, looked me in the eye and told me he knew *who* had bought *my* backbar from the festering mess Jim Ness. And for how much—three thousand. I had no plans to bother the new *owners* of my backbar. I was, however, determined to make Ness's life miserable until I got my money back.

Jesse Jones was yet another auctioneer and he and I often worked each other's sales. Soon, maybe two weeks, after I had made it clear to Tennessee Jim my undying intentions to collect, I was due to be a ring man and spotter for Jesse's auction, just up the road from Ness, at Brooklake Community Center.

Bob Warner was a younger friend of mine who had agreed to work for Jesse this auction, so he rode up with me from Lacey to Federal Way. We left way early enough to afford time enough to stop and pressure Ness for my money. A good hour to spare.

After demanding my $1,250, I got the exact response from him I expected. "Those two guys gotcher *bar*! Those hippies."

"Listen, you dumb hillbilly! I know where it *is*! I know who bought it! And I know how much you sold it for—three grand! I should make you pay me all three grand, but I doubt if you've got that much. You are sure *as hell* gonna pay me what you took from me! 'Cause we're not leavin' 'til ya do!" an empty bluff, but he had no way to know we had a sale to work. We went outside and sat—leaned on his car's front fenders, feet up on the tall curb and sidewalk; like we had all night.

Maybe twenty minutes into that charade, the young oafish "lumper" who worked there came out and handed me a check. I scanned it quickly and just as quickly registered that this big kid—maybe 20-22—has not moved. His big boots are still pointed at me. I looked up just in time to see his right fist up next to his right ear. Still "sitting," I shot my left hand up with palm open and stiff-armed his hand and held it there. I was surprised how effective that was. He was too. When I realized he was shifting his feet to dive on me, I ducked. He threw his upper body over my head and shoulders to wrap his arms around my chest. I'm looking at a big "camel" cigarette silver belt buckle. We slid off the fender, still on our feet, onto the gravel. He was doing his best to take me down; I was equally determined to not let that happen. I was wearing "good" clothes. Nice slacks and a new tan "velour" shirt and shiny leather-soled loafers. *I* wanted to take *him* down, to be the one on top; I didn't want to get dirty.

The large plow horse boots he wore gave him plenty of purchase in this loose gravel. I had none. With my legs spread out I kept him from throwing us to the ground sideways, although he outweighed me by thirty pounds or more, he could only plow me around in the gravel my shoes surfed on. This went on for a while.

My arms were free, but I couldn't do much. Knowing his head is up there somewhere, I swung up, best I could, towards my shoulder blades. When I knew I'd hit the back of this bonehead's skull, I switched hands, looking to land one or two onto something softer. When I did, I felt him loosen his bearhug somewhat; I was able to pull my upper torso closer to vertical. He would not let go. I was trying my damnedest to get slightly sideways of him to throw my right leg behind his.

When my right calf hit the back of his knee, he buckled backwards and down we went. He let go then. But he rolled over too fast for me to get in any face punches. I landed a couple ineffective ones on the back of this numbskull's head. He got up and ran to his pickup forty feet away. But he wasn't done yet.

He soon returned, brandishing a broken bloody nose and face as well as a steel bar about eighteen inches long.

"Bob, I need something real heavy, really quick."

About the time Bob picked up the corner chunk of a broken cinder block Ness used as a doorstop, he dropped it. Ness had come outside to play; he jammed a double barrel 12-gauge shotgun into Bob's back. The oaf ran past them—playtime over.

With hands up we backed away to climb in my van. Right across Highway 99 from where we were I saw the King County Sheriff's car at "Secoma Lanes" bowling alley.

This poor hungry cop had an enormous and delicious-looking cheeseburger halfway up for his first juicy bite when I ran up to his booth. He held it there while listening. He kept looking at it. "*When did this happen?*"

"Just now! Right there!" Then he said one very bad word and put down his dinner.

Within six minutes the three of us were joined by eight or ten more county and state cops.

Ness would *not* come out. When the S.W.A.T. team showed up we were told to leave.

So we went to work. Four hours later, after the auction, Jesse asks me privately if I was okay. "Yeah, why?"

"Everybody is concerned. Did you tear some stitches or something? Your back had been bleeding all night."

"Oh. That's not my blood. I had to break someone's nose on the way up here, down at that mongrel Jim Ness's place."

"Have anything to do with that backbar I heard about?" And he took a big drag off his smoke and laughed it all out—shaking his head, coughing.

* * * * * *

Jesse later would join the ranks of several other auctioneers that died of throat cancer, from smoking.

65

Act I—Soccer Hooligans

A long time ago (1976) in a land far away (London) I was on an antique buying trip and had purchased an early '60s Van Den Plas (it's a car) at a vehicle auction. While driving it one day I also picked up a nice young clean-cut hitchhiker. Noticing his shiny black shoes, I somewhat assumed he was on his way to work. "No. I'm *looking* for work. Hey, I know London pretty well and I'm a good driver—if you can use one."

Not real keen on driving on the "wrong" side of the road—I'd been doing it a few days with no issues, but…so I asked him his name.

When I found out his name was "Clive," I hired him on the spot; I mean, how could I not?

"Your dad's name wouldn't be 'Jeeves' by any chance, would it?"

"No. Why?"

We fell into a nice routine; I would have Clive pick me up at the Heathrow airport Holiday Inn restaurant every morning at seven o'clock and we'd go junkin' all over London. For five weeks I would be spending money like a drunken sailor, then after securing trucks and crew I was to fill two forty-foot containers for export to Seattle and Tacoma.

After very quickly learning that nobody wanted American Express travelers checks I also learned they only wanted English pounds. Period. And that's how it went—coin of the realm.

My West Coast bank was named after our regional and majestic mountain: "Rainier" Bank—with a satellite Rainier bank in downtown London—making $10,000 wire transfers to myself quite handy. Clive and I were making our way to visit "my" bank in the center of the banking district; we'd been there a few times before but not this early in the morning—too early.

Being as astute and knowledgeable as he'd said he was, Clive announced he knew of a posh place where all the rich bankers and fancy people ate. Being's how I now have my own driver—with shiny shoes—and I own my own black limousine (well, it was black)—I thought maybe I should sit behind him when we're on our way to someplace posh. I sat up straight, trying to look fancy.

The place was posh, at least the outside of it. But they weren't open yet either; we had started out too early; half an hour to go. "Just drive around for a while." I wanted to look important. I started clearing my throat unnecessarily—to *sound* important, or at least high maintenance and privileged. "Are you catching a cold?" from Clive.

What a considerate and thoughtful hitchhiker I had scored for myself. So empathetic. And I *deserved* him.

"No. When we stop, I think I'll grab some gum or something. Hey, Clive, what's going on up there?" Up at the very end of a quite broad thoroughfare—with not *one* vehicle on it—was a coliseum or stadium of some kind. No cars to be seen. Anywhere, *only* pedestrians.

After *proudly* informing me the name of it, he says, "You want to take a look at it?" "Sure. Why not? And what's with the spectators' colors; *all* the blue and white on one sidewalk and *all* the red and white on the other sidewalk?" No one was in the road other than Clive and myself on the pavement. Both camps were slowly meandering up their respective sidewalk, laden with thermoses, lunch bags, lunchboxes, and the like. Hundreds of people on each side.

Clive now informs me that "on one side, we have Manchester United and on the other we've got Leicester City." (And if those aren't the right names that day, it doesn't matter—you get the picture.)

Given what little I know now about fanatical football fans in England, they probably had *laws preventing* them mingling on the tarmac or the sidewalks; because of what happened next, they *should* have.

"Which one is on this side, our side?"

"That's Leicester City."

"Okay, Clive; now drive real slow," as I rolled down my window and stuck my head out, I began hollering, "Go, Manchester United! Go, Manchester United! Yay! Manchester's gonna kick yer ass!"

Apples, oranges, full cans of soda pop, thermoses and insults were hurled at us. Some hit my "limo." Clive made a U-turn up near the stadium entrance and I did exactly the same thing going down to where we'd started. "Yay, Leicester City! Go, Leicester City! Yer gonna be sorry you ever took on Leicester City! Yay! Losers!"

More oranges, bananas, apples, cans, thermoses and threats. Clive was laughing so hard I thought he would pass out. (This was not the only hearty gut-busting laugh he would have this day.) It was time for breakfast. Nobody had left the sidewalk.

66

ACT II—LET'S MAKE A DEAL

Clive had been right; it was a nice posh breakfast (note to self: next time eat at the Holiday Inn). And when I paid, I picked up a big fat pack of Wrigley's Juicy Fruit gum.

I've really never been much of a gum chewer; back then I would succumb to the occasional lure of a fifteen-pack of flavored chewable sugar. Nowadays my jowls are too loose and floppy to keep them— my inner jowls—away from my teeth. So I've stopped chewing both the gum *and* my inner cheeks.

I've always loved sugar, and I'm impatient (actually I'm very patient—just not for very long!). So I would cram the sticks into my cakehole one after another, maybe two minutes apart.

And there I was, driving/riding along on the M-1, London's outskirts, sitting behind Clive, after leaving Rainier bank, patting my pockets bulging with twenty-pound bank notes while digesting something that was "posh." Life was good. Weather equally lovely. Chewing away. Looking over Clive's left shoulder in front of us, I saw the unmistakable square back of a small station wagon type motorcar. Only a vintage Morris Minor has the very recognizable classy—wrapped in oak—back end with the cute little rounded rear fenders. "Hey, Clive, catch up with that car—I want a better look." And I gave myself a nice loud sugary "slurp." Right into Clive's ear.

I've always loved them—these adorable little "woodies" being what we Americans called them—"woody wagons." And since arriving in London, I'd kept one eye out for one for sale. Oh, I had found a few, not many, some on used car lots. But they, for some reason, all suffered from the same malady: all of them had severe rust on the front fenders. ALL of them, and a bit more than I wanted to pay in the first place.

I had all but given up after asking, about maybe five car salesmen, "Why do they all seem to have this rust problem?" when one finally explained, "Sir, we live on an island. In the middle of the sea. If you can show me one without the rust, *I'll pay off our national debt!!*" And I watched Clive nod in agreement.

He pulled up next to the single occupant and matched his speed, 50 or 60 mph, so that I could, from the distance of a lane—four feet or so—eyeball the front fender and, by the way, they're called "wings" in England—"wings." My cursory inspection told me this was a *good* one—some rust, but nothing like what I'd seen on the resale lots.

This is when everything kicks in at once: my "posh" breakfast with lots of English tea, the half-pound of Wrigley's Juicy Fruit I'm swallowing, the fresh wads of cash in *most* of my pockets, my very own driver in my very own black limo (although dented now). And a cute little car I've *always wanted! I must have* that car!

Salivating like "David over Bathsheba," I rolled down my window for a second time that morning (and for a completely different reason), and caught the driver's eye, "Hey, ya wanna sell that car?"

A youngish middle-aged hippie type guy (gray hair and ponytail) looks up at me and, both hands on the wheel, smiles all smug like, and shakes his head. Like this car's "not for sale at any price." Suddenly I didn't feel very important anymore. I really did not appreciate his "this car's mine, not yours" attitude. Chomping away at my gum while deeply feeling the erosion of my American ego, I made one more attempt at Bathsheba. I must have her!!

When I rolled down my window again, a cross breeze caught all the silver crinkly-edged tinfoil wrappers as well as all of the yellow Juicy Fruit jacket papers, whipping them into a tornado inside my "limo." Some went out the window.

Mustering the best American diplomacy I could on foreign soil, I jammed one hand full of money out the window towards the nice man and hollered, "How the hell you know it's not for sale? Look! I have *cash*!" I could feel gum slobber roll across my cheek and into my hair. Paper money chattering away in the wind.

Upon seeing all the colorful coinage of the queen fluttering at 55 mph—in American terms, the money was around three thousand dollars—his eyes got all saucer-like and he motioned toward the shoulder of the road. He began to slow.

Now what have I done? I thought to myself. He's not getting' this whole wad for that piece of shit, if that's what he's thinkin'. I wasn't born yesterday. I mean, just look at me; I even have my own driver.

As I walked up to his car, all cool and business-like with all fifteen sticks of gum balled up in my left cheek, I barely realized I couldn't blink with my right eye. My eyelashes on that eye had congealed with my eyebrow, thanks to the fruit-flavored corn syrup and saliva. He stared at me like I had a glass eye. Both hands still on the wheel; now they're tapping lightly. "How much did you have in mind?" he asks, in eager anticipation.

I thought to myself, "Not so fast there—lemmee look this ol' mare over a bit. She's kinda long in the tooth." But I hadn't said anything yet; mainly 'cause my gob of gum had hardened and I needed to pry it out. I strolled slowly around the car I'd salivated over since I first saw one. I think he saw me in his rearview mirror as I got two fingers behind the impacted wad and flung it earthward, glancing off the rear bumper. I kicked it into the ditch, wiped my mouth with the back of my hand, and came back around to the driver's side, satisfied that it was in very good shape; he still had both hands on top of the steering wheel. That's when I assumed this poor old hippie had been taught by the cops to keep his hands where they could be seen at all times.

Again he asks, "So, what are you thinking?"

While we had been pulling over to negotiate, I'd already separated the amount I wanted to pay, 800 pounds, from the main attraction

I had earlier brandished. Plus another 200 pounds; for what I *would* pay. Thousand pounds total. I held up 800 pounds, and said, "Eight hundred pounds."

His hands finally came unglued from the wheel. As he raises them up in the air and keeps them there for a moment or two while he ponders blankly through his windshield. To anyone driving past, this looks like a holdup, I thought. Assuming that I'd insulted him, I was readying the other 200 when he says, "No. No. Nope." And he's shaking his head slowly but thoughtfully. I thought about offering *another* two hundred, but before I could, he concludes with: "It's just not worth it—I'll take four hundred." Just like that, with a straight face and an "I'm not backing down" attitude.

So now I'm sure that this car is stolen. I knew this was gonna be too good to be true; I wish I hadn't thrown my gum away. I wondered if I could find it. "Do you have the title?" knowing full well he does not.

"Sure. It's at the house—couple miles up. Would you care to follow?"

As I climbed in behind Clive I heard him moaning incoherently. From his vantage point, sitting behind the wheel of our car, he'd been watching in the mirror the transaction—or near transaction because no cash had changed hands yet—he had a pretty good idea, because I had returned to the car all smiles. But when I told him what had just transpired—that's when my rather straightlaced driver *lost* it. He fell over in the front seat *convulsing* with laughter. And then when he could talk, through his tears he announces, "Alan, you have just fulfilled every Britisher's depiction of a *gum-chewing money-waving American!!*" We got to the guy's house and he produced a clear title. He, of course, offered me tea. I declined. I wanted to get the hell out of there before his wife came home from her walk or whatever and said, "Where's my car?"

Maybe he sold it to me that cheap because he felt sorry for me 'cause I had a glass eye.

EPILOGUE

I drove that sweet little woody all over England. I bought brand-new "wings" for the front as my plan was to ship it home to drive it. My "blokes" as they refer to themselves were instructed to include it in the second forty-foot container of antiques I had gathered. I'd overseen—as in done it myself—the loading and packing of the first one, but I needed more muscle and brawn on the second one—I was running out of time. My "blokes," of course, did not load it. They didn't even try. They claimed they had no way to get it into the container. That's what loading dock platforms are for, I told them. But it was too late. The container was filled and shipped sans my vintage woody. They said they left it where I had: the Heathrow Holiday Inn parking lot.

Those rat-bastards are probably sitting in it right now, guzzling beer and telling stale old stories about the old days.

The "Van Den Plas Rolls," as I called it, I had purchased to drive, but when it was announced at the auction that it had a Rolls Royce engine and transmission, my plan was to, when finished with it, have the "blokes" ship that running gear as well. Well, that never happened. After five weeks of dealing with these clowns I knew they were good at two things: finding antiques and drinking beer. Guess which one they excelled at. I gave the Rolls Royce limousine Van Den Plas to Clive—ugly square lookin' tank anyway—not Clive, the car. I did have another vehicle that bears mentioning during this saga. A small step side diesel "Commer" deliver lorry—think old-time bread or milk truck, open on the sides, two doors in the back—great for picking up smaller loads all over England and dropping off at my loading docks. I was to give that to the "blokes" when I was done, and I did. But first, I drove it all over England, too; and I never had any feared traffic instances regarding the American arguments over who drives on the "wrong side of the road." All went well. No altercations. No fouls. No horns or fingers—well, none that I heard or saw—'cept one time, parallel parking on a city street in an area of

London I wasn't too familiar with, a slight mishap occurred. Getting lined up next to a parked Mercedes—late model, of *course*—I'd misjudged slightly the distance between as I slowly turned to start backing up my bread truck.

Sssqweeeakk! "DAMMIT!"

I straightened it up, got it parked and grabbed a pen and some paper preparing to write down all my pertinent information which, in polite America is: "All the onlookers that watched me destroy your car believe I am giving you my insurance information, driver's license number and phone number. I am not. Have a nice day." Then you put it under the wiper blade and drive away. That's how we do it.

Before I could get started with my "info," a guy came trotting from down and across the street, nice slacks and shirt, huffing a little bit, slightly out of shape. Typical Mercedes-Benz owner.

"Hey, hey! Why'd you hit my car?" I'm thinking that's a dumb question—does he think people aim for parked cars?—like I did it on purpose? From him puffing at me I knew he'd been drinking, so now I thought I could negotiate without going through the whole—you know—rigamarole. (Do they have rigamaroles in Great Britain? I bet they've got a lot of 'em.) Then he asks me another brain teaser: "How didja do that?"

So he wants an explanation. Not having any blackboards nor chalk to diagram it for him, I realize he wants me to plead my case, so I threw myself at the mercy of the court. I began whining how they've got me in a strange land—everything's all backwards—you got me driving on the wrong side of the car, wrong side of the street and… and that's when I realized I was talking too long, and he was starting to sober up. The time to act was now!

"How about I give you two hundred pounds cash, right now. That'll buy a lotta drinks and then you can turn It in as a hit-and-run to your insurance company.

The very next thing out of his mouth is—thankfully *not* another question. He says, "Nah, just give me twenty pounds. That'll pay for three or four drinks."

I recently told that story to a couple of friends of mine and they got a good laugh. Pat, who's a prosecutor, laughed the longest and when he stopped laughing, he said, ever so kindly, "Alan, that was not his car."

67

SCRUFALUMPUS INTERRUPTUS

If you thought for one minute I was done talking about our cat Scruffy, well...I just don't know what to say...I mean, how could I not talk about one of the coolest "people" that ever crossed our path—Cheryl's and mine.

You know those times when you said, "God, I wish I had a camera!"? We had a few of those; the following is a perfect example of not having a recording device of *some* kind.   He and Cheryl used to hide from each other, then jump out and chase one another around. The cat was, more often than not, the one who initiated these hilarious escapades. If she was on bended knee washing the front glass of a showcase, for example, this goofy cat would run up her back, swat her on both sides of her head, jump down, and take off running.

She'd be in hot pursuit. After he'd outrun her, they'd both stop, and he'd turn to face her. That's when she knew it was her turn— and off *she'd* go—squealing her head off. But here's the best part: this goofy feline would chase her all over the shop *on his back legs*! Standing straight UPRIGHT with his "arms" pumping in unison with his stride like the hundred-yard-dash track star that he was. Some of the few people who were lucky enough to witness this frivolity would laugh, shake their heads in disbelief, and say something like, ". . . never saw anything like that in my *life*."

* * * * * *

Then there was the "cat and moose show." If you remember seeing "Northern Exposure" on T.V. you'll recall the big bull moose head mounted on the wall of "The Brick" saloon in Roselyn, Washington. We had sold some of the set decorations to the series, so when time came to liquidate, they chose us to auction it off.

We got $500 for that mangy old moose head. One year later the guy brought it back. "Yah, my wife said if I brought it into the house, she'd throw us *both* out. And it takes up half our garage." So we sold it again; for $300 [Just what in blazes does that have to do with their supernaturally insane cat?—Ed.]

And we did have another full-blown, full-size bull moose in the shop. But we weren't allowed to go near it. Not if our cat had anything to say about it. The moose was on our middle floor at the top of the ramp.

If, when going down, or up, from whichever of our three floors we were on, we would pass that giant hairy moose, and *IF* accompanied by the slightly warped shop cat, we'd be in danger. You remember when "Rambo" said, "The park is mine!"?

Our *very* possessive kitty had early on claimed "Bullwinkle" to be *his* property; "The moose is mine." He would race on over, leap up onto him in eager anticipation of our passing by. We've all seen squirrels scamper around on the bark of a large three trunk. We had one squirrely cat who just loved to skitter around on his buddy Bullwinkle's thick trunk, face and antlers hoping for someone to come within striking distance. If someone made the mistake of befriending our adorable and frisky squirrel cat by reaching out to him, he'd nail 'em. One big fat thorny swat later, they'd decided to *NOT* do that again. It was his game, and he loved it.

Of course, *we knew* to not go near him when he was jumping around on that moose, but he was *so* irresistible to customers; our cash register is directly above where Bullwinkle and the cat of ten thorns hung out, so we knew when he'd found a new playmate.

"Geeyoww!! Dammit! This cat just tried to take my hand off! He looked so cute a second ago—he was just waiting for me to stick my hand out! He baited me! Lookit him—he's celebrating!" All of which was true. Whenever I heard someone scream in pain on the next floor down, I would simply go turn the shop's radio way up.

He was very annoyed when we sold Bullwinkle.

* * * * * *

After we lost our little apartment calico cat, "Peanut," the time had come to move Scruffy into our apartment before he killed somebody. And this was the period of time when he could no longer wallow in dust bunnies or sawdust in my workshop—hence becoming pure white—retaining, however, the same name—"Scruffy."

My wife and I have always agreed that any and all animals need to have another of their *own kind* for companionship. Camels, geese, guppies, whatever. But we knew that a female cat will not accept another cat *cheerfully* into its residence, and we hadn't tried. So Scruff now had our apartment to himself—well, he *did* allow us to stay there.

Our friend "Abby" who ran a wine shop out of our building was on her way home one night when she spotted a "dumped" calico sitting near a cardboard box on the side of the road. When she went to examine the unopened box, the cat jumped into the car. A small hole in the side of the box showed how the mother cat had repeatedly gnawed—clawed her way out, leaving one very tiny starving black-and-white kitten inside.

Scruffy's solo existence was soon to never be the same.

My mom had told me a male cat will kill any new kittens that show up unannounced, so I was sure we had two new "shop" cats who would never see the inside of our apartment where Scruff now lived.

While at the vet's getting their shots and whatnot, I reluctantly asked Dr. Smith about a male cat's acceptance of a new kitten, I couldn't believe my ears when he said "Oh, about a thousand percent."

He could not have been more right. My mom was wrong, at least about housecats. Scruffy was lying on his side when we placed a softball size bi-color fuzzball under his puzzled gaze and chin. He sniffed at it and immediately curled his right arm around it, drew it closer and began vigorously washing "Buster," our new—*HIS* new—kitten. Uncle Scruffy would raise him up to be the wonderful cat he is now; same size as Scruff. Introducing "Sweetie" and Scruff was a little more work, but it all went well. It would be months before we realized that with Scruffy's very *own* little boy to raise, love, and wrestle with, he hadn't swatted or chewed on either one of us. We had given him a companion. He was now happier than ever, and he never lashed out at anybody again.

* * * * * *

You recall when I earlier mentioned the sudden yearning for a camera that's nonexistent or out of reach? Please read on.

As Buster grew, he was lovingly tutored by his Uncle Scruff how to lie, cheat, steal Cheryl's jewelry and my turkey as well as my do-nut, and best of all, how to cope when Cheryl and I were traveling. We knew he had slight abandonment issues as I mentioned, but I'd noticed after awhile how he handled it: by opening a heavy mirrored sliding closet door and squeezing in between some towels or bed-sheets. Something he *never* did when we were there.

Returning from a trip is always a pleasant surprise for the kitties because guess what? They *never know* when we are coming back. Why? 'Cause they can't read a calendar or answer a phone! So they're tick-led pink when we show up.

If we can find them. This is when we realized Scruffy had been tutoring Buster on how to deal with the trauma of our being gone.

Essentially Scruffy had created his own little "safe room" in-side our linen closet. After sliding open the heavy mirrored door, he scooted our towels around and burrowed a nice dark corner up on a shelf. And he only did this in our absence of several consecutive days. This time he took Buster with him; and by now they are the same size.

Sweetie came running as soon as Cheryl called for them. "Sweetie! Buster! Scruffy!— We're home!"

No Buster. No Scruffy. We're worried. This had *never* happened. After five minutes of both of us calling and searching, we went out into the shop, hollering for them. Cheryl kept on. I checked up on our large rooftop garden. I am scared. Cheryl is crying. Nothing means more to us than these damn cats.

Then I remembered Scruff's little hideaway. "Scruffy! Buster! Are you in *here?*" As I slid the door open, I wasn't hollering, but I was not quiet. Light filled the dark closet, illuminating two full-grown tomcats who had obviously been sent to the local taxidermist for the full procedure. Our cats had died! And our cat sitter had had them stuffed! I'm yelling for my wife, as I see one eye—no other movement—open; ever so slightly. They're not dead! They're paralyzed! Dammit! We've got two quadriplegic cats!

Before I can continue, I must describe how our two mysteriously crippled, comatose, catatonic cats are positioned.

They are sitting upright! Each of them is in full bear-hug embrace of the other! Each passed-out cat has his back pressed against a vertical wall corner of the closet. Each cat has his chin on the shoulder of the other, sitting *straight* up. Two hibernating cats glued together for eternity from all appearances.

As I snatch for my camera which hung by a strap around my neck to grab a couple quick photos for proof of the impossible scene before me, I realize it's not there! It's gone! Why is it gone?

It's gone because it was *never* there. Not only that, I have *NEVER* owned a camera that hung around my neck! But at that moment I wanted one *SO BADLY* I grabbed for a camera which was non-existent—talk about grasping for straws! I've never *really* owned a camera in the first place.

I don't much *ever* get headaches, but this stressful ordeal caused the two mastoid lobes in the base of my skull just above the nape of my neck to throb mercilessly for the next four hours after these cats unwrapped from one another while we celebrated their slow miraculous resurrection.

Little by little, a paw here, a paw there, a tiny ear twitch, then a *full* cat—bleary eyeball reveal—small movements of actual *life* proved they weren't dead *or* paralyzed. Our kitties were fine.

Cats *CAN'T* sleep like that! But they had been; until I showed up to release them from whatever death grip spell they were under. I still can't believe how "far gone" they were.

* * * * * *

Scrufalumpus Hopalong Kerplop is a dream now. We lost our boy two years ago. His kidneys failed, even though he was only eleven. One kidney was misshapen from being kicked before he came to us. We had each other for ten years, the three of us—Cheryl, Scruffy and me. By my math, that's thirty years.

Buster is happy, but he keeps hoping he'll find his Uncle Scruff somewhere.

ACKNOWLEDGEMENTS:

My wife Cheryl, for telling me which stories to *not* write, all of which I wrote anyway; and for buying me a new sofa to sleep on.

Ron Powers, for writing his excellent biography of Mark Twain, which inspired me to resume writing after seven years of mock sobriety.

Val Dummond, editor and publisher of my first two books, as well as author of many printings on grammar, punctuation, and a lotta other stuff I don't care about.

All my typists who struggled valiantly to translate my cuneiform/Sanskrit hand-printed gibberish into English: Vicky Smith, Jenny Aarde, Megan, Christa, Amber, Amber's imaginary sister, Tasha, Sara Zahran, Kelsey, Derek, Alex, Carol Bucholz, Judy Voelker for proofing, and my favorite prosecutor, Patrick Hammond, who advised me in case I forgot somebody, to just say "Donner, Blitzen, Dancer, Prancer and Sneezy."

And Mani, who helped me spell "acknowledgement."

And who is this [Ed.] guy?

9 7 9 8 9 8 9 1 8 6 9 0 7